Beginning postcolonialism

MANCHESTER
UNIVERSITY PRESS

Beginnings
Series editors: Peter Barry and Claire Buck

'**Beginnings**' is a series of books designed to give practical help to students beginning to tackle recent developments in English, Literary Studies and Cultural Studies. The books in the series will:

- demonstrate and encourage a questioning engagement with the new;
- give essential information about the context and history of each topic covered;
- show how to develop a practice which is up-to-date and informed by theory.

Each book will focus uncompromisingly upon the needs of its readers, who have the right to expect lucidity and clarity to be the distinctive feature of a book which includes the word 'beginning' in its title.

Each will aim to lay a firm foundation of well understood initial principles as a basis for further study and will be committed to explaining new aspects of the discipline without over-simplification, but in a manner appropriate to the needs of beginners.

Each book, finally, will aim to be both an introduction and a contribution to the topic area it discusses.

Also in the series

Beginning theory
Peter Barry

Beginning postmodernism
Tim Woods

Forthcoming titles

Beginning romanticism
Michael Baron

Beginning postcolonialism

John McLeod

Manchester University Press
Manchester and New York

Distributed exclusively in the USA by St. Martin's Press

Published by Manchester University Press
Oxford Road, Manchester M13 9NR, UK
and Room 400, 175 Fifth Avenue, New York, NY 10010, USA
http://www.man.ac.uk/mup

Distributed exclusively in the USA by
St. Martin's Press, Inc., 175 Fifth Avenue, New York, NY 10010, USA

Distributed exclusively in Canada by
UBC Press, University of British Columbia, 6344 Memorial Road,
Vancouver, BC, Canada V6T 1Z2

British Library Cataloguing-in-Publication Data
A catalogue record for this book is available from the British Library

Library of Congress Cataloging-in-Publication Data applied for

ISBN 0 7190 5208 4 *hardback*
     0 7190 5209 2 *paperback*

First published 2000

07 06 05 04 03 02 01 00   10 9 8 7 6 5 4 3 2 1

Typeset in Ehrhardt
by Northern Phototypesetting Co Ltd, Bolton

Printed in Great Britain
by Bell & Bain Ltd, Glasgow

for my parents,
Veronica and James McLeod

Contents

Acknowledgements

I owe my greatest debt to Shirley Chew, under whose expert guidance I made my own beginnings in the field of Commonwealth and postcolonial literatures. Her generosity with knowledge and the sharpness of her criticism have inspired me throughout my career, and often sent me back to the 'drawing-board' to think again. Professor Chew must share in any success which this book may merit (of course, its shortcomings are entirely my own). I am also very grateful to my colleagues Fiona Becket, Elleke Boehmer, Tracy Hargreaves, Lynette Hunter and especially David Richards. Their help with materials, expertise, and words of encouragement proved invaluable to me in the writing of this book. A special thank you is due to Sally Keenan, with whom I taught a course on 'Postcolonial Literatures' at LSU (now New College), Southampton. The organisation of this book is based on the module Sally and I designed together, and I learned a great deal while working as her colleague. I remain especially indebted to Peter Barry for putting his faith in me and involving me in the *Beginnings* series.

I am also grateful to the following for their support: Nigel Anderton, Mark Batty, Jerry Brotton, Tom Cheesman, Stuart Davies, Terence Ebberston, Peter Ekstein, Shirley Ekstein, David Fairer, Marie Gillespie, Ingrid Gunby, John Huntriss, Rick Jones, Vivien Jones, David Lindley, Nigel Mapp, Gail Marshall, Richard Napier, Alex Nield, Matthew Pateman, Kate Pettifer, Fiona Richards, Mark

Robson, Simon Ross, Martin Rushworth, Richard Salmon, Alison
Sellers, Alistair Stead, Victoria Stewart, Geoff Waggott, John
Whale and David Williams. Thanks to Matthew Frost and Lauren
McAllister at Manchester University Press for their help and
patience.

My work would not have been possible without the love, care and
encouragement of my parents, Veronica and James McLeod. This
book is dedicated to them. I have also received much lively support
from the aptly-named Joys: Linda, Brian, Caitlin, Lydia and
Madeleine.

Finally, loving thanks are due to Liz Ekstein, for her support,
patience and proof-reading skills – and for showing me during the
course of writing this book just how vital and exciting new beginnings can be.

Rudyard Kipling's 'The Overland Mail' is reproduced with per-
mission from Wordsworth Editions, *The Poems of Rudyard Kipling*
(1994).

John McLeod
University of Leeds

Introduction

Beginning

Any new beginning poses several important questions. Exactly what am I beginning, and what am I about to encounter? How shall I best proceed? Where might be the most appropriate position to start from? Beginnings are exciting things, inviting us to explore that which we may not have previously visited; but they also expose us to the unfamiliarity and inevitable disorientation of doing something new.

Beginning Postcolonialism is an attempt to help you to make your own beginnings in one of the most exciting and challenging fields of study that has emerged in recent years. It is a book primarily concerned with reading practices. It aims to introduce you to the various ways that we can approach, perhaps for the first time, literatures in English produced by writers who either come from, or have an ancestral purchase upon, countries with a history of colonialism. In addition, we will reconsider our approaches to older, more familiar literary works that seem to have little to do with the fortunes of Empire. By the end of this book you will have encountered many new concepts which will help you build and develop your readings of the range of literatures which preoccupy postcolonialism.

That said, we should also be clear what this book is *not*. It will not be attempting to offer a full history of the various literatures often considered 'postcolonial'. There already exists some excellent work which narrates the emergence and fortunes of postcolonial literatures throughout the twentieth century. Neither should we presume that the literary texts we consider in this book are typical of, or adequately represent, the wide-ranging field of postcolonial writing. The choice of texts in the chapters that follow is informed on the whole by my experience of teaching many of them to undergraduate students, and will inevitably reflect some of my own areas of interest. They have served in undergraduate seminars to stimulate successfully the reading strategies which are the primary concern of this book. But they are not the only texts we could choose, and we should not treat them as paradigmatic of postcolonialism.

I hope that this book will assist in kindling your excitement and enthusiasm for the texts and the approaches we cover, and will stabilise to an extent some of the disorientation that is inevitable with any new departure. Yet, disorientation is also very much a productive and valuable sensation, and it is fair to say that many of the reading and writing practices often considered 'postcolonial' achieve much of their effectiveness from derailing accustomed trains of thought. For many of us, postcolonialism challenges us to think again and question some of the assumptions that underpin both *what* we read and *how* we read. So it is important that, throughout this book, some of this valuable disorientation will be maintained.

Postcolonialism?

It is fair to say that beginning postcolonialism is an especially challenging procedure because it is particularly difficult to answer those questions with which we started. Such is the variety of activities often called 'postcolonial' that it is not very easy to find an appropriate point of departure. For example, the literatures of nations such as Canada, Australia, New Zealand, Nigeria, Kenya, India, Pakistan, Jamaica and Ireland have been called 'postcolonial'. Are they all 'postcolonial' in the same way? What is the best way to begin reading them? Could such a 'best way' of reading ever exist, one that is appropriate to all these literatures (and should we be looking for it)? In addition, readings of postcolonial literatures sometimes are resourced by concepts taken from many other critical practices, such as poststructuralism, feminism, Marxism, psychoanalysis and linguistics. Such variety creates both discord and conflict within the field, to the extent that there seems no one critical procedure that we might identify as typically 'postcolonial'.

Due to the variety and wide range of our field, it is worth considering if we can ever really talk of a 'postcolonial*ism*', with all the coherency that this term implies. Rather than using an umbrella term that lets in so much, it might be better for us to begin by questioning 'postcolonialism' as a meaningful concept and seeking better ways of accounting for its prevailing, manifold subject matter and myriad reading strategies.

These are persisting questions for postcolonial critics and writers alike, and we shall be returning to the issues they raise. But it is important that we do not become transfixed by these questions as we try to make our beginnings, to the extent that we cannot proceed at all. For better or for worse, the term 'postcolonialism' does have a history. It has entered common parlance and is frequently used by critics, teachers and writers. It is important that we understand the *variety* of what the term signifies if we want to begin to use it self-consciously and productively. The range of issues covered by the term is indeed huge, as are the kinds of readings performed in its name. By using the term 'postcolonialism' in this book when describing such various activities, I by no means want to suggest that either the diverse and culturally specific literatures, or our readings of them, can be readily homogenised. There is no one singular postcolonial*ism*. But one of the fundamental arguments of this book is that 'postcolonialism' can be articulated in different ways as an enabling concept, despite the difficulties we encounter when trying to define it. As we are about to see, 'postcolonialism' is not a word we can render precisely. But out of its very variety comes possibility, vitality, challenge. 'Postcolonialism', then, is a term we will use in this book to help us with our beginnings, a term we can begin with; but I hope by the end of reading this book you will be using it with a healthy degree of self-consciousness and suspicion.

In order to bear witness to the enabling possibilities of postcolonialism, each chapter of the book concerns a specific issue - such as 'colonial discourses', 'the nation in question', 'diaspora identities'. They are designed to introduce the major areas of enquiry within postcolonialism, as well as offer concrete examples of various kinds of relevant reading and writing practices. But it is also the intention that we read *across* the chapters too. Many of the issues which are raised in each chapter can be relevant in other related areas, and I will endeavour to signal some useful points of connection and contrast as we proceed. It is vital that we take into account the cultural specificity of writers when we read them, and consider the dynamic relationship between a writer and the culture(s) about which he or she writes. But it is also true that similar issues can and do preoccupy readers, writers and critics in different areas, and the skills we collect from each chapter will offer productive ways of approaching many texts, not just the small selection we encounter in this book.

In order to enable us to think critically about the ideas and concepts raised in *Beginning Postcolonialism*, I have at times inserted small sections under the heading 'STOP and THINK'. In these sections we review the ideas we have been exploring so far in the chapter, and pose a series of questions about them. The responses to these questions will, of course, be your own. The 'STOP and THINK' sections are designed to assist you in making your own conclusions about the ideas raised within postcolonialism – and, ultimately, the notion of postcolonialism itself. In introducing several debates within the field throughout this book, my intention is to enable you to enter *actively* into these debates. I will not be providing definitive conclusions or answers to the questions we raise (although I cannot pretend to remain neutral either). So, in order to help you begin your active participation in the field, the 'STOP and THINK' sections will identify focal points of debate for you to pursue critically; either with others with whom you may be studying postcolonialism, or in your own further reading. As regards this latter activity, each chapter concludes with a selected reading list which points you in the direction of some of the key texts that concern each chapter, as well as other texts in which the particular issues we are exploring have received more prolonged, sophisticated attention.

A note on terminology

In Chapter 1 we will define the terms 'colonialism' and 'postcolonialism' in some detail. But before we begin, we need to make some provisional decisions about the *form* of words such as 'postcolonial' and 'postcolonialism'. As we will see, these terms have attracted much debate among scholars who often use them in contrary and confusing ways, and this makes it difficult to fix the meaning of these terms. Indeed, critics often cannot even agree how to spell 'post-colonialism': with a hyphen (as in 'post-colonialism') or without?

So, let us be clear from the start: throughout *Beginning Postcolonialism* we will *not* use the hyphen but spell the term as a single word: 'postcolonialism'. There is a particular reason for this choice of spelling and it concerns the *different meanings* of 'post-colonial' and 'postcolonial'. The hyphenated term 'post-colonial' seems more appropriate to denote a particular *historical period* or *epoch*, like those suggested by phrases such as 'after colonialism', 'after independence' or 'after the end of Empire'. However, for much of this book we will be thinking about postcolonialism not just in terms of strict historical periodisation, but as referring to disparate forms of *representations*, *reading practices* and *values*. These can circulate *across* the barrier between colonial rule and national independence. Postcolonialism is not contained by the tidy categories of historical periods or dates, although it remains firmly bound up with historical experiences.

To keep confusion to a minimum as we begin, let us use the phrases 'once-colonised countries' or 'countries with a history of colonialism' (rather than 'post-colonial countries') when dealing in strictly *historical* terms with those nations which were previously part of the British Empire. When quoting from other critics we must, of course, preserve their own habits of spelling 'postcolonial'. But, for the duration of *Beginning Postcolonialism*, 'postcolonial' and 'postcolonialism' will be used when talking about historically situated forms of representation, reading practices and values which range across both the *past* and *present*. How and why this is the case will be the subject of the first chapter.

1

From 'Commonwealth' to 'postcolonial'

Introduction

The purpose of this chapter is to approach a flexible but solid definition of the word 'postcolonialism'. In order to think about the range and variety of the term, we need to place it in two contexts. The first regards the historical experiences of decolonisation that have occurred chiefly in the twentieth century. The second concerns relevant intellectual developments in the latter part of the twentieth century, especially the shift from the study of 'Commonwealth literature' to 'postcolonialism'. After looking at each, we will be in a position at the end of this chapter to make some statements about how we might define 'postcolonialism'.

Colonialism and decolonisation

At the turn of the twentieth century, the British Empire covered a vast area of the earth that included parts of Africa, Asia, Australasia, Canada, the Caribbean and Ireland. At the turn of the twenty-first century, there remains a small number of British colonies. The phrase 'the British Empire' is most commonly used these days in the past tense, signifying a historical period and set of relationships which are no longer current. In short, the twentieth century has been the century of colonial demise, and of decolonisation for millions of people who were once subject to the authority of the British crown.

Yet, at the start of the twenty-first century Britain remains a colonial power, with several possessions in (for example) the Caribbean and the South Atlantic. In addition, the material and imaginative legacies of both colonialism and decolonisation remain fundamentally important constitutive elements in a variety of contemporary domains, such as anthropology, economics, art, global politics, international capitalism, the mass-media and – as we shall be exploring in this book – literature.

Colonialism has taken many different forms and has engendered diverse effects around the world, but we must be as precise as we can when defining its meaning. This can be gauged by thinking first about its relationship with two other terms: 'capitalism' and 'imperialism'. Let us take each in turn. As Denis Judd argues in his book *Empire: The British Imperial Experience from 1765 to the Present* (HarperCollins, 1996), '[n]o one can doubt that the desire for profitable trade, plunder and enrichment was the primary force that led to the establishment of the imperial structure' (p. 3). Judd argues that colonialism was first and foremost part of the commercial venture of the Western nations that developed from the late seventeenth and early eighteenth centuries (although others date its origins to the European 'voyages of discovery' in the fifteenth and sixteenth centuries, such as those of Christopher Columbus). The seizing of 'foreign' lands for government and settlement was in part motivated by the desire to create and control markets abroad for Western goods, as well as securing the natural resources and labour-power of different lands and peoples at the lowest possible cost. Colonialism was a lucrative commercial operation, bringing wealth and riches to Western nations through the economic exploitation of others. It was pursued for economic profit, reward and riches. Hence, colonialism and capitalism share a mutually supportive relationship with each other.

'Colonialism' is sometimes used interchangeably with 'imperialism', but in truth the terms mean different things. As Peter Childs and Patrick Williams argue, imperialism is an ideological concept which upholds the legitimacy of the economic and military control of one nation by another. Colonialism, however, is only *one form of practice* which results from the ideology of imperialism, and specifically concerns the *settlement* of one group of people in a new location. Imperialism is not strictly concerned with the issue of settlement; it does not demand the settlement of different places in order to work. Childs and Williams define imperialism as 'the extension and expansion of trade and commerce under the protection of political, legal, and military controls' (*An Introduction to Post-Colonial Theory*, Harvester Wheatsheaf, 1997, p. 227). Note how imperialism does *not* require the settling of communities from the imperial nation in another location. In these terms, colonialism is one historically specific experience of how imperialism can work through the act of settlement, but it is not the only way of pursuing imperialist ideals. Hence, it could be argued that while *colonialism* is virtually over today, *imperialism* continues apace as Western nations such as America are still engaged in imperial acts, securing wealth and power through the continuing economic exploitation of other nations. Thus, as Benita Parry puts it, colonialism is 'a specific, and the most spectacular, mode of imperialism's many and mutable states, one which preceded the rule of international finance capitalism and whose formal ending imperialism has survived' ('Problems in Current Theories of Colonial Discourse', *Oxford Literary Review*, 9 (1–2), 1987, p. 34).

To recap: colonialism is a particular historical manifestation of imperialism, specific to certain places and times. Similarly, we can regard the British Empire as one form of an imperial economic and political structure. Thus, we can endorse Elleke Boehmer's judicious definition of colonialism in her book *Colonial and Postcolonial Literature* (Oxford University Press, 1995) as the 'settlement of territory, the exploitation or development of resources, and the attempt to govern the indigenous inhabitants of occupied lands' (p. 2). Note in this definition (a) the emphasis on the *settlement* of land, (b) the *economic* relationship at the heart of colonialism, and (c) *the unequal relations of power* which colonialism constructs.

Boehmer's phrase 'the attempt to govern' hints at the ways in which British colonialism was not always fully successful in securing its aims, and met with acts of resistance from the outset by indigenous inhabitants of colonised lands, as well as members of the European communities who had settled overseas and no longer wished to defer power and authority to the imperial 'motherland'. As regards the imperial venture of the British Empire, there are three distinct periods of *decolonisation* when the colonised nations won the right to govern their own affairs. The first was the loss of the American colonies and declaration of American independence in the late eighteenth century. The second period spans the end of the nineteenth century to the first decade of the twentieth century, and concerns the creation of the 'dominions'. This was the term used to describe the nations of Canada, Australia, New Zealand and South Africa. These nations (today referred to as 'settler' nations) consisted of large European populations that had settled overseas, often violently displacing or destroying the indigenous peoples of these lands – Native Indians in Canada, Aboriginal communities in Australia and New Zealand, black African peoples in South Africa. The 'settler' peoples of these nations agitated for forms of self-government which they achieved as dominions of the British Empire. Yet, as a 'dominion' each still recognised and pledged allegiance to the ultimate authority of Britain as the 'mother country'. Canada was the first to achieve a form of political autonomy in 1867; Australia followed suit in 1900, New Zealand similarly in 1907, and South Africa in 1909. Slightly after this period, Ireland won self-rule in 1922, although the country was partitioned and six counties in the North East remained under British control. In 1931 the Statute of Westminster removed the obligation for the dominions to defer ultimate authority to the British crown and gave them full governmental control.

The third period of decolonisation occurred in the decades immediately following the end of the Second World War. Unlike the self-governing settler dominions, the colonised lands in South Asia, Africa and the Caribbean did not become sites of mass European migration, and tended to feature larger dispossessed populations settled by small British colonial elites. The achievement of independence in these locations occurred mainly after the Second World War, often as a consequence of indigenous anti-colonial nationalism and military struggle. India and Pakistan gained independence in 1947, Ceylon (now Sri Lanka) in 1948. In 1957 Ghana became the first 'majority-rule' independent African country, followed by Nigeria in 1960. In 1962, Jamaica and Trinidad and Tobago in the Caribbean followed suit. The decades of the 1960s and 1970s saw busy decolonisation throughout the declining Empire. So, with the passing of Hong Kong from Britain to China on 1 July 1997, the numbers of those living overseas under British rule fell below one million for the first time in centuries – a far cry from the days when British colonialism subjected millions around the globe.

There were, of course, as many reasons for decolonisation as there were once-colonised nations. One fundamental reason was due in many ways to the growth of various nationalist movements in both the 'settler' and 'settled' colonies which mounted resistance to British colonial authority. In addition, particularly after the Second World War, Britain's status as a world economic power rapidly declined, while America and the Soviet Union became the military superpowers of the post-war era. The British Empire was becoming increasingly expensive to administer, and it made economic sense to hand over the costly administration of colonial affairs to its people, whether or not the colonised peoples were prepared (economically or otherwise) for the shift of power.

The emergence of 'Commonwealth literature'

Let us move from this very brief history of colonialism and decolonisation to the intellectual contexts of postcolonialism. In particular, we need to look at two areas of intellectual study that have come to influence its emergence: 'Commonwealth literature' and 'theories of colonial discourses'. This will equip us with a useful historical understanding of how postcolonialism has developed in recent years, while indicating its particular, if wide-ranging, scope. Of course, I do not wish to imply that the narrative which follows is a full account or representative of all the work that has occurred in the field; far from it. But in pointing to a few key developments we can begin to understand the intellectual scope and focus of postcolonialism as it is understood today.

One important antecedent for postcolonialism was the growth of the study of Commonwealth literature. 'Commonwealth literature' was a term literary critics began to use from the 1950s to describe literatures in English emerging from a selection of countries with a history of colonialism. It incorporated the study of writers from the predominantly European settler communities, as well as writers belonging to those countries which were in the process of gaining independence from British rule, such as those from the African, Caribbean and South Asian nations. Literary critics began to distinguish a fast-growing body of literature written in English which included work by such figures as R. K. Narayan (India), George Lamming (Barbados), Katherine Mansfield (New Zealand) and Chinua Achebe (Nigeria). The creation of the category of 'Commonwealth literature' as a special area of study was an attempt to identify and locate this vigorous literary activity, and to consider via a comparative approach the common concerns and attributes that these manifold literary voices might have. Significantly, neither American nor Irish literature were included in early formulations of the field. 'Commonwealth literature', then, was associated exclusively with *selected* countries with a history of colonialism.

The term 'Commonwealth literature' is important in the associations it beckons, and these associations have historical roots. One consequence of the decline of the British Empire in the twentieth century was the establishment of – to use its original title – the British Commonwealth of Nations. At first, this term was used to refer collectively to the special status of the dominions within the Empire and their continuing allegiance to Britain. However, as the relationship between Britain and the dominions changed in the first half of the century (with the term 'dominions' being gradually dropped) a different meaning of 'Commonwealth' emerged. In the early decades, Britain hosted frequent 'colonial conferences' which gathered together the Governors of the colonies and heads of the dominions. In 1907 these meetings were re-named 'imperial conferences' in recognition of the fact that the dominions were no longer strictly British colonies. After the Second World War, these meetings became 'Commonwealth conferences' and featured the Heads of State of the newly independent nations. The British monarch was recognised as the head of the Commonwealth *in symbolic terms only*; the British crown held no political authority over other Commonwealth nations, and the word 'British' was abandoned altogether. Thus, 'Commonwealth' became redefined after the war in more equitable terms, as meaning an association of sovereign nations without deference to a single authority. Today, the Commonwealth of Nations as a body exists in name only. It has no constitution nor any legal authority, and its membership – although based on the old map of Empire – is not compulsory for the independent nations (Ireland and Burma elected to leave the Commonwealth in 1948).

This shift from 'colonial' to 'Commonwealth' perhaps suggests a particular version of history in which the status of the colonised countries happily changes from subservience to equality. But we must avoid subscribing to this selective view, not least because the economic and political relations between Britain and the Common-wealth nations have remained far from equal. The identification and study of 'Commonwealth literature' certainly echoed the tenor of the specifically benign usage of 'Commonwealth', but it also had its own problems. In general the term suggested a shared, valuable lit-erary inheritance between disparate and variable nations. It dis-tinctly promoted unity in diversity – revealingly, the plural term 'Commonwealth *literatures*' was rarely used. However, that common inheritance arguably served to reinforce the primacy of Britain among the Commonwealth nations. As A. Norman Jeffares declared in 1964, addressing the first conference of Commonwealth literature at the University of Leeds in England, 'one reads [Commonwealth writers] because they bring new ideas, new interpretations of life to us' (*Commonwealth Literature: Unity and Diversity in a Common Culture*, ed. John Press, Heinemann, 1965, p. xiv). It is not clear whether the 'us' in this sentence referred to the diverse audience at the conference comprising writers and academics from many Com-monwealth nations, or specifically British (or, more widely, Western) readers in particular. 'Commonwealth literature' may well have been created in an attempt to bring together writings from around the world on an equal footing, yet the assumption remained that these texts were addressed primarily to a Western English-speaking read-ership. The 'Commonwealth' in 'Commonwealth literature' was never fully free from the older, more imperious connotations of the term.

One of the fundamental assumptions held by the first Western critics of Commonwealth literature concerned the relationship between literature and the nation. In the introduction to a collection of essays *The Commonwealth Pen: An Introduction to the Literature of the British Commonwealth* (Cornell, 1961), the editor A. L. McLeod (no relation!) proposed that '[t]he genesis of a local literature in the Commonwealth countries has almost always been contemporaneous with the development of a truly nationalist sentiment: the larger British colonies such as Fiji, Hong Kong and Malta, where there are relatively large English-speaking populations, have produced no literature, even in the broadest sense of the term. The reason probably lies in the fact that they have, as yet, no sense of national identity, no cause to follow, no common goal' (p. 8). Many agreed that the 'novel' ideas and new 'interpretations of life' in Commonwealth literature owed much to the ways that writers were forging their own sense of national and cultural identity. This was certainly one of the functions of the texts regarded as 'Commonwealth literature', and we shall be examining closely the relationship between literature and nationalist representations in Chapters 3 and 4.

However, the attention to the alleged nationalist purposes of much Commonwealth literature often played second fiddle to more abstract concerns which distracted attention away from specific national contexts. Many critics were primarily preoccupied with identifying a common goal shared among writers from many different nations that went beyond more 'local' affairs. Just as the idea of a Commonwealth of nations suggested a diverse community with a common set of concerns, Commonwealth literature – whether produced in India, Australia or the Caribbean – was assumed to reach across national borders and deal with universal concerns. Commonwealth literature certainly dealt with national and cultural issues, but the best writing possessed the mysterious power to transcend them too.

Witness the editorial to the first edition of the *Journal of Commonwealth Literature* published in September 1965. The editorial saw the need to recognise the important cultural differences between writers from divergent locations. But it also revealed the ways in which literature from Commonwealth countries was unified through the category of 'Commonwealth literature':

> The name of the journal is simply a piece of convenient shorthand, which should on no account be construed as a perverse underwriting of any concept of a single, culturally homogeneous body of writings to be thought of as 'Commonwealth Literature'. ... Clearly, all writing ... takes its place within the body of English literature, and becomes subject to the *criteria of excellence by which literary works in English are judged*, but the *pressures* that act upon a Canadian writing in English differ significantly from those operating upon an Indian using a language not his mother tongue, just as both kinds differ from those that

affect an Englishman. (*Journal of Commonwealth Literature*, 1 (1), 1965, p. v – my emphasis)

Such 'pressures' were presumably the historical and cultural influences of each writer that differed across time and space. How, then, could one account for the *common* wealth of these writings? As the editorial claims, because the texts studied as Commonwealth literature were written ostensibly in English, they were to be evaluated *in relation to* English literature, with the same criteria used to account for the literary value of the age-old English 'classics'. Commonwealth literature at its best was comparable with the English literary canon which functioned as the means of measuring its value. It was able to transcend its regional affiliations and produce work of *permanent* and *universal* relevance. As A. Norman Jeffares put it, a Commonwealth writer of value 'wants ultimately to be judged not because he [*sic*] gives us a picture of life in a particular place, in a particular situation, but by the universal, lasting quality of his writings, judged by neither local nor yet national standards. Good writing is something which transcends borders, whether local or national, whether of the mind or of the spirit' (*Commonwealth Literature*, p. vxiii).

Commonwealth literature, then, was really a sub-set of canonical English literature, evaluated in terms derived from the conventional study of English that stressed the values of timelessness and universality. For example, consider the following moment from William Walsh's book *Commonwealth Literature* (Oxford University Press, 1973), when Walsh is discussing a novel by George Lamming. Lamming is from Barbados in the Caribbean and has African ancestry. This is what Walsh made of Lamming's novel *Season of Adventure* (1960):

> In this novel the African theme and connection become stronger and more positive, although it is never allowed to puff into a merely abstract existence. Indeed, Lamming's achievement is to make us hear the scream of the humiliated and persecuted and to make it simultaneously a metaphor for the damage *universal in mankind*. (p. 53 – my emphasis)

Walsh identifies 'African' elements in the novel that bear witness to the context of Lamming's position as a writer. But Africa is only a 'theme' and not allowed to be the *primary* focus of the work, which is the novel's attention to the 'damage universal in mankind'. Later in his book Walsh reads the Australian Patrick White's novel *Voss* (1957) in similar terms, as 'a powerful and humane work coloured with the light and soaked with the sweat and personality of Australia' (p. 134). So, for critics like Walsh, Commonwealth literature dealt fundamentally with the same preoccupations with the human condition as did Jane Austen or George Eliot. National differences were certainly important, adding the novelty of 'personality', 'light' and 'colour'; but ultimately these 'national' specifics were secondary to the fundamental universal meaning of the work.

Today this kind of critical approach that makes secondary the historical contexts that inform a work of literature is often described as 'liberal humanist' (for a discussion of this term, see Peter Barry, *Beginning Theory*, Manchester University Press, 1995, pp. 11–38). For liberal humanists the most 'literary' texts always transcend the provincial contexts of their initial production and deal with moral preoccupations relevant to people of all times and places. In retrospect, many critics of Commonwealth literature appear very much like liberal humanists. Unlike later critics, they did not always think how the texts they read so enthusiastically might resist their reading practices and challenge the assumptions of universality and timelessness that legitimated the criteria of 'good writing'. Indeed, one of the fundamental differences that many postcolonial critics today have from their Commonwealth predecessors is their insistence that historical, geographical and cultural specifics are *vital* to both the writing and the reading of a text, and cannot be so easily bracketed as secondary colouring or background. But for many critics of Commonwealth literature, these texts conformed to a critical *status quo*. They were not considered especially radical or oppositional; nor were they seen to challenge the Western criteria of excellence used to read them. Their experimental elements, their novelty and local focus made them exciting to read and helped depict the nation with which they were concerned. But their potential differences were contained by the identification within them of universal themes that bound texts safely inside the aesthetic criteria of the West. For postcolonial critics the *different* preoccupations and contexts of texts were to become more important than their alleged *similar* abstract qualities.

However, it would be a travesty to condemn or dismiss the work of a previous generation of critics of Commonwealth literature, on the grounds that it does not fit the current critical climate. True, critics like Jeffares and Walsh belong to an earlier phase of literary criticism that was soon to be radically challenged in the latter decades of the century. But they and others were instrumental in securing Commonwealth literature as an important category of artistic endeavour and as a viable area of academic study. In isolating the liberal assumptions of these critics' reading practices it can be too easily forgotten that the attention they gave to Commonwealth literature, and the space they cleared for it on university English courses in the West, constituted a fundamentally important political act. Such critics assisted in ensuring that these literatures were not a minor area of curiosity but a major field that merited serious attention on the same terms as the 'classics' of English literature. What might today look like a liberal humanist enterprise was at the time also an important political investment in these new literatures as significant, despite the limitations we have considered. The patient, detailed and enthusiastic readings of Commonwealth literature laid the foundations for the various postcolonial criticisms that were to follow, and to which much postcolonial critical activity remains indebted.

As Shirley Chew has explained, 'a paradox sits at the heart of the Commonwealth: described as a free association of equal and mutually cooperating nations, it is nevertheless drawn together by a shared history of colonial exploitation, dependence and interchange' ('The Commonwealth: Pedestal or Pyre?', *New Statesman and Society*, 21 July 1995, p. 32). If the study of Commonwealth literature was pursued in the philanthropic spirit of the first side of this paradox, the critical activity of postcolonialism was to concentrate more on the other, darker side of exploitation and dependence. In the late 1970s and 1980s many critics endeavoured to discard the liberal humanist bias perceived in critics of Commonwealth literature, and to read the literature in new ways. In order to understand how and why this happened we need to look briefly at the second chief antecedent to postcolonialism: theories of 'colonial discourses'.

Theories of colonial discourses: Frantz Fanon and Edward Said

Theories of colonial discourses have been hugely influential in the development of postcolonialism. In general, they explore the ways that *representations* and *modes of perception* are used as fundamental weapons of colonial power to keep colonised peoples subservient to colonial rule. Colonial discourses have been rigorously explored in recent years by critics working with developments in critical theory, and we shall be looking more closely at these ideas in Chapter 2.

A good introduction to the issues involved in the identification and study of colonial discourses can be made by considering the following statement by the Trinidadian writer Sam Selvon. At the beginning of his 1979 lecture, 'Three Into One Can't Go – East Indian, Trinidadian, West Indian', Selvon recalls an Indian fisherman who used to visit his street in San Fernando, Trinidad, when he was a child. The fisherman, Sammy, was partly paralysed and was often a figure of ridicule by the children. One day Sammy brought a white assistant on his round with him, apparently an escaped convict. Selvon records his utter fury at Sammy for employing the white man as an assistant. This, it seemed to the young Selvon, was not the way life was organised: the white man should be the master, not Sammy. Selvon admits he felt sympathy and dismay for the white assistant, feelings he never had for the lame Sammy. He uses this anecdote to exemplify how as a child he had learned always to regard non-Westerners as inferior: the idea of a white assistant to the Indian Sammy was an affront to his sense of order. This example of the *internalising* of certain expectations about human relationships speaks volumes about how colonialism operates, as Selvon notes:

> When one talks of colonial indoctrination, it is usually about oppression or subjugation, or waving little Union Jacks on Empire Day and singing 'God Save the King'. But this gut feeling I had as a child, that the Indian was just a piece of cane trash while the white man was to be honoured and respected – where had it come from? I don't consciously remember being brainwashed to hold this view either at home or at school. (In *Foreday Morning: Selected Prose*, Longman, 1989, p. 211)

Where indeed? Much work has been done in recent years that could provide an answer to Selvon's question. Many writers have striven to demonstrate how colonialism suggests certain ways of seeing, specific modes of understanding the world and one's place in it that assist in justifying the subservience of colonised peoples to the (oft-assumed) 'superior', civilised order of the British colonisers. These ways of seeing are at the root of the study of colonial discourses.

Colonialism is perpetuated in part by justifying to those in the colonising nation the idea that it is right and proper to rule over other peoples, and by getting colonised people to accept their lower ranking in the colonial order of things – a process we can call 'colonising the mind'. It operates by persuading people to internalise its logic and speak its language; to perpetuate the values and assumptions of the colonisers as regards the ways they perceive and represent the world. Theories of colonial discourses call attention to the role language plays in getting people to succumb to a particular way of seeing that results in the kind of situation Selvon describes. Although the term is often used in the singular, it is more accurate to talk of colonial *discourses* rather than 'colonial discourse' due to its multifarious varieties and operations which differ in time and space. We shall use the plural term throughout this book to keep this fact firmly in mind.

Colonial discourses form the intersections where language and power meet. Language, let us remember, is more than simply a means of communication; it constitutes our world-view by cutting up and ordering reality into meaningful units. The meanings we attach to things tell us which values we consider are important, and how we learn or choose to differentiate between superior or inferior qualities. Listen to Kenyan novelist Ngugi wa Thiong'o on this point:

> Language carries culture, and culture carries, particularly through orature and literature, the entire body of values by which we come to perceive ourselves and our place in the world. How people perceive themselves affects how they look at their culture, at their politics and at the social production of wealth, at their entire relationship to nature and to other human beings. Language is thus inseparable from ourselves as a community of human beings with a specific form and character, a specific history, a specific relationship to the world.

> (*Decolonising the Mind: The Politics of Language in African Literature*,
> James Currey, 1986, p. 16)

As Ngugi stresses, language does not just passively reflect reality; it also goes a long way towards creating a person's understanding of their world, and it houses the values by which we (either willingly or through force) live our lives. Under colonialism, a colonised people are made subservient to ways of regarding the world which reflect and support colonialist values. A particular value–system is taught as the best, truest world-view. The cultural values of the colonised peoples are deemed as lacking in value, or even as being 'uncivilised', from which they must be rescued. To be blunt, the British Empire did not rule by military and physical force alone. It endured by getting *both colonising and colonised people* to see their world and themselves in a particular way, internalising the language of Empire as representing the natural, true order of life. Selvon's anecdote reveals just how far-reaching the invidious effects of inter-nalising colonial assumptions about the 'inferiority' of certain peoples can be.

If the internalisation of colonial sets of values was to a degree, as Selvon's example shows, an effective way of disempowering people, it was also the source of trauma for colonised peoples who were taught to look negatively upon their people, their culture and them-selves. In the 1950s there emerged much important work that attempted to record the psychological damage suffered by colonised peoples who internalised these colonial discourses. Prominent was the psychologist Frantz Fanon, who wrote widely and passionately about the damage French colonialism had wreaked upon millions of people who suffered its power. Fanon is an important figure in the field of postcolonialism and we shall be meeting his work again later in this book. He was born in the French Antilles in 1925 and edu-cated in Martinique and France. His experience of racism while being educated by and working for the French affected him deeply; in Algeria in 1954 he resigned his post as head of the Psychiatric Department in Blida-Joinville Hospital and joined with the Alger-ian rebels fighting against the French occupation of the country. Influenced by contemporary philosophers and poets such as Jean-Paul Sartre and Aimé Césaire, Fanon's publications include two polemical books – *Black Skin, White Masks* (trans. Charles Lam

Markmann, Pluto [1952] 1986) and *The Wretched of the Earth* (trans. Constance Farrington, Penguin [1961] 1967) – that deal angrily with the mechanics of colonialism and its effects on those it ensnared. *Black Skin, White Masks* examined in the main the psychological effects of colonialism, drawing upon Fanon's experience as a psychoanalyst. In a narrative both inspiring and distressing, Fanon looked at the cost to the individual who lives in a world where due to the colour of his or her skin, he or she is rendered peculiar, an object of derision, an aberration. In the chapter 'The Fact of Blackness' he remembers how he felt when in France white strangers pointed out his blackness, his difference with derogatory phrases such as 'dirty nigger!' or 'look, a Negro!':

> On that day, completely dislocated, unable to be abroad with the other, the white man, who unmercifully imprisoned me, I took myself far off from my own presence, far indeed, and made myself an object. What else could it be for me but an amputation, an excision, a haemorrhage that spattered my whole body with black blood? But I did not want this revision, this thematisation. All I wanted was to be a man among other men. I wanted to come lithe and young into a world that was ours and to help to build it together. (*Black Skin, White Masks*, pp. 112–13)

In this scenario, Fanon's identity is defined in negative terms by those in a position of power. He is forced to see himself not as a human *subject*, with his own wants and needs as indicated at the end of the quotation, but an *object*, a peculiarity at the mercy of a group that identifies him as inferior, less than fully-human, placed at the mercy of their definitions and representations. The violence of this 'revision' of his identity is conveyed powerfully in the image of amputation. Fanon feels abbreviated, violated, imprisoned by a way of seeing him that denies him the right to define his own identity as a subject. Identity is something that the French *make for him*, and in so doing they commit a violence that splits his very sense of self. The power of description, of naming, is not to be underestimated. The relationship between language and power is far-reaching and fundamental.

Black Skin, White Masks explains the consequences of identity formation for the colonised subject who is forced into the internalisation of the self as an 'other'. The 'Negro' is deemed to epitomise everything that the colonising French are not. The colonisers are civilised, rational, intelligent: the 'Negro' remains 'other' to all these qualities against which colonising peoples derive their sense of superiority and normality. *Black Skin, White Masks* depicts those colonised by French imperialism doomed to hold a traumatic belief in their own inferiority. One response to such trauma is to strive to escape it by embracing the 'civilised' ideals of the French 'motherland'. But however hard the colonised try to accept the education, values and language of France – to don the white mask of civilisation that will cover up the 'uncivilised' nature indexed by their black skins – they are never accepted on equal terms. 'The white world', writes Fanon, 'the only honourable one, barred me from all participation. A man was expected to behave like a man. I was expected to behave like a black man' (*Black Skin, White Masks*, p. 114). That imaginative distinction that differentiates between 'man' (self) with 'black man' (other) is an important, devastating part of the armoury of colonial domination, one that imprisons the mind as securely as chains imprison the body. For Fanon, the end of colonialism meant not just political and economic change, but psychological change too. Colonialism is destroyed only once this way of thinking about identity is successfully challenged.

In 1978 Edward W. Said's *Orientalism* was published. *Orientalism* is considered to be one of the most influential books of the late twentieth century. Said also looked at the divisive relationship between the coloniser and the colonised, but from a different angle. He, like Fanon, explored the extent to which colonialism created a way of seeing the world, an order of things that was to be learned as true and proper; but Said paid attention more to the colonisers than the colonised. *Orientalism* draws upon developments in Marxist theories of power, especially the political philosophy of the Italian intellectual Antonio Gramsci and France's Michel Foucault. We will be looking in detail at *Orientalism* in Chapter 2, and how it helps us read texts. Briefly, Said examined how the knowledge that the Western imperial powers formed about their colonies helped continually to justify their subjugation. Western nations like France and Britain, he argued, spent an immense amount of time producing knowledge about the locations they dominated. Looking in particular at representations of Egypt and the Middle East in a variety of

written materials, Said pointed out that rarely did Western travellers in these regions ever try to learn much about, or from, the
native peoples they encountered. Instead, they recorded their
observations based upon commonly-held *assumptions* about 'the
Orient' as a mythic place of exoticism, moral laxity, sexual degeneracy and so forth. These observations (which were not really observations at all) were presented as scientific truths that, in their turn,
functioned to justify the very propriety of colonial domination.
Thus colonialism continuously perpetuated itself. Colonial power
was buttressed by the production of knowledge about colonised cultures which endlessly produced a degenerate image of the Orient for
those in the West, or Occident.

This is a cursory summary of Said's work, and we will flesh it out
in the next chapter. But at this stage we need to note that the work of
Fanon and Said inspired a new generation of literary critics in the
1980s keen to apply their ideas to the reading of literary texts. What
critics learned from the work of people like Fanon and Said was the
simultaneously candid and complex fact that Empires colonise imag-
inations. Fanon shows how this works at a psychological level for the
oppressed, while Said demonstrates the legitimation of Empire for
the oppressor. Overturning colonialism, then, is not just about hand-
ing land back to its dispossessed peoples, returning power to those
who were once ruled by Empire. It is also a process of overturning
the dominant ways of seeing the world, and representing reality in
ways which do *not* replicate colonialist values. If colonialism involves
colonising the mind, then resistance to it requires, in Ngugi's phrase,
'decolonising the mind'. This is very much an issue of language. The
Anglo–Indian novelist Salman Rushdie puts it this way: 'The language, like so much else in the colonies, needs to be decolonised, to
be remade in other images, if those of us who use it from positions
outside Anglo–Saxon culture are to be more than artistic Uncle
Toms' (*The Times* 3 July 1982, p. 8).

So, freedom from colonialism comes not just from the signing of
declarations of independence and the lowering and raising of flags.
There must also be a change in the minds, a challenge to the dominant ways of seeing. This is a challenge to those from both the
colonised and *colonising* nations. People from all parts of the Empire
need to refuse the dominant languages of power that have divided

them into master and slave, the ruler and the ruled, if progressive and lasting change is to be achieved. As Fanon wrote, '[a] man who has a language consequently possesses the world expressed and implied by that language' (*Black Skin, White Masks*, p. 18). The ability to read and write *otherwise*, to rethink our understanding of the order of things, contributes to the possibility of change. Indeed, in order to challenge the colonial order of things, some of us may need to re-examine our received assumptions of what we have been taught as 'natural' or 'true'.

The turn to 'theory' in the 1980s

It would be grossly reductive to assert that Edward Said is the instigator of postcolonialism, not least because this would ignore the important anti-colonial critiques prior to 1978 of Fanon, Ngugi and others who we will be meeting later in this book. However, it is perhaps reasonable to suggest that, institutionally, the success of *Orientalism* did much to encourage new kinds of study. Sensitised by the work of Said and others to the operations of colonial discourses, a new generation of critics turned to more 'theoretical' materials in their work. This was probably the beginning of postcolonialism as we understand it today and marked a major departure from the earlier, humanist approaches which characterised criticism of Commonwealth literature. Emerging in the 1980s were dynamic, excitingly new forms of textual analysis notable for their eclecticism and interdisciplinarity, combining the insights of feminism, philosophy, psychology, politics, anthropology and literary theory in provocative and energetic ways.

Three forms of textual analysis in particular became popular in the wake of *Orientalism*. One involved *re-reading canonical English literature* in order to examine if past texts perpetuated or questioned the latent assumptions of colonial discourses. This form of textual analysis proceeded along two avenues. In one direction, critics looked at writers who dealt manifestly with colonial themes and argued about whether their work was supportive or critical of colonial discourses. One example is Joseph Conrad's novel about colonialism in Africa, *Heart of Darkness* (1899). Critics debated whether Conrad's novel perpetuated colonialist views of the alleged inferiority of other peoples, or if it questioned the entire colonial project, dissenting from colonial discourses. In another direction, texts that seemingly had little to do with colonialism, such as Jane Austen's *Mansfield Park* (1814) or Charlotte Brontë's *Jane Eyre* (1847), were also re-read provocatively in terms of colonial discourses, as we shall explore more fully in Chapter 5.

Second, a group of critics who worked in the main with the post-structuralist thought of Jacques Derrida, Michel Foucault and Jacques Lacan began to enquire in particular into *the representation of colonised subjects* in a variety of colonial texts, not just literary ones. If, as Said claimed, the West produced knowledge about other peoples in order to prove the 'truth' of their 'inferiority', was it possible to read these texts *against the grain* and discover in them moments when the colonised subject *resisted* being represented with recourse to colonial values? This issue was pursued in different ways during the 1980s by two of the leading and most controversial postcolonial theorists, Homi K. Bhabha and Gayatri Chakravorty Spivak, as well as the *Subaltern Studies* scholars based in India. In his work on 'mimicry', Bhabha explored the possibility of reading colonialist discourses as endlessly ambivalent, split and unstable, never able to install securely the colonial values they seemed to support. In her influential essays 'Subaltern Studies: Deconstructing Historiography' (in *In Other Worlds: Essays in Cultural Politics*, Routledge, 1988) and 'Can the Subaltern Speak?' (in Patrick Williams and Laura Chrisman (eds), *Colonial Discourse and Post-Colonial Theory*, Harvester Wheatsheaf, 1993), Spivak explored the problem of whether or not it was possible to recover the voices of those who had been made subjects of colonial representations, particularly women, and read them as potentially disruptive and subversive. Since the 1980s, Said, Bhabha and Spivak have opened a wide variety of theoretical issues central to postcolonialism and we shall be exploring their ideas on several occasions in this book. They have also, for better or worse, emerged (in Robert Young's unfortunate phrase) as the 'Holy Trinity' of critics working in the field (*Colonial Desire*, Routledge, 1995, p. 163) and their predominance can sometimes be at the expense of other equally important voices.

The Empire 'writes back'

The third form of literary analysis engendered by the turn to theory brought together some of the insights gained by theories of colonial discourses with readings of the new literatures from countries with a history of colonialism. Using the work of Fanon and Said, and later Bhabha and Spivak, it became popular to argue that these texts were primarily concerned with *writing back to the centre*, actively engaged in a process of questioning and travestying colonial discourses in their work. The nomenclature of 'Commonwealth' was dropped in preference for 'postcolonial' in describing these writers and their work, as if to signal a new generation of critics' repudiation of older attitudes in preference of the newer, more interdisciplinary approaches. The imperious overtones of 'Commonwealth literature' made this term fall increasingly out of favour from the 1980s. In stark contrast to liberal humanist readings by critics of Commonwealth literature, the (newly re-christened) 'postcolonial literatures' were at a stroke regarded as politically radical and locally situated, rather than universally relevant. They were deemed to pose direct challenges to the colonial centre from the colonised margins, negotiating new ways of seeing that both contested the dominant mode and gave voice and expression to colonised and once-colonised peoples. Postcolonial literatures were actively engaged in the act of decolonising the mind.

This approach was crystallised in an important book that appeared at the end of the decade titled *The Empire Writes Back: Theory and Practice in Post-Colonial Literatures* (Routledge, 1989), co-authored by three critics from Australia: Bill Ashcroft, Gareth Griffiths and Helen Tiffin. Inspired by Rushdie's argument concerning the need to decolonise the English language, *The Empire Writes Back* orchestrated the issues we have been exploring into a coherent critical practice. It epitomised the increasingly popular view that literature from the once-colonised countries was fundamentally concerned with challenging the language of colonial power, unlearning its worldview, and producing new modes of representation. Its authors looked at the fortunes of the English language in countries with a history of colonialism, noting how writers were expressing their own sense of identity by refashioning English in order to enable it to accommodate their experiences. English was being displaced by 'different linguistic communities in the post-colonial world' (p. 8) who were remaking it as an attempt to challenge the colonial value-system it enshrined, and bear witness to these communities' sense of cultural difference. In a tone often more prescriptive than descriptive, they expressed the belief that the 'crucial function of language as a medium of power demands that post-colonial writing define itself by seizing the language of the centre and replacing it in a discourse fully adapted to the colonised place' (p. 38).

This refashioning worked in several ways. Ashcroft, Griffiths and Tiffin claimed that writers were creating new 'englishes' (the lack of a capital 'E' is deliberate) through various strategies: inserting untranslatable words into their texts; by glossing seemingly obscure terms; by refusing to follow standard English syntax and using structures derived from other languages; of incorporating many different creolised versions of English into their texts. Each of these strategies was demonstrated operating in a variety of postcolonial texts, and in each the emphasis was on the writer's attempt to subvert and refashion standard English into various new forms of 'english', as a way of jettisoning the colonialist values which standard English housed.

The Empire Writes Back asserted that postcolonial writing was always written out of 'the abrogation [i.e. discontinuing] of the received English which speaks from the centre, and the act of appropriation [i.e. seizure] which brings it under the influence of a vernacular tongue, the complex of speech habits which characterise the local language' (p. 39). The new 'english' of the colonised place was ultimately, irredeemably different from the language at the colonial centre, separated by an unbridgeable gap: 'This absence, or gap, is not negative but positive in its effect. It presents the difference through which an identity (created or recovered) can be expressed' (p. 62). The new 'englishes' could not be converted into standard English because they have surpassed its limits, broken its rules. As a consequence of this irredeemable difference, new values, identities and value-systems were expressed, and old colonial values wholeheartedly rejected.

Widely influential in discussions of postcolonial literature in university classrooms in the early 1990s, *The Empire Writes Back* made a valuable contribution to literary studies in the field. It shifted the approach to literatures from the once-colonised nations away from the abstract issue of a text's universal and timeless value and towards a more politicised approach which analysed texts primarily within historical and geographical contexts. For Ashcroft, Griffiths and Tiffin, postcolonial writing challenged generally-held values rather than confirmed them. Their 'local' concerns were fundamental to their meanings, not of secondary importance.

However, several criticisms have been made of this important book, the chief one being that it is remarkably totalising in its representation of how literatures from many different areas function according to the same agenda. Throughout *Beginning Postcolonialism* we will pause to consider the problems with postcolonialism as a term, and in Chapter 8 we will review some of the chief complaints made about the term. But it is useful to flag at this early stage some of the potential problems with postcolonialism which we can hold in our minds throughout this book. Three criticisms of *The Empire Writes Back* are useful to list here because they can serve as warnings to some of the problems within postcolonialism as a whole. It is important that we remain on our guard against some of the dangers with the term:

1. *Gender differences*. *The Empire Writes Back* neglects gender differences between writers. How does gender impact on these issues? As Anne McClintock argues in her essay 'The Angel of Progress: Pitfalls of the Term "Post-Colonialism"' (in *Colonial Discourse/Postcolonial Theory*, ed. Barker, Hulme and Iversen, Manchester University Press, 1994, pp. 253–66), and as we shall explore in Chapter 6, 'women and men do not live "postcoloniality" in the same way' (p. 261). This must affect a writer's relationship to language. Ashcroft, Griffiths and Tiffin offer us little way of accounting for gender differences in their theory of the uses of language in postcolonial texts. Exactly the same can be said for class differences. Important social facts of a writer's identity are passed over by the authors in an attempt to isolate an identifiable, common mode of postcolonial writing.

2. *National differences*. Similarly, there is little attempt to differentiate within or between writings from divergent nations. Did colonialism happen in the same manner in divergent locations?

Can we assume that the writing from countries with such different historical and cultural relationships with the 'centre' functions in the same way? What status would we give to writings of Maori peoples in New Zealand or First Nations peoples of the American sub-continent, who might view white settler communities more as neo-colonial than postcolonial?

3. *Is 'writing back' really so prevalent?* Some critics have voiced their concern with the assumption that *all* writing from once-colonised locations is writing against colonial discourses. Arun P. Mukherjee makes the important point in an essay called 'Whose Post-Colonialism and Whose Postmodernism?' that this assumption 'leaves us only one modality, one discursive position. We are forever forced to interrogate European discourses, of only one particular kind, the ones that degrade and deny our humanity. I would like to respond that our cultural productions are created in response to our own needs ...' (*World Literature Written in English*, 30 (2), 1990, p. 6). The issues surrounding colonialism and postcolonialism may be only *one* part of a wider set of concerns – albeit a fundamentally important part – that preoccupy those writers often regarded as 'postcolonial' due to their cultural or national position. It is vitally important to be clear at the beginning of our readings that we do not assume that all writing from countries with a history of colonialism is primarily concerned with colonial history, colonial discourses and 'decolonising the mind'.

Thus, for all its good intentions, *The Empire Writes Back* ultimately created as many problems as it solved. As Vijay Mishra and Bob Hodge argue convincingly in their essay 'What is Post(-)colonialism?' (in *Colonial Discourse and Post-Colonial Theory*, ed. Patrick Williams and Laura Chrisman, Harvester, 1993, pp. 276–90), Ashcroft, Griffiths and Tiffin collapse together a diverse and plural body of literatures from many places, neglecting to think carefully about the *differences* between the literatures they examine. The book creates a 'grand theory of post-colonialism' that ignores the historical and cultural differences between writers; thus, 'particularities are homogenised ... into a more or less unproblematic theory of the Other' (p. 278). Diversity and variety are ultimately denied. So, we should be alert to the fact that theories of postcolonialism might not be so remote from the homogenising and generalising tendencies often asserted today as the central weakness of the field of 'Commonwealth literature'.

Postcolonialism at the millennium

In the 1990s, postcolonialism has become increasingly busy and academically fashionable. In a literary context, a peculiar splitting of the field has been in danger of occurring between critical work which explores postcolonial theory, and textual criticism of postcolonial literatures. We saw above how in *The Empire Writes Back*, Ashcroft, Griffiths and Tiffin attempted, albeit problematically, to bring theoretical insights to bear on readings of postcolonial texts. However, in recent years the 'Holy Trinity' of Said, Spivak and Bhabha has become the focus for much commentary and debate in postcolonialism, not least because several aspects of the work of Spivak and Bhabha can seem pretty impenetrable at first sight. Collectively, this has helped create 'postcolonial theory' almost as a separate discipline in its own right, sometimes at the expense of criticism of postcolonial literature. (For a more detailed version of this argument, see Bart Moore-Gilbert, *Postcolonial Theory: Contexts, Practices, Politics*, Verso, 1997.)

The most useful surveys of postcolonial theory, not least because they go beyond the Said-Spivak-Bhabha triad, tend to be collections of essays rather than critical texts. *Colonial Discourse and Post-Colonial Theory*, edited by Patrick Williams and Laura Chrisman (Harvester, 1993) features extracts from the work of the 'Holy Trinity' as well as many other important voices. By including some excellent introductory sections, the editors give a full and wide-ranging sense of the variety and excitement of postcolonial theory. There is a sense of this too in *The Post-Colonial Studies Reader*, edited by Ashcroft, Griffiths and Tiffin (Routledge, 1995), although the editors choose to give short extracts from longer pieces and little commentary, making this book seem rather threadbare. Another collection, *Colonial Discourse/Postcolonial Theory*, edited by Francis Barker, Peter Hulme and Margaret Iversen includes several essays which question many of the key assumptions of postcolonial theory, although the complexity of the criticism it includes makes it a text to be

approached once you have made your beginnings in postcolonialism. We shall be referring to material in each of these useful collections throughout *Beginning Postcolonialism*.

As for prolonged critiques of Said, Bhabha and Spivak, the two
most useful are Robert Young's *White Mythologies: Writing History
and the West* (Routledge, 1990) and Bart Moore-Gilbert's *Postcolonial Theory*, mentioned above. Robert Young offers useful explana-
tions of the work of the 'Holy Trinity' and situates their work
within a wider exploration of poststructuralist approaches to history. Bart Moore-Gilbert's book gives perhaps the fullest and rich-
est work to date on postcolonial theory, and usefully situates it in
relation both to 'Commonwealth literature' and the work of other
postcolonial writers (although Said, Spivak and Bhabha remain his
primary subject-matter). Moore-Gilbert's prolonged attention to
the nuances of postcolonial theory is highly impressive and
extremely useful, although once again this means his is not really an
introductory text.

There are specifically introductory guides to postcolonial theory,
but they often struggle to deal adequately with postcolonial literatures; a surprising fact, perhaps, when one considers that their
authors tend to work primarily in literary studies. Peter Childs and
Patrick Williams's *An Introduction to Post-Colonial Theory* (Harvester Wheatsheaf, 1997) is certainly the most stimulating in that it
deals with much more than Said, Spivak and Bhabha, and in clear
and helpful terms, although once again the 'Holy Trinity' remains
paramount. Ania Loomba's *Colonialism/Postcolonialism* (Routledge,
1998) is detailed yet rather too often concerned with colonial rather
than postcolonial representations. Leela Gandhi's *Postcolonial
Theory: A Critical Introduction* (Edinburgh, 1998) is less successful,
rendering the work of postcolonial theorists in an often synoptic and
disorganised fashion; but at least she devotes a chapter to the problems and possibilities of reading postcolonial literatures with
recourse to theoretical developments. But too few texts which deal
with postcolonial theory pay this kind of attention to literature.
Hence, postcolonialism can appear from one perspective as inward-
looking and theoretically preoccupied with the privileged work of
Said, Spivak and Bhabha. In its less sophisticated versions, narratives of postcolonial theory can sensitise readers to the Derridean

influences in Spivak's work or Bhabha's use of Lacanian psycho-analysis, but not much else.

Readings of postcolonial literatures in terms of new theoretical insights might not always be found in fashionable discussions of postcolonial theory, but they certainly *do* exist. It is fair to say that the many critics who do produce such readings have remained wary of producing the kind of wide-ranging and homogenising works of criticism that characterised critical texts on Commonwealth literature. Instead, more recent critical activity has attended more closely to the cultural and historical specifics of literature from particular locations in the light of important theoretical developments. Some randomly chosen examples would include Michael Chapman's *Southern African Literatures* (Longman, 1996) and Ato Quayson's *Strategic Transformations in Nigerian Writing* (James Currey, 1997). This kind of attention to the specifics of location is, as we have seen, vital to postcolonialism.

But there is also the risk that a more *comparative* approach to postcolonial literatures is lost, as well as a sense of how intellectual and artistic activity in one part of the world has been influential in others. However, several good comparative texts do exist. The best example is Edward Said's *Culture and Imperialism* (Vintage, 1993), which we will be looking at in Chapter 5. Two further books also attempt a wide-ranging and comparative approach in a strictly literary context. Elleke Boehmer's *Colonial and Postcolonial Literature* surveys a wealth of writing in a variety of locations both before and after colonialism. Boehmer skilfully identifies the salient literary themes and preconceptions that have crossed both time and space, without sacrificing an awareness of local and historical contexts. However, although she creates a sophisticated and critical comparative account of the variety of postcolonial literatures, some of the theoretical questions concerning *how* we read them do not always inflect Boehmer's authoritative scholarship. Dennis Walder also attempts to bring the two together in his *Post-Colonial Literatures in English* (Blackwell, 1998), which looks in particular at 'Indo-Anglian fiction', Caribbean and Black British Poetry, and recent South African literature. His attention to these 'case studies' exemplifies the necessity and rewards of reading texts closely in context, although he cannot always offer the range of Boehmer's study.

'Postcolonialism': definitions and dangers

Having looked at the historical and intellectual contexts for post-colonialism, we are now in a position to make some definitions.

First and foremost, we need to be very precise in how we understand the relationship between 'colonialism' and 'postcolonialism'. As theories of colonial discourses argue, colonialism fundamentally affects modes of *representation*. Language carries with it a set of assumptions about the 'proper order of things' that is taught as 'truth' or 'reality'. It is by no means safe to assume that colonialism conveniently stops when a colony formally achieves its independence. The hoisting of a newly independent colony's flag might promise a crucial moment when governmental power shifts to those in the newly independent nation, yet it is crucial to realise that colonial values do not simply evaporate on the first day of independence. As Stuart Hall argues in his essay 'When Was "the Post-Colonial"?: Thinking at the Limit' (in *The Post-Colonial Question: Common Skies, Divided Horizons*, ed. Iain Chambers and Lidia Curti, Routledge, 1996, pp. 242–60), life after independence in many ways 'is characterised by the persistence of many of the effects of colonisation' (p. 248). Colonialism's *representations, reading practices* and *values* are not so easily dislodged. Is it possible to speak about a 'postcolonial' era if colonialism's various assumptions, opinions and knowledges remain unchallenged?

Postcolonialism, as we have seen, in part involves the *challenge* to colonial ways of knowing, 'writing back' in opposition to such views. But colonial ways of knowing still circulate and have agency in the present; unfortunately, they have not magically disappeared as the Empire has declined. Thus, one of Carole Boyce Davies's reservations about 'postcolonialism' is the impression it may give that colonial relationships no longer exist. In her book *Black Women, Writing and Identity* (Routledge, 1994) she argues that we must remember the 'numerous peoples that are still existing in a colonial relationship' around the world, as well as those 'people within certain nations who have been colonised with the former/colonies (Native Americans, African-Americans, South Africans, Palestinians, Aboriginal Australians)' (p. 83). This comment raises the issue of *internal colonialism* which persists in many once-colonised countries; for such peoples, colonial oppression is far from over. This is why we should beware using 'postcolonialism' strictly as marking a historical moment or period, as I argued in the Introduction, and reserve it for talking about aesthetic practices.

So, the term 'postcolonialism' is *not* the same as 'after colonialism', as if colonial values are no longer to be reckoned with. It does *not* define a radically new historical era, nor does it herald a brave new world where all the ills of the colonial past have been cured. Rather, 'postcolonialism' recognises both historical *continuity* and *change*. On the one hand, it acknowledges that the material realities and modes of representation common to colonialism are still very much with us today, even if the political map of the world has changed through decolonisation. But on the other hand, it asserts the promise, the possibility, and the continuing necessity of change, while also recognising that important challenges and changes have already been achieved.

So, with this firmly in our minds, we can proceed to make some decisions about what is gathered under our umbrella-term 'postcolonialism'. Keeping in mind the disquiet with the range that the term often covers, we can identify at least three salient areas that fall within its remit. Very basically, and in a literary context, postcolonialism involves one or more of the following:

- Reading texts produced by writers from countries with a history of colonialism, primarily those texts concerned with the workings and legacy of colonialism in either the past or the present.
- Reading texts produced by those that have migrated from countries with a history of colonialism, or those descended from migrant families, which deal in the main with diaspora experience and its many consequences.
- In the light of theories of colonial discourses, re-reading texts produced during colonialism; both those that directly address the experiences of Empire, and those that seem not to.

A central term in each is 'reading'. The act of reading in postcolonial contexts is by no means a neutral activity. *How* we read is just as important as *what* we read. As we shall see throughout this book, the ideas we encounter within postcolonialism and the issues they raise demand that conventional reading methods and models of interpretation need to be rethought if our reading practices are to contribute to the contestation of colonial discourses to which post-colonialism aspires. Rethinking conventional modes of reading is fundamental to postcolonialism.

Of course, making distinctions like the ones above always involves a certain degree of generalisation. It would be impossible, as well as wrong, to unify these three areas into a single coherent 'postcolonialism' with a common manifesto. Single-sentence definitions are impossible and unwise. In addition, we must be aware that each area *is itself* diverse and heterogeneous. For example, colonial discourses can function in particular ways for different peoples at different times. We should not presume consensus and totality where there is instead heterogeneity. A sense of the variable nature of the field will be reinforced, I hope, as you read through this book.

One last word of warning. Postcolonialism may well *aim* to oppose colonial representation and values, but whether it *fulfils* these aims remains a hotly debated issue in the field. Postcolonialism may bring new possibilities, but, as we shall see, it is not free from problems of its own. So, in beginning postcolonialism, it is important that we maintain an element of suspicion too.

Selected reading on 'what is postcolonialism?'

Ahmad, Aijaz, 'The Politics of Literary Postcoloniality' in Padmini Mongia (ed.), *Contemporary Postcolonial Theory: A Reader* (Edward Arnold, 1996), pp. 274–93.

An essay highly critical of the ways in which postcolonialism has been enthusiastically discoursed upon in literary studies.

Ashcroft, Bill, Gareth Griffiths and Helen Tiffin, *The Empire Writes Back: Theory and Practice in Post-Colonial Literatures* (Routledge, 1989).

A ground-breaking work of criticism, still influential today, although many of its arguments have been questioned by several critics (see the essay by Mishra and Hodge cited below).

Ashcroft, Bill, Gareth Griffiths and Helen Tiffin, *Key Concepts in Post-Colonial Studies* (Routledge, 1998).

A very productive reference guide which includes useful definitions of many of the key terms in the field, as well as suggestions for further reading.

Boehmer, Elleke, *Colonial and Postcolonial Literature* (Oxford University Press, 1995).

An informative and wide-ranging comparative account of the literary activity in countries with a history of colonialism, which begins with some very useful definitions.

Childs, Peter and Patrick Williams, *An Introduction to Post-Colonial Theory* (Harvester Wheatsheaf, 1997).

The introduction, 'Points of Departure', offers an excellent and highly recommended account of the different ways of thinking about postcolonialism which emerge from debates within literary theory.

Hall, Stuart, 'When Was "the Post-Colonial"?: Thinking at the Limit' in Iain Chambers and Lidia Curti (eds), *The Post-Colonial Question: Common Skies, Divided Horizons* (Routledge, 1996), pp. 242–60.

This is a complex but highly useful discussion of 'the postcolonial', and an excellent place to start your deliberations concerning the usefulness of this and related terms. But work through it slowly.

Loomba, Ania, *Colonialism/Postcolonialism* (Routledge, 1998).

The first section of this book, 'Situating Colonial and Postcolonial Studies', explores usefully some of the origins of postcolonialism in post-war developments in Western literary and cultural theory.

Mishra Vijay, and Bob Hodge, 'What is Post(-)colonialism?' in Patrick Williams and Laura Chrisman (eds), *Colonial Discourse and Post-Colonial Theory* (Harvester Wheatsheaf, 1993), pp. 276–90.

An excellent critique of *The Empire Writes Back* which also raises several of the problems and possibilities of postcolonialism.

Moore-Gilbert, Bart, *Postcolonial Theory: Contexts, Practices, Politics* (Verso, 1997).

The opening chapter, 'Postcolonial Criticism or Postcolonial Theory?', has an excellent and detailed account of the shift from 'Commonwealth literature' to 'postcolonialism' in literary studies.

Tiffin, Chris and Alan Lawson (eds), *De-Scribing Empire: Post-Colonialism and Textuality* (Routledge, 1994).

The introduction, 'The Textuality of Empire', offers several illuminating points concerning the supportive relationship between colonialism and forms of representation, and their significance to postcolonialism.

Walder, Dennis, *Post-Colonial Literatures in English* (Blackwell, 1998).

The first half of this book offers a clear and illuminating discussion of postcolonialism in relation to history, language and theory. Very readable.

Walsh, William, *Commonwealth Literature* (Oxford University Press, 1973).
   A typical example of the older, 'liberal humanist' criticism of Commonwealth literature which surveys the field region by region.

Reading colonial discourses

Reading and politics

In Chapter 1 we touched briefly upon some of the issues raised by the study of 'colonial discourses'. Colonialism was certainly dependent upon the use of force and physical coercion, but it could not occur without the existence of a set of beliefs that are held to justify the possession and continuing occupation of other peoples' lands. These beliefs are encoded into the language which the colonisers speak and to which the colonised peoples are subjected. This results in the circulation of a variety of popularly held assumptions about the relative differences between peoples of allegedly dissimilar cultures. As Chris Tiffin and Alan Lawson explain, 'Colonialism (like its counterpart, racism), then, is an operation of discourse, and as an operation of discourse it interpellates colonial subjects by incorporating them in a system of representation' (*De-Scribing Empire*, Routledge, 1994, p. 3). Their use of the term 'interpellates' is derived from Louis Althusser's work on the important role of interpellation in the functioning of ideology. Very basically, 'interpellation' means 'calling'; the idea is that ideology calls us, and we turn and recognise who we are. In the previous chapter we looked at Fanon's memory of being called a 'dirty nigger' while in France, and the damaging effect this had on his sense of identity. This is a vivid example of interpellation in action. Fanon is *called* by others, and this makes him suddenly consider himself in terms of the racist ideology which informs how others see him. Ideology assigns him a role and an identity which he is made to recognise as his own. Or, to put it another way, the ideology of racism is calling to him through the mouths of the white French who tell him who he is.

Although this example highlights the *pain* of being represented by other people, interpellation also works through *pleasure*: by inviting individuals to regard themselves in flattering ways. Some would argue that it is easier to make a person act according to your wishes by making them feel valuable or special, rather than bereft or contemptuous, as this fulfills an individual's sense of worth and makes them happy with the identity that has been written for them. Indeed, we might consider that colonial discourses have been successful because they make the colonisers feel important, valuable and superior to others; as well as gaining the complicity of the colonised by enabling them to derive a new sense of self-worth through their participation in the furthering the 'progress' of 'civilisation' (represented, of course, squarely in Western terms). So, the central point to grasp from the outset is that theories of colonial discourses are predicated upon the important mutually supportive relationship between the *material practices* of colonialism and the *representations* it fashions in order for it to work.

Reading literature in the context of colonial discourses serves several purposes. First, this reading approach, sometimes called 'colonial discourse analysis', refuses the humanist assumption that literary texts exist above and beyond their historical contexts. It situates texts in history by exposing how historical contexts influence the production of meaning within literary texts, and how literary representations themselves have the power to influence their historical moment. Second, and more specifically, criticism of colonial discourses dares to point out the extent to which the (presumed) 'very best' of Western high culture – be it opera, art, literature, classical music – is caught up in the sordid history of colonial exploitation and dispossession. Third, the attention to the machinery of colonial discourses in the *past* can act as a means of resisting the continuation in the *present* of colonial representations which survive after formal colonisation has come to an end: a situation often referred to as 'neo-colonialism'. In understanding how colonial discourses have functioned historically we are in a better position to refuse their prevailing assumptions and participate in the vital process of 'decolonising the mind'. So at the local level of literary study, our reading practices can constitute a political act. Reading practices are never politically neutral; how we wish to read a text will always tell us something about the values we hold, or oppose.

In this chapter we will look first at Edward W. Said's influential book *Orientalism* (Penguin, 1978). Although Said was not the first writer interested in colonial discourses, as evidenced by our brief glance at Fanon's work in the previous chapter, his definition of Orientalism has been important in instigating postcolonial studies today, and it remains highly influential. Next, we shall survey some of the important criticisms of his work in order to gain a sense of how the study of colonial discourses has developed. The chapter concludes with an example of writing from the colonial period that directly addresses colonial life, as we consider Rudyard Kipling's poem 'The Overland Mail' in the light of the reading strategies we have explored.

Reading *Orientalism*

Although our doorway into colonial discourses is through Said's definition of Orientalism, let us be quite clear at the outset that Orientalism and colonial discourses do *not* amount to the same thing. They are not interchangeable terms. As I shall explain, colonial discourses are more complex and variable than Said's model of Orientalism; they encapsulate Orientalism, to be sure, but go beyond it.

Said's *Orientalism* is a study of how the Western colonial powers of Britain and France represented North African and Middle Eastern lands in the late nineteenth and early twentieth centuries, although Said draws upon other historical moments too. 'The Orient' is the collective noun Said uses to refer to these places (although it is also sometimes used by others when discussing Far Eastern lands). 'Orientalism' refers to the sum of the *West's* representations of the Orient. In the book's later chapters, Said looks at how Orientalism still survives today in Western media reports of Eastern, especially Arab, lands, despite formal decolonisation for many countries. This reinforces the point made previously that the machinery of colonialism does not simply disappear as soon as the colonies become independent. Indeed, Said shows how the modes of representation common to colonialism have continued after decolonisation and are still very much a part of the contemporary world.

One of *Orientalism*'s many commendable qualities is its readability. Although a lengthy academic work that draws upon some complex scholarship, particularly the political theories of Antonio Gramsci and Michel Foucault, Said's written style is accessible and noted for its clarity and lucidity. None the less, it raises many challenging ideas and issues, and you may well profit by looking closely in the first instance at an extract or two, rather than initially attempting the book in its entirety. Several editions of collected essays concerning postcolonialism include useful excerpts that can be used to experience the tenor and substance of *Orientalism* – such as *The Post-Colonial Studies Reader* (eds Ashcroft, Griffiths and Tiffin, pp. 87–91) and *Colonial Discourse and Post-Colonial Theory* (eds Williams and Chrisman, pp. 132–49). Alternatively, the introductory chapter to *Orientalism* (pp. 1–28) contains many of the points Said elaborates in his book, and is worth getting to grips with before proceeding to the body of the text.

Let us look at a brief outline of Said's definition of Orientalism that should help us begin. To support your study, choose one of these three extracts suggested above and spend time working through the ideas it contains in the light of my outline, allowing your understanding of Orientalism to build gradually to a suitable and productive level of sophistication. I have divided the outline into two sections: the first highlights the general *shape* of Orientalism and its manifold manifestations as defined by Said, while the second looks in a little more detail at the *stereotypical* assumptions about cultural difference that it constructs. The salient points are summarised under a series of sub-headings.

The shape of Orientalism

1. *Orientalism constructs binary divisions*. Fundamental to the view of the world asserted by Orientalism is the binary division it makes between the Orient and the Occident (the West). Each is assumed to exist in opposition to the other: the Orient is conceived as being everything that the West is *not*, its 'alter ego'.

However, this is not an opposition of equal partners. The Orient is frequently described in a series of *negative* terms that serve to buttress a sense of the West's superiority and strength. If the West is assumed as the seat of knowledge and learning, then it will follow that the Orient is the place of ignorance and naiveté. Thus in Orientalism, East and West are positioned through the construction of an *unequal* dichotomy. The West occupies a superior rank while the Orient is its 'other', in a subservient position. This makes the relations between them asymmetrical.

Orientalism reveals by proxy more about *those that describe the Orient* than the peoples and places that are being 'described'. As David Richards points out in *Masks of Difference: Cultural Representations in Literature, Anthropology and Art*, (Cambridge University Press, 1994), '[t]he representation of other cultures invariably entails the presentation of self-portraits, in that those people who are observed are overshadowed or eclipsed by the observer' (p. 289). Said stresses in the introduction to *Orientalism* that the Orient has been fundamental in defining the West 'as its contrasting image, idea, personality, experience' (*Orientalism*, p. 2). The West comes to know itself *by proclaiming via Orientalism everything it believes it is not*. Consequently, Said claims that 'European culture gained in strength and identity by setting itself off against the Orient as a sort of surrogate and even underground self' (p. 3).

2. *Orientalism is a Western fantasy*. It is important to grasp Said's argument that Western views of the Orient are not based on what is observed to exist in Oriental lands, but often result from the West's dreams, fantasies and assumptions about what this radically different, contrasting place contains. Orientalism is first and foremost a *fabricated* construct, a series of *images* that come to stand as the Orient's 'reality' for those in the West. This contrived 'reality' in no way reflects what may or may not actually be there in the Orient itself; it does not exist outside of the representations made about it by Westerners. It is not 'an inert fact of nature' (p. 4) but 'man-made' (p. 5), a creation fashioned by those who presume to rule. So, Orientalism *imposes* upon the Orient specifically Western views of its 'reality'. But crucially, its creation from the stuff of fantasy does not make it any less

remote from the world. Orientalism may be fundamentally *imaginative*, but *material effects* result from its advent.

3. *Orientalism is an institution*. The imaginative assumptions of Orientalism are often taken as hard facts. They find their way into, and make possible, a whole institutional structure where opinions, views and theses about the Orient circulate as objective knowledges, wholly reliable truths. These are some of its material effects. As Rana Kabbani argues in *Imperial Fictions: Europe's Myths of Orient* (Pandora, rev. 1994), 'the ideology of Empire was hardly ever a brute jingoism; rather, it made subtle use of reason, and recruited science and history to serve its ends' (p. 6). The Orient, writes Said, became an object 'suitable for study in the academy, for display in the museum, for reconstruction in the colonial office, for theoretical illustration in anthropological, biological, linguistic, racial and historical theses about mankind and the universe, for instances of economic and sociological theories of development, revolution, cultural personality, national religious character' (*Orientalism*, pp. 7–8). Such a dizzying, exhaustive list underlines just how far-reaching Orientalism was, the large part it played in helping those in the West formulate their knowledge of the world, and their (superior) place therein, in a variety of disciplines from anthropology to zoology.

In these terms, the Western project of Enlightenment that aimed to secure the progress of humanity through developments in scientific and other 'objective' knowledges is deemed to be tainted by the subjective fantasies of the Orient upon which Western 'rational' knowledge rests. The variety of institutions, academic or otherwise, mentioned above indicates how ingrained Orientalism was (and, arguably, still is) in the imagination and institutions of daily life in the West, and its central contribution to intellectual and daily life.

4. *Orientalism is literary*. If Orientalism suffuses a vast institutional network, it similarly influences the multitude of literary (and non-literary) writings. Said identifies 'philology [the study of the history of languages], lexicography [dictionary-making], history, biology, political and economic theory, novel-writing and lyric poetry' (p. 15) as coming to the service of Orientalism. Orientalism also made possible new forms of writing that

enshrined and often celebrated Western experience abroad, such as the heroic boys' adventure story popular during the Victorian period (see Joseph Bristow, *Empire Boys: Adventures in a Man's World*, HarperCollins, 1991). These various kinds of writing are all influenced by the structures, assumptions, and stereotypes of Orientalism, reminding us that Western culture is inextricably bound up with Western colonialism.

5. *Orientalism is legitimating.* All these points underline the important detail that Orientalism is a far-reaching system of representations bound to a structure of political domination. Orientalist representations function to justify the propriety of Western colonial rule of Eastern lands. They are an important part of the arsenal of Empire. They legitimate the domination of other peoples and lubricate the political and judicial structures which maintain colonial rule through physical coercion.

6. *There is 'latent' and 'manifest' Orientalism.* In order to emphasise the connection between the imaginative assumptions of Orientalism and its material effects, Said divides Orientalism into two. Borrowing some terms from Freud, he posits a *latent* Orientalism and a *manifest* Orientalism. Latent Orientalism describes the dreams and fantasies about the Orient that, in Said's view, remain relatively constant over time. Manifest Orientalism refers to the myriad examples of Orientalist knowledge produced at different historical junctures. Said's argument proposes that while the manifestations of Orientalism will be different, due to reasons of historical specifics and individual style or perspective, their underlying or latent premises will always be the same. For example, a Victorian travel writer and Edwardian journalist might produce texts about the Orient which on the surface appear to differ, but their assumptions about the division between East and West and the character of the Orient (and of Orientals) will, at a deeper level, be alike.

Latent Orientalism, then, is like a blueprint; manifest Orientalism is the many different versions that can built from fundamentally the same design. When a writer or painter makes an Orientalist representation, they will be drawing upon the same assumptions regardless of the differing styles or forms they may choose to adopt.

Stereotypes of the Orient

1. *The Orient is timeless*. If the West was considered the place of historical progress and scientific development, then the Orient was
   deemed remote from the influence of historical change. 'Orientalism assumed an unchanging Orient' (p. 96), it is argued. It
   was considered to be essentially no different in the twelfth century than it was in the eighteenth, trapped in antiquity far
   behind the modern developments of the 'Enlightened' West.
   Conceived in this way, the Orient was often considered as 'primitive' or 'backwards'. A Westerner travelling to Oriental lands
   was not just moving in *space* from one location to the other;
   potentially they were also travelling back in *time* to an earlier
   world. Hence in Orientalism, the Orient exists as a timeless
   place, changeless and static, cut off from the progress of Western history.

2. *The Orient is strange*. Crucial to Orientalism was the stereotype
   of the Orient's peculiarity. The Orient is not just different; it is
   oddly different – unusual, fantastic, bizarre. Westerners could
   meet all manner of spectacle there, wonders that would beggar
   belief and make them doubt their Western eyes. The Orient's
   eccentricity often functioned as a source of mirth, marvel and
   curiosity for Western writers and artists; but ultimately its radical oddness was considered evidence enough of the Orient's
   inferiority. If the Occident was rational, sensible and familiar,
   the Orient was irrational, extraordinary, abnormal.

3. *Orientalism makes assumptions about 'race'*. Oriental peoples
   often appeared in Western representations as examples of various invidious racial stereotypes. Assumptions were often made
   about the inherent 'racial' characteristics of Orientals: stock-
   figures included the murderous and violent Arab, the lazy
   Indian and the inscrutable Chinaman. The Oriental's 'race'
   somehow summed up what kind of person he or she was likely to
   be, despite their individual qualities and failings. So racialising
   categories like 'Arabian' and 'Indian' were defined within the
   general negative representational framework typical of Orientalism, and provided Orientalism with a set of generalised types
   (*all* Arabs were violent, *all* Indians were lazy). The Orient was

where those in the West would encounter races considered inferior to them – which helped, of course, to buttress the West's sense of itself as inherently superior and civil.

4. *Orientalism makes assumptions about gender.* Similarly, popular gendered stereotypes circulated, such as the effeminate Oriental male or the sexually promiscuous exotic Oriental female. The Oriental male was frequently deemed insufficiently 'manly' and displayed a luxuriousness and foppishness that made him appear a grotesque parody of the (itself stereotyped) 'gentler' female sex. The exoticised Oriental female, often depicted nude or partially–clothed in hundreds of Western works of art during the colonial period, was presented as an immodest, active creature of sexual pleasure who held the key to a myriad of mysterious erotic delights. In both examples, the Oriental is deemed as failing to live up to received gender codes: men, by Western standards, are meant to be active, courageous, strong; by the same token, women are meant to be passive, moral, chaste. But Oriental men and women do not comply with these gender roles; their gender identity is transgressive. This adds to the general sense of oddness and abnormality ascribed to the Orient.

5. *The Orient is feminine.* In addition to the gendering of individuals in Orientalism was the more general gendering of the opposition of the Occident and the Orient as one between rigidly stereotypical versions of masculinity and femininity. In Orientalism, the East as a whole is 'feminised', deemed passive, submissive, exotic, luxurious, sexually mysterious and tempting; while the West becomes 'masculine' – that is, active, dominant, heroic, rational, self-controlled and ascetic. This trope makes way for a specifically sexual vocabulary available to those from the West when describing their encounters: the Orient is 'penetrated' by the traveller whose 'passions' it rouses, it is 'possessed', 'ravished', 'embraced' ... and ultimately 'domesticated' by the muscular coloniser. According to Said, this is in part a result of the fact that Orientalism was 'an exclusively male province' (p. 207). So it responded to and buttressed the discourses of heroic, muscular masculinity common in the Western colonial nations.

It is worth considering the extent to which this vocabulary of sexual possession common to Orientalism reveals the Orient as a site of perverse *desire* on the part of many male colonisers. Projected onto the Orient are fantasies of the West concerning supposed moral degeneracy, confused and rampant sexualities. These fantasies did much to stimulate the domination of the Orient, but also its continuing fascination for many in the West. It seemed deliciously to offer Western men the opportunity to sample an untrammelled life free from the prohibitions of society back home. Travellers to the Orient might think they were going to a place where moral codes of behaviour did not function, and where they could indulge in forms of sexual excess. The fantasy of the Orient as the desirable repository of all that is constrained by Western civilisation acted as a continual stimulus for those that studied it or travelled through it. So, as we noted previously, in writing 'about' the Orient, they were actually writing about themselves, putting on the page their own desires, fantasies and fears.

6. *The Oriental is degenerate.* Compositely, Oriental stereotypes fixed typical weaknesses as (amongst others) cowardliness, laziness, untrustworthiness, fickleness, laxity, violence and lust. Oriental peoples were often considered as possessing a tenuous moral sense and the readiness to indulge themselves in the more dubious aspects of human behaviour. In other words, Orientalism posited the notion that Oriental peoples needed to be civilised and made to conform to the perceived higher moral standards upheld in the West. So, once again, in creating these stereotypes, Orientalism justified the propriety of colonialism by claiming that Oriental peoples needed saving from themselves.

Criticisms of *Orientalism*

With a sense of what is involved in Said's theory of Orientalism, let us turn next to look at the various critiques of *Orientalism* which have been voiced since its publication. In so doing, we will gain a fuller sense of how colonial discourses operate. These criticisms do not invalidate Said's ground-breaking study, but they do invite us to think more flexibly about the operations of colonial discourses.

1. Orientalism *is ahistorical*. The major criticism of *Orientalism*, from which several of the others stem, concerns its capacity to make totalising assumptions about a vast, varied expanse of representations over a very long period of history. As Dennis Porter describes it in his essay of 1983, '*Orientalism* and its Problems' (in *Colonial Discourse and Post-Colonial Theory*, ed. Williams and Chrisman, pp. 150–61), Said posits the 'unified character of Western discourse on the Orient over some two millennia, a unity derived from a common and continuing experience of fascination with and threat from the East, of its irreducible otherness' (p. 152). Said's examples of Orientalist writing range from the Italian poet Dante writing in the early fourteenth century up to twentieth-century writers. Can it be true that they *all* hold essentially the same latent assumptions? Can such a massive archive of materials be so readily homogenised? Has nothing changed? Said's view takes in a broad, generalising sweep of history but attends little to *individual* historical moments, their anomalies and specifics. As John MacKenzie points out in his book *Orientalism: History, Theory and the Arts* (Manchester University Press, 1995), Said's history of Orientalism is perhaps 'in itself essentially ahistorical' because it glosses over the variable factors that make historical moments unique, such as the 'contrasting economic and social circumstances of different territories' (p. 11).

   In these terms, we could say that Said privileges latent Orientalism over manifest Orientalism by neglecting to think whether the representations of the Orient made by those in the West at particular moments might modify or challenge the enduring assumptions of the Orient. MacKenzie argues that Western artists have approached the Orient at various moments with perfectly honourable intentions and 'genuine respect' (p. 60) for other peoples, in order to learn from and value their cultures. Not everybody looked down upon the Orient so crudely. This was no doubt true in some cases. However, in fairness to Said, MacKenzie is too trusting of the examples of 'benign' Orientalist art he reproduces and fails to grasp the point that even the most gracious and respectful artist may *unwittingly* reproduce Orientalist assumptions. If Said's work privileges the latent aspect of Orientalism, MacKenzie pays it too scant attention and forgets that the road to hell is often paved with good intentions. It does not necessarily follow that a sympathetic representation of the Orient or the Oriental will automatically be free from the latent assumptions of Orientalism.

2. *Said ignores resistance by the colonised*. This is another major criticism of *Orientalism*. If Said is to be believed, Orientalism moves in one direction from the active West to the passive East. But he rarely stops to examine how Oriental peoples *received* these representations, nor how these representations circulated in the colonies themselves. In what ways did the colonised peoples respond to Orientalist representations? Did they readily submit to the colonisers' view of themselves? How might they have *contested* Orientalism and brought it to crisis? As Patrick Williams and Laura Chrisman have argued in their introduction to *Colonial Discourse and Post-Colonial Theory*, there is little notion of the colonised subject as a *constitutive* agent (p. 16) with the capacity for political resistance. And in the words of Aijaz Ahmad, one of Said's fiercest critics, Said never thinks about how Western representations 'might have been received, accepted, modified, challenged, overthrown or reproduced by the intelligentsias of the colonised countries' (*In Theory: Classes, Nations, Literatures*, Verso, 1992, p. 172). In these terms, Said stands accused of writing out the agency and the voice of colonised peoples from history as he never stops to consider the challenges made to dominant discourses. In so doing, his work is in danger of being just as 'Orientalist' as the field he is describing by not considering alternative representations made by those subject to colonialism.

3. *Said ignores resistance within the West*. According to Said, 'every European, in what he could say about the Orient, was consequently a racist, an imperialist, and almost totally ethnocentric' (*Orientalism*, p. 204). This is certainly a sweeping statement. What about those within the West who opposed colonialism and were horrified by the treatment of colonised peoples? As Dennis Porter argues, *Orientalism* leaves no room to accommodate what he calls, adapting a term from Antonio Gramsci, 'counter-hegemonic thought' ('*Orientalism* and its Problems', p. 152); that

is, opinions contrary to the dominant views within the West which contest the authority of Orientalist representations.

4. *Said ignores gender differences.* As we noted previously, Said argues that Orientalist representations were made in the main by men. This explains why the Orient is a specifically *male* fantasy and is often represented in feminine terms. Said maintains that in Orientalist writing 'women are usually the creatures of a male power-fantasy. They express unlimited sensuality, they are more or less stupid, and above all they arc willing' (*Orientalism*, p. 207). But did Western women write about the Orient? And if they did, did they also resort to the same stereotypes? As Sara Mills has argued importantly in *Discourses of Difference: An Analysis of Women's Travel Writing and Colonialism* (Routledge, 1992), many women travelled to the colonies and made their own observations in a variety of writings, but Said rarely looks at women's writing in *Orientalism*.

However, it is not just a case of 'adding in' women's writing to Said's theory in order to fill the gaps in his more male-centred study. Mills points out that the position of women in relation to Orientalism is often different to that of men because of the tensions between the discourses of colonialism and the discourses of gender. Looking at late Victorian and early twentieth-century travel writing by Western women, Mills maintains that these women were, at one level, *empowered* by colonialism due to the superior position they perceived themselves to hold in relation to colonised peoples. Yet, not unlike colonised peoples, women were *disempowered* due to the inferior position they were placed in in relation to Western men. This might make available, if only fleetingly, a partial and problematic accord between the Western woman traveller and thc colonised peoples she encountered. Her position in relation to the colonised is not the same as the Western male. Hence, the intersection of colonial and patriarchal discourses often places Western women in a contradictory position. They occupy a dominant position due to colonialism, but a subordinate place in patriarchy. Women 'cannot be said to speak from outside colonial discourse, but their relation to [it] is problematic because of its conflict with the discourses of "femininity", which were operating on them in an equal, and sometimes stronger, measure. Because of these discursive pressures, their work

exhibits contradictory elements which may act as a critique of some
of the components of other colonial writings' (*Discourses of Difference*, p. 63). Women's writing about the colonies may not be so readily explained with recourse to Said's theory of Orientalism due to its
particular contradictions borne out of the contrary positions frequently held by women. (We will consider these issues again in
Chapter 6.)

As Sara Mills's argument above suggests, the various criticisms of
Said's work collectively give the impression that colonial discourses
are multiple, precarious and more ambivalent than Said presumes in
Orientalism. They do not function with the smoothness or the com-
plete success that he awards the totalising concept of Orientalism.
Colonial discourses were in constant confrontation with resistances
and contrary views of various kinds, in the colonies and in the West.
Colonial discourses, then, are by no means homogeneous or unitary.
Said is certainly right to identify a series of representations about the
Orient which functioned to justify and perpetuate the propriety of
colonial rule, but these representations were not monolithic, static
and uncontested.

In these terms, we can propose that Orientalism as defined by
Said describes the operations of colonial discourses *up to a point*.
The institutionalised system of asymmetrical, repetitive stereotypes
tells only part of the story of how colonial discourses function in the
world. To be fair, Said has responded positively to some of the criticism of *Orientalism*, especially the argument that he ignores insurgency, although he disagrees with certain of the charges made
against him such as the accusation that his work is ultimately ahistorical (see Said's 'Afterword' to the 1995 Penguin edition of *Orientalism*). In recent years he has looked more closely at the resistance
to Orientalism, as well as its continuing presence in the contemporary world. These are some of the major preoccupations of his more
recent book *Culture and Imperialism* (Vintage, 1993). None the less,
we should not underestimate the power which Orientalist representations clearly achieved when holding Said's theory up for questioning. Just because these representations were more volatile than Said
assumes, it does not mean that they were (and are) without substan-
tial power and influence in Westerners' views of other peoples. This,
the central premise of *Orientalism*, must not be underestimated.

'Ambivalence' and 'mimicry' in colonial discourses

Let us probe further into how colonial discourses are not always so sure of themselves as might be presumed. In '*Orientalism* and its Problems', Dennis Porter argues that even the most seemingly Orientalist text can include within itself moments when Orientalist assumptions come up against alternative views that throw their authority into question. Texts rarely embody just one view. Often they will bring into play several different ways of seeing without always deciding which is the true or most appropriate one.

An example Porter gives is T. E. Lawrence's *The Seven Pillars of Wisdom* (1922). Sure, he admits, this text might seem a fairly robust example of Orientalism. But there can be identified moments when Lawrence seems to depart from an Orientalist position and articulates *alternative* ways of thinking about the differences between East and West. Porter concludes with the important point that 'literary texts may in their play establish distance from the ideologies they seem to be reproducing' ('*Orientalism* and its Problems', p. 160). Even the most seemingly Orientalist text can articulate 'counter-hegemonic' views within itself. As Porter usefully reminds us in his use of the phrase 'in their play', literary texts are mobile and often contradictory affairs, positing several opinions rather than just one. Cross-currents of 'Orientalist' or 'counter-Orientalist' thinking can exist simultaneously within a single text.

The lack of conviction within colonial discourses is also the concern of Homi K. Bhabha. Like Said, Bhabha has become one of the leading voices in postcolonialism since the early 1980s; but unlike Said, his work is often very difficult to understand at a first reading because of his compact and complex written style. In his essay 'The Postcolonial Aura: Third World Criticism in the Age of Global Capitalism' (in *Critical Inquiry*, 20, 1994, pp. 328–56), Arif Dirlik argues that Bhabha is 'something of a master of political mystification and theoretical obfuscation' (p. 333) and attacks his incomprehensibleness. Bhabha is difficult to read, to be sure, but he is not completely incomprehensible and his ideas can be some of the most thought-provoking within postcolonialism. Whereas Said draws upon more materialist theoretical work in his thinking, Bhabha is indebted to psychoanalysis and is influenced by Sigmund Freud, the poststructuralist Jacques Lacan, and the Fanon of *Black Skin, White Masks*. The first of Bhabha's essays we refer to in this section constitutes Chapter 3 of his book *The Location of Culture* (Routledge, 1994), and is called 'The Other Question: Stereotype, Discrimination and the Discourse of Colonialism'. The second essay, 'Of Mimicry and Man: The Ambivalence of Colonial Discourse', constitutes Chapter 4 of the same book. I suggest that you approach Bhabha's essays slowly in the light of the abridged accounts we meet below, which necessarily sacrifice some of his ingeniousness and suggestiveness for the sake of clarity. The accounts I will give bear scant witness to the sophistication and theoretical innovation – as well as frustration – of his work, but it is hoped that they will prove useful guides as you begin reading Bhabha. The purpose of looking at Bhabha's work is to construct a working knowledge of his concepts of 'ambivalence' and 'mimicry' in the operations of colonial discourses.

Let's take 'ambivalence' first. Like Said, Bhabha argues that colonialism is informed by a series of assumptions which aim to legitimate its view of other lands and peoples. 'The objective of colonial discourse', writes Bhabha, 'is to construe the colonised as a population of degenerate types on the basis of racial origin, in order to justify conquest and to establish systems of administration and instruction' (*The Location of Culture*, p. 70); hence, as we have seen, the emergence of colonial stereotypes that represent colonised peoples in various derogatory ways. However, in an inspired departure from Said's concept of Orientalism, Bhabha argues that this important aim is *never fully met*. This is because the 'discourse of colonialism' (we'll have to use Bhabha's problematic singular term for the time being) does not function according to plan because it is always pulling in two *contrary* directions at once.

On the one hand, the discourse of colonialism would have it that the Oriental (or, in Bhabha's parlance, the 'colonised subject') is a radically strange creature whose bizarre and eccentric nature is the cause for both curiosity and concern. The colonised are considered the 'other' of the Westerner (or the 'colonising subject'), essentially *outside* Western culture and civilisation. Yet, on the other hand, the discourse of colonialism attempts to domesticate colonised subjects and abolish their radical 'otherness', bringing them *inside* Western understanding through the Orientalist project of constructing knowledge about them. The construction of 'otherness' is thus *split* by the contradictory positioning of the colonised simultaneously inside and outside Western knowledge. Hence, in Bhabha's terms, 'colonial discourse produces the colonised as a social reality which is at once an "other" and yet entirely knowable and visible' (pp. 70–1).

So, on the one hand, stereotypes translate the unfamiliar into coherent terms by seeming to account for the strangeness of other peoples: the Irish are inevitably stupid; the Chinese are always inscrutable; the Arabs essentially are violent. The distance between the colonisers and the colonised is *lessened*, as the colonised are brought within the boundaries of Western knowledge. But, on the other hand, colonial stereotypes also function contrariwise to *maintain* this sense of distance. The colonisers must never admit that other peoples are not really very different from themselves, as this would undercut the legitimacy of colonialism.

Probing Said's argument that Western representations of the East are based primarily on fantasies, desires and imaginings, Bhabha points out that the fantasies of the colonial stereotype often appear as horrors. The discourse of colonialism is frequently populated with '*terrifying* stereotypes of savagery, cannibalism, lust and anarchy' (p. 72 – my italics). Any attempt to subdue the radical otherness of the colonised is perpetually offset by the alarming fantasies that are projected onto them. This indicates how, in the discourse of colonialism, colonised subjects are split between contrary positions. They are domesticated, harmless, knowable; but also *at the same time* wild, harmful, mysterious. Bhabha argues that, as a consequence, in colonialist representations the colonised subject is always in motion, sliding *ambivalently* between the polarities of similarity and difference; he or she simply will not stand still. Because of this slippery motion, *stereotypes* are deployed as a means to arrest the ambivalence of the colonised subject by describing him or her in static terms. But this fixing of the colonised's subject position always fails to secure the colonised subject into place. Hence, stereotypes must be *frequently repeated* in an anxious, imperfect attempt to secure the colonised subject in the discourse of colonialism. As Bhabha argues, 'the *same old* stories of the Negro's animality, the Coolie's inscrutability or the stupidity of the Irish *must* be told (compulsively) again and afresh, and are differently gratifying and terrifying each time' (p. 77). The *repetition* of the colonial stereotype is an attempt to secure the colonised in a fixed position, but also an acknowledgement that this can never be achieved.

Thus, to sum up, Bhabha's 'discourse of colonialism' is characterised by both *ambivalence* and *anxious repetition*. In trying to do two things at once – construing the colonised as both *similar* to and the *other* of the colonisers – it ends up doing neither properly. Instead it is condemned to be at war with itself, positing radical otherness between peoples while simultaneously trying to lessen the degree of otherness. Although the aim is to fix knowledge about other peoples once and for all, this goal is always deferred. The best it can do is set in motion the anxious repetition of the colonised subject's stereotypical attributes that attempt to fix it in a stable position. But the very fact that stereotypes *must* be endlessly repeated reveals that this fixity is never achieved.

In his essay 'Of Mimicry and Man', Bhabha builds on these ideas and explores how the ambivalence of the colonised subject becomes a direct threat to the authority of the colonisers through the effects of 'mimicry'. Bhabha describes mimicry as 'one of the most elusive and effective strategies of colonial power and knowledge' (p. 85). He focuses on the fact that in colonised nations such as India, the British authorities required native peoples to work on their behalf and thus had to teach them the English language. An example is Macaulay's infamous 'Minute' (in Bill Ashcroft, Gareth Griffiths and Helen Tiffin (eds), *The Post-Colonial Studies Reader*, Routledge, 1995) on Indian education of 1835, in which Macaulay argued that the British in India needed to create a class of Indians capable of taking on English opinions, morals and intellect (we will taking a longer look at this 'Minute' in Chapter 5). These figures, comparable to Fanon's French–educated colonials depicted in *Black Skin, White Masks*, are described as 'mimic men' who learn to act English but do not look English nor are accepted as such. As Bhabha puts it, 'to be Anglicised is *emphatically* not to be English' (p. 87).

However, these mimic men are *not* the disempowered, slavish individuals required by the British in India. Bhabha argues that they are invested with the power to *menace* the colonisers because they threaten to disclose the ambivalence of the discourse of colonialism which the use of stereotypes anxiously tries to conceal. Hearing their language returning through the mouths of the colonised, the colonisers are faced with the *worrying threat of resemblance* between coloniser and colonised. This threatens to collapse the Orientalist structure of knowledge in which such oppositional distinctions are made. The ambivalent position of the colonised mimic men in rela tion to the colonisers – '*almost the same but not quite*' (p. 89) – is, in Bhabha's thinking, a source of anti-colonial resistance in that it presents an unconquerable challenge to the entire structure of the discourse of colonialism. By speaking English, the colonised have *not* succumbed to the power of the colonised. Contrariwise, they challenge the representations which attempt to fix and define them.

This is a different assertion to Said's model of Orientalism, which does not consider how colonial discourses generate the possibilities of their own critique. Previously, the notion of mimicry had been seen as a condition of the colonised's subservience and crisis, the measure of their powerlessness. We can find this view at times in Fanon's *Black Skin, White Masks*; its most famous expression is perhaps the Trinidadian V. S. Naipaul's novel *The Mimic Men* (1967). But Bhabha refuses the defeatism in Naipaul's work and offers a much more positive, active and insurgent model of mimicry. So, by revealing that the discourse of colonialism is forever embattled and split by ambivalence and mimicry, always doomed to failure in its attempt to represent the colonised, Bhabha avoids the criticisms of Said's work by attending to the ways in which colonial discourses are problematised by the very people they claim to represent.

STOP and THINK

As his critical vocabulary might suggest, Bhabha deals with the (singular) discourse of colonialism at a very abstract level. Terms like 'colonising subject', 'the colonial stereotype', even 'colonial discourse' itself are rather transcendent and absolute. As Nicholas Thomas argues, Bhabha's work is weakened by its 'generalising strategy' (*Colonialism's Culture: Anthropology,*

Travel and Government, Polity, 1994, p. 43). To what extent do you think Bhabha makes an attempt to think about differences of gender or social class as complicating the discourse of colonialism? Some of the criticisms made against Said could also be applied to Bhabha, particularly those concerned with gender difference; Bhabha's 'colonising' and 'colonised' subjects are problematically gender-free.

Also, Bhabha's writing, dazzling and inspiring in many respects, is notoriously difficult partly because he wilfully writes at an abstruse, highly theoretical level – often it is hard see the intellectual wood for the linguistic trees. This is not accidental: Bhabha has chosen to present his ideas in a certain manner. What is your attitude to Bhabha's style? What might he hope to achieve in writing in such a compact and challenging way? (You might want to compare his style to Said's, and consider what kinds of readership each figure might be aiming to engage with.)

For better or worse, Bhabha's work on the 'discourse of colonialism' contributes much in its attention to ambivalence, not least because he shows how colonial discourses make possible the conditions of their own critique. So if he is right, even the most fiercely argued Orientalist tract will never be able fully to secure the colonised as essentially 'other'. This view avoids some of the pitfalls of Said's notion of Orientalism, especially the charge that Said offers no ways of accounting for resistance to it.

However, if colonial discourses are endlessly split, anxiously repetitive and menaced by mimicry, as Bhabha would have it, we might want to ask: how could colonialism survive for as long as it did?

Taking the criticisms of *Orientalism* made by Bhabha and others into account, we are now in a position to recap the key elements of colonial discourses that can be used as part of our reading practices. We have seen how colonial discourses are characterised *in part* by their attempts to construct and perpetuate a sense of difference between the Western colonisers and their colonised subjects. But this attempt rarely happens smoothly. According to Bhabha, its functioning is buckled by its internal contradictions that make it a profoundly ambivalent affair. And as Porter and Mills point out, rarely does it occur without meeting opposition or encountering different, contrary ways of seeing the relationship between the colonisers and the colonised. These different ways of seeing can appear within seemingly Orientalist writings.

Colonial discourses and Rudyard Kipling: reading 'The Overland Mail'

Let us turn to a literary example in order to put into practice some of the ideas we have gathered. In this concluding section we will look at a poem by Rudyard Kipling called 'The Overland Mail'. The poem is reproduced in the Appendix, and you should read it a couple of times before continuing.

Why Kipling, and why this poem in particular? Kipling was born in Bombay in 1865 and, although educated in England, spent much of his time as a young man in the country of his birth, which was also at the same time Britain's largest colony in the Empire. His life coincides with a period of time when the Empire was at its zenith in the late nineteenth and early twentieth centuries. In addition to India, he lived in and travelled among many colonial locations, such as Canada, New Zealand and South Africa. His literary works speak often of the countries he witnessed, the people he met, the colonial administrations and shipping lines that kept the wheel of Empire turning.

Kipling died in 1936. Although extremely popular in his time, his reputation today is less secure. Said quotes his work in *Orientalism* as exemplifying colonial attitudes to Oriental peoples. Whereas some have agreed with Said, others have not, and have used Kipling's work to point up some of the problems with Said's concept of Orientalism (see, for example, Bart Moore-Gilbert, *Kipling and 'Orientalism'*, Croom Helm, 1986). Kipling's work is appropriate for this chapter as it has been used both to prove and to question Said's argument.

First published in 1886 in the second edition of his collection *Departmental Ditties*, 'The Overland Mail' concerns the transportation of letters to British exiles in India who are residing in the Indian hill–stations. These were popular retreats for those who found the Indian climate intolerable during the summer months. The most popular, in Simla, often grew to three times its population when the British beat their annual retreat from the heat. Kipling's poem looks in particular at the 'foot–service to the hills', the journeys under-taken by Indian runners employed to carry mail from the railway stations to the exiles.

I have chosen to examine this poem for several reasons (not least because it is short). First, it makes interesting remarks about the Indian landscape through which the Indian runner who carries the mail must move. Second, its subject is in part the Indian runner himself, the 'colonised subject' of colonial discourses. Third, in Peter Keating's opinion, 'The Overland Mail' is not 'simply a cele-bration of the postal service: it is also one of Kipling's most unashamedly joyful endorsements of imperial endeavour, with the postal activity offered as a microcosm of the far–flung Empire' (Keating, *Kipling the Poet*, Secker and Warburg, 1994, p. 21); so it would seem ripe for reading as a manifestation of Orientalism. How-ever, using the insights of Homi Bhabha, I want to examine how even this seemingly 'joyful endorsement' of Empire is more anxious and ambivalent than Keating suggests.

Let us deal first with the descriptions of the Indian landscape. The poem begins as dusk falls. The Indian runner has received the post from the railway and will be undertaking his foot–journey to the hills at night, in darkness. In the first stanza there is created the sense that the landscape which lies ahead is not especially hospitable. It is referred to bluntly as a 'Jungle' (l. 2), and the poet warns of 'rob-bers' and 'tigers' that must 'make way' for the mail to be delivered in the 'Name of the Empress of India', Queen Victoria. India is repre-sented as containing formidable obstacles to the delivery of the mail from the homeland to the exiles in the hills, which must be overcome if the messages are safely to get through.

But once the runner's journey gets underway, even more chal-lenges appear to bar the passage of the mail. In the third stanza tor-rents of water threaten the runner's path, rainfall has the potential to destroy the roads, and the possibility of tempests is also enter-tained. Nature is represented as destructive, a malignant force, haz-ardous and unaccommodating. The higher the runner ventures, the more precarious his surroundings seem, as evidenced in the fourth stanza. From the less threatening locations that feature rose-oaks and fir trees, he journeys upwards to the more precarious rock-ridge and spur. A less menacing, arduous landscape is reached only in the last stanza, when the mail is delivered to the exiles in the hill-station. Now 'the world is awake and the clouds are aglow' (l. 28), and the sun has come out to shine on the successful runner. Everything is calm again. The disconcerting tigers and Lords of the Jungle that mysteriously 'roam' in the first stanza are, in the final one, substituted by the comparatively less sinister 'scuffle above in the monkey's abode' (l. 27). The journey has been completed successfully.

Using the observations of Said and others, there are at least three significant observations we can make about the landscape. First, it is remarkably empty. Where is everyone? Apart from the roaming Lords of the Jungle and the odd tiger turning tail, the only human characters mentioned are the Empress of India (who is present as a symbolic invocation in name only), a vague body of 'we exiles', the retreating robber, and the runner himself. This is a depopulated landscape. The only figures that appear are those significant to the British in the Indian hills and the smooth running of their postal service. In presenting this part of India as a wilderness of obstacles, an ominous, anonymous jungle, Kipling virtually empties it of any indigenous Indians. This is landscape as metaphor, not as reality.

Second, and following on from the previous point, until we reach the calm of the British in the hills the following morning, India seems wild and out of control. It appears in the main as dark, menacing, and dangerous; full of tempests and floods where even the roads are vulnerable. The association of the exiles in the hills with the break of day, and an untamed India with the dangerous night, is exactly the kind of opposition Said suggests is common to Orientalism: where there is Western civilisation there is daylight, but a sinister darkness resides otherwise.

Third, as we might expect in a poem about a foot-service to the hills, the landscape progressively rises, taking the runner up higher and higher. Reading this figuratively, we could argue that the poem's movement up through the landscape rehearses in microcosm the conquest of India by the British. In the poem, India's various wild aspects stand in the way of an easy passage; yet, on the other side of the rivers, ravines and rock-ridges we find the exiles waiting patiently for their mail. The landscape may be troublesome, but ulti- mately it has not stopped the ascent of the British up the hills. They have already defeated these imposing surroundings, have met in the past the challenges presented by the landscape and overcome them, challenges that the Indian runner rehearses every time he delivers the mail. The exiles' residence in the hills seems all the more impressive when one realises what has been successfully negotiated in order to establish it. Similarly, the geography of the poem seems to applaud the conquering British. If, like the runner, one moves 'up, up through the night' of a wild, dark undomesticated India, one comes to the civil daylight of British colonial rule. The hill station sits above the surrounding landscape like the Empress of India sits above her subjects, looking out over a landscape that may be wild, yet has been conquered and is under British command.

So, we can detect a pattern of asymmetrical oppositions under- pinning the landscape: night vs. day, wild vs. civilised, below vs. above. The first term is associated negatively with India, the second with the civilising presence of the British. These oppositions would seem to support Said's argument that Orientalism divides the world into two opposing sides, in which the colonial location comes off the worst.

Let us turn next to the characters of the poem. There are at least two important figures we can consider. The first, referred to fleet- ingly, is the 'robber' in line 5; the second is the Indian runner. Although he is mentioned just the once, the robber is not the mar- ginal figure in this poem that he seems. At an immediate level, he appears as one of the various dangers of the wild landscape of India that the runner must avoid when delivering the mail to the exiles. If we presume that the robber is also an Indian (although the poem does not explicitly state this), here, then, are the split positions com- monly available to the 'colonised subject' in colonial discourses. The colonised is either the brigandly *other* of colonialism, challenging the order of Empire by threatening to steal the mail; or he is the *obe- dient* servant of the Empire, like the runner who provides the foot- service to the hills. No other positions are recognised (hence, perhaps, the depopulated landscape).

At first glance, it might seem that the runner is represented in a sympathetic light. He lets nothing bar the delivery of his mail. He seems competent, reliable, and trustworthy. Here perhaps is a sympathetic representation of a colonised subject which, as John MacKenzie argued, Said's *Orientalism* ignores. Indeed, there is certainly a sense of camaraderie between the speaker of the poem and the Indian runner. But let us probe more closely the relationship between the speaker and his subject. The runner is given no name of his own, save that of the important baggage he delivers. He is significant only as the facilitator of the Overland Mail; he has no other purpose. Furthermore, notice how in the vocabulary of the poem the runner is made subservient to the compulsion of the exiles. In the third stanza, the speaker repeats 'must' on three occasions when describing the travail through the foreboding landscape. The runner 'must' ford the river, he 'must' climb the cliff, and he 'must bear without fail' the Overland Mail. Any fortitude on the part of the runner is seen not to be due to his own virtues, but the product of the colonial service that commands him to perform his actions. Indeed, the speaker anticipates the runner to be a rather pusillanimous creature in his statement that 'the service admits not a "but" or an "if"'' (l. 16), almost as if he is expecting the runner to complain about his task. The suggestion is, perhaps, that the true nature of the runner tends towards faint-heartedness; only his service to the Empire makes him an admirable fellow capable of performing laudable feats. Furthermore, this service is a life-sentence, as suggested by the sinister phrase: 'While the breath's in his mouth, he must bear without fail ...' (l. 17). The runner is compelled to undertake his duties, it seems, so long as he has life in his body.

In these terms, the poem enacts the disciplining power of colonialism by rehearsing the runner's subservience to the will of the exiles. This point is cemented by the poem's final line, when the runner hails the exiles with "In the Name of the Empress, the Overland Mail!" (l. 30). In declaring his arrival, the hail repeats in part the poem's opening line and thus underlines the extent to which he is perpetuating through his own mouth the exiled speaker's language by upholding the authority of the Empress of India. Read in this way, the runner has been thoroughly domesticated as the obedient servant of the Empire.

So far, in looking at the landscape and the Indian runner, we have read 'The Overland Mail' as exemplifying various Orientalist assumptions and strategies of representation. But as we remarked when holding Said's notion of Orientalism up to question, colonial discourses are often more ambivalent than resolute in their aims. Despite Keating's claims about it, we can perhaps identify certain anxieties in Kipling's poem that threaten to make its endorsement of Empire rather unsteady.

In order to make this argument, let us draw upon Bhabha's argument concerning the ambivalence of representations of colonised subjects which results from the simultaneous attempt to reduce *and* maintain their seeming otherness in relation to the colonisers. In the poem, this double movement is indexed by the contrast between the runner and the robber we glimpse in the first paragraph. As we noted, in the robber we have the colonised who exists as *other* to the West, threatening by his very occupation to disobey its rules, while the runner signifies the domesticated colonised subject. Significantly, the beginning of the poem attempts to banish the robber from the landscape by referring to him retreating into the anonymity of the 'Jungle'. Yet, we could argue that the threat of the robber is *never entirely banished*, but instead haunts the speaker's representation of the runner throughout the poem. Runner and robber threaten to merge. The messages entrusted to the colonised need not get given back to the British. The speaker anxiously recognises that the colonised have the potential for subversion – a recognition which he attempts to disavow.

The day-to-day business of the Empire commands the obedience of the Indian subjects, requiring that they become trusted runners, not untrustworthy robbers. The mail could not get delivered without them and messages would not get through. In these terms, the speaker's repeated demand that the runner 'must' ford, 'must' climb and 'must bear without fail' the Overland Mail *so long as there is breath in his very body* seems over-stated to say the least. These repetitions reveal perhaps a half-hidden anxiety that the civilised runner has the potential to slip into another, less civil, role. Paradoxically, in stating that the service 'admits not a "but" or an "if"' to be uttered by the runner, the speaker acknowledges the very possibility of disobedience that threatens the exiles' survival abroad. This acknowledgement serves, on the one hand, to justify the runner's subservience to Empire, but on the other, it makes the unsavoury recognition that the runner has the potential to subvert order. Thus, he has to be *repeatedly* told what to do and how to behave. Hence, the repetition of the speaker's commands ('must' ... 'must' ... 'must') in the third stanza is an anxious attempt to fix the obedience of the colonised subject and jettison these uncertainties – but one that unavoidably reveals the capacity for disobedience.

Note too that the runner's travails mimics the journey of the British into the hills, and his cry 'In the Name of the Empress, the Overland Mail!' (l. 30) also mimics the speaker's lines which conclude stanzas 1 and 3. There is, perhaps, something menacing in the duplication of the colonisers' journey to the hills of Simla, exposing as it does the resemblance of the Indian's endeavours with that of the British. That final cry of 'the Overland Mail!' which merges the runner's voice with the speaker's, conflicts with those aspects of the poem that attempt to separate out one from the other through the disciplinary strategies we noted above. Exactly what kind of message is the runner delivering at the end of the poem? Is he endorsing the superiority of the British or revealing the similarity between them? Does he bring a menacing moment of resemblance which is uneasily disavowed, or is he the domesticated mimic man – almost the same, *but not quite* – completely at the mercy of British authority? Note that by the final stanza, the runner's body has been almost removed from the vista of the poem. He has become a 'dot' or a 'speck', barely visible to the eye. Yet the jingle of his bells and his voice remain, perhaps to menace and mock the civility of the British in the hills who cannot receive their messages without his actions. Ultimately, *he* brings the name of the 'Empress of India' to *them*, reversing and mocking the power relations between the colonising British and the colonised runner.

So, following Bhabha, we might argue that the runner is an ambivalent figure in the poem, both praised and commanded, congratulated yet disciplined, elided yet audible. His presence is vital to the exiles' survival in the hills, but also creates anxieties because of the threat he poses to its smooth running. These anxieties emerge in the repetition of the speaker's commands which, in both acknowledging and disqualifying the runner's potential for disorder, ultimately split

the authority and confidence of the speaking voice. The threat to
authority epitomised by the robber is not as easily banished as the
poem would prefer. Read in this way, Kipling's seeming celebration
of the obedient colonised subject begins to seem begotten by anxieties
that result from the recognition and disavowal of the colonised's
capacity for *disobedience*. Although an 'Orientalist' reading of the
poem might usefully expose its deployment of latent Orientalist
views, the latter points we have considered attend to those moments
when colonial discourses malfunction and short-circuit. Resisting the
(continuing) agency of colonial discourses to define the world
requires that we expose their contradictions and shortcomings, and
show how their seemingly 'factual' pictures of the world result from
half-hidden fears and fantasies. Thus, our critical comments of 'The
Overland Mail' constitute a specifically *postcolonial* reading practice.

Selected reading

Ahmad, Aijaz, *In Theory: Classes, Nations, Literatures* (Verso, 1992).
    Chapter 5, 'Orientalism and After', is an extended critique of Said's
    thought from a staunchly Marxist position.
Bhabha, Homi K., *The Location of Culture* (Routledge, 1994).
    Chapter 3, 'The Other Question: Stereotype, Discrimination and the
    Discourse of Colonialism', is Bhabha's critique of Said's *Orientalism* and
    one of his most influential statements concerning the work of ambiva-
    lence; while Chapter 4, 'Of Mimicry and Man', theorises the subversive
    propensities of mimicry. Proceed with patience.
Childs, Peter and Patrick Williams, *An Introduction to Post-Colonial Theory*
    (Harvester Wheatsheaf, 1997).
    Features two clear and up-to-date chapters on the work of Said and
    Bhabha.
Kabbani, Rana, *Imperial Fictions: Europe's Myths of Orient* (Pandora,
    revised 1994).
    An excellent study of travel writing and painting which details the
    centrality of gender in Orientalist representations.
MacKenzie, John M., *Orientalism: History, Theory and the Arts* (Man-
    chester University Press, 1995).
    A highly sceptical critique of *Orientalism* which argues that East/West
    encounters were not always part of the unequal power-relations of

colonialism. MacKenzie illustrates his argument with a wealth of different aesthetic materials ranging from art to theatre.

Mills, Sara, *Discourses of Difference: An Analysis of Women's Travel Writing
and Colonialism* (Routledge, 1992).

Gives a useful theoretical critique of Said's *Orientalism* and offers close
analyses of women's travel writing in relation to Orientalist representations.

Moore-Gilbert, Bart, *Kipling and 'Orientalism'* (Croom Helm, 1986).

A consideration of Kipling's Indian writing which is used to problematise some of the assumptions of Said's *Orientalism*.

Moore-Gilbert, Bart, *Postcolonial Theory: Contexts, Practices, Politics*
(Verso, 1997).

Includes long, detailed and critical chapters on both Said and Bhabha
which explore their shifting affiliations with different critical theorists.
Highly recommended.

Parry, Benita, 'Problems in Current Theories of Colonial Discourse',
Oxford Literary Review, 9 (1–2), 1987, pp. 27–58.

A complex and challenging essay that appraises the work of Bhabha in
relation to Gayatri Chakravorty Spivak and others.

Porter, Dennis, '*Orientalism* and its Problems' in Patrick Williams and
Laura Chrisman (eds), *Colonial Discourse and Post-Colonial Theory*,
(Harvester Wheatsheaf, 1993), pp. 150–61.

An early but still highly influential critique of *Orientalism* which should
be 'required reading' for all those exploring Said's work.

Richards, Thomas, *The Imperial Archive: Knowledge and the Fantasy of
Empire* (Verso, 1993).

An illuminating and often challenging book which explores the theme
of gathering knowledge about the Empire and its impact on literature,
with specific reference to the work of Kipling, Bram Stoker and H. G.
Wells.

Said, Edward W., *Orientalism* (second edition) (Penguin [1978] 1995).

The second edition includes an important 'Afterword' in which Said
addresses the major criticisms of his work and discusses the relationship
between *Orientalism* and postcolonialism.

Said, Edward W., 'Orientalism Reconsidered' in *Europe and Its Others*, Vol.
1, ed. Barker, Hulme, Iversen and Loxley (University of Essex, 1985), pp.
14–27.

An early response to the academic reception of *Orientalism*.

Thomas, Nicholas, *Colonialism's Culture: Anthropology, Travel and Govern-ment* (Polity, 1994).

    Chapter 2, 'Culture and Rule: Theories of Colonial Discourse', includes a far-reaching critique of Bhabha's thinking on the grounds of its lack of attention to specific historical and geographical contexts.

Young, Robert, *White Mythologies: Writing History and the West* (Routledge, 1990).

    Although a little out of date, this useful book offers a helpful and clear critique of both Said and Bhabha in terms of their relation to Marxism and poststructuralism. Highly recommended.

Nationalist representations

Introduction

In the previous chapter we examined colonial discourses in relation to writings from the colonial period. In this and several of the following chapters we will explore many of the different strategies with which the authority of colonial discourses has been combated. This chapter and the next are concerned with representations related to anti-colonial nationalism and their impact upon political, social, cultural and literary contexts. Attitudes to nationalism in postcolonialism are wide-ranging and conflictual. As our immediate concern is to become sensitised to the problems surrounding nationalist representations when reading postcolonial literatures, we need to examine some of the different views which have emerged.

In this chapter we will approach various attitudes towards nationalist representations in literary and other writings during the busy third stage of decolonisation in the 1950s and 1960s. There were, of course, nationalist representations in previous periods, particularly in the settler colonies, such as those by the Australian writers Henry Lawson and A. B. 'Banjo' Patterson in the 1890s (see *Empire Writing: An Anthology of Colonial Literature*, 1870–1918, ed. Elleke Boehmer, Oxford World's Classics, 1998, which gathers together a variety of writing about Empire from several contrasting perspectives during the period of 'high imperialism' in the late nineteenth and early twentieth centuries). However, we will confine ourselves to post-war discussions of nationalism because several of the most salient writings on nationalism from this period in particular have been of critical significance to postcolonial theory. In the following chapter, 'The Nation in Question', we shall examine some critical perspectives of nationalist representations in the light of the mixed fortunes of many countries with a history of colonialism since achieving independence.

But first, let us think about the nation in more general, abstract terms before examining its use as a profitable idea mobilised by many struggling to free themselves from colonial authority. This will allow us to explore at the end of this chapter Ngugi wa Thiong'o's novel *A Grain of Wheat* (1967) as a postcolonial nationalist representation.

Imagining the nation: forging tradition and history

Nations are not like trees or plants: they are not a naturally occurring phenomenon. Yet the nation has become one of the most important modes of social and political organisation in the modern world and we perhaps assume that they are simply 'just there'. Most commentators agree that the idea of the nation is Western in origin. It emerged with the growth of Western capitalism and industrialisation and was a fundamental component of imperialist expansion. It is almost second nature these days to map the world as a collection of different nations, each separated from the other by a border. But borders between nations do not happen by accident. They are constructed, defended and (in too many tragic cases) bloodily contested by groups of people. It is important that we try to think about nations fundamentally as *fabrications*. As Ernest Gellner argues in his book *Nations and Nationalism* (Blackwell, 1983), '[n]ations are not inscribed into the nature of things' (p. 49). Nations, like buildings, are planned by people and built upon particular foundations – which also means that, like buildings, they can both rise and fall.

So, the nation is primarily an idea. It is customary these days to talk about the 'myth of the nation' in recognition of this. In his influential book *Imagined Communities: Reflections on the Origins and Spread of Nationalism* (Verso, 1983), Benedict Anderson defines the nation first and foremost as 'an imagined political community' (p. 6).

This is because 'the members of even the smallest nation will never know most of their fellow-members, meet them, or even hear of them, yet in the minds of each lives the image of their communion' (p. 6). Individuals *think* they are part of a greater collective, that they share a 'deep, horizontal comradeship' (p. 7) with many others. In a similar vein Timothy Brennan points out in his essay 'The National Longing for Form' (in *Nation and Narration*, ed. Homi K. Bhabha, Routledge, 1990, pp. 44–70) that the nation refers 'both to the modern nation-state and to something more ancient and nebulous – the "*natio*" – a local community, domicile, family, condition of belonging' (p. 45). So, central to the idea of the nation are notions of collectivity and belonging, a *mutual* sense of community that a group of individuals imagines it shares. These feelings of community are the emotive foundation for the organisation, administration and membership of the 'state', the political agency which enforces the social order of the nation.

It is often pointed out that a sense of mutual, national belonging is manufactured by the performance of various *narratives*, *rituals* and *symbols* which stimulate an individual's sense of being a member of a select group. As Eric Hobsbawm has argued, the nation depends upon the invention of national traditions which are made manifest through the repetition of specific symbols or icons. The performance of national traditions keeps in place an important sense of *continuity* between the nation's present and its past, and helps concoct the unique sense of the *shared history* and *common origins* of its people. Nations often traffic in highly revered symbols that help forge a sense of its particular, idiosyncratic identity in which the nation's people emotionally invest. Reviewing the history of European nations since the eighteenth century, Hobsbawm notes that

> entirely new symbols and devices came into existence as part of national movements and states, such as the national anthem (of which the British in 1740 seems to be the earliest), the national flag (still largely a variation on the French revolutionary tricolour, evolved 1790–4), or the personification of 'the nation' in symbol or image, either official, as with Marianne and Germania, or unofficial, as in the cartoon stereotypes of John Bull, the lean Yankee Uncle Sam or the 'German Michel'. (Eric Hobsbawm, 'Introduction: Inventing

Traditions' in *The Invention of Tradition*, ed. E. Hobsbawm and
T. Ranger, Cambridge University Press, 1983, p. 7)

The emergence of national symbols such as the flag or the national
anthem are part of the 'invention of tradition' in which all nations
participate: the repeated performance of rituals, events or symbols
which take on an emotive and semi-sacred character for the people.
Think of how the public burning of a nation's flag as a form of
protest is often a highly provocative act. Such idiosyncratic and
emotive symbols serve as focal points around which a large number
of people gather as a single, national body.

If the invention of tradition is central to the nation, then so is the
narration of *history*. Nations are often underwritten by the positing
of a common historical archive that enshrines the common past of a
collective 'people'. The nation has its own historical narrative which
posits and explains its origins, its individual character and the victories won in its name. In reality, there are as many different versions
of history as there are narrators; but a national history makes *one*
particular version of the past the only version worthy of study. In
many national histories, certain events are ritually celebrated as fundamental to the nation's past fortunes and present identity, which
directly connect the narration of history with the repeated performance of those symbols and icons mentioned a moment ago. Think
about the annual commemoration of events such as Thanksgiving in
America or Guy Fawkes Night in Britain. Each looks back to an
occasion that is considered a defining moment in the history of the
nation, the celebration of which helps cement the people's relationship with their past as well as highlight their togetherness in the present by gathering them around one emotive symbol, such as the
burning of the Guy on the bonfire. Similarly, individual figures are
identified as the chief actors and actresses in the story of the nation:
great leaders, scientists, martyrs, writers, generals or admirals.
These figures both come from the people yet stand apart from the
crowd due to their extraordinary or inspirational qualities. Thus, a
national history functions like a 'story of the tribe', providing the
people with a sense of shared origins, a common past and a collective identity in the present.

An excellent example of these processes in action is provided by
the Jamaican writer Mervyn Morris in his essay 'Feeling, Affection,

Respect' (in *Disappointed Guests: Essays by African, Asian and West Indian Students*, ed. H. Tajfel and J. L. Dawson, Oxford University Press, 1965, pp. 5–26) in which he remembers his first visit to England in the 1960s:

> I learnt the fundamental lesson of nationalism … half an hour away from England, approaching the cliffs of Dover. There was excitement among the English on board [the boat]. I looked, but the cliffs seemed very ordinary to me. And then I realised that of course the cliffs are not cliffs: to the Englishmen they are a symbol of something greater, of the return from a land of strangers, of the return home. Nothing is more important in nationalism than the feeling of ownership. (pp. 25–6)

As Morris points out, the symbolic suggestiveness of the cliffs functions to bond the travelling coincidence of the English, who all respond similarly to what they see. The same emotive reaction occurs throughout a coincident body of people because it is customary for them to associate the 'ordinary' cliffs with 'something greater'. The cliffs of Dover have long been an important symbol in the imagination of the English nation, and their symbolic importance was heightened in particular during the Second World War (as in Vera Lynn's popular song, 'There'll be bluebirds over the white cliffs of Dover'). When viewing the cliffs in the 1960s, the English 'see' more than inert, blank chalk. United for a moment by the sight they share before them, they are in the presence of an important aspect of the national imaginary. Additionally, the cliffs also function as a border, a 'first sight' of England that marks the distinction between the world outside and inside the nation. Because of his vantage point at one remove from all the excitement as a Jamaican visiting a foreign country, Morris does not see at first sight what is so obviously 'there' for the English, and his recollection of the incident reminds us that the wonder of the cliffs is entirely mythic. The cliffs of Dover are, after all, just cliffs.

In addition, of equal importance is the way the symbol helps nurture the feeling of ownership that Morris argues is important to nationalist sentiment. On the one hand, the symbolic associations of the cliffs of Dover make the English feel that *they belong to the land*, and, on the other, that *the land belongs to them*. Community, belonging, a sense of rootedness in the land, home – each is relevant to the construction and purpose of nationalist representations. As this example of the excited English evidences, the production of symbols is important to the construction of the myth of the nation, the function of which is to unite *many* individuals into *one people*.

STOP and THINK

Draw a time line that represents the last three hundred years. What events of 'national importance' would you include on it? What defining moments would you wish to highlight? Why are these events significant in the history of your nation? Where did you learn them, and how are they publicly remembered?

In a similar fashion, choose a nation and make a list of five symbols that are commonly used to conjure its identity. What do these symbols relate to? Can you discover how they were produced? How do a nation's people revere such symbols? Have any new ones appeared in recent years?

National time and space

As Benedict Anderson argues in *Imagined Communities*, a defining feature of the nation is the standardisation of *one unitary language* that all of its members can understand. Although people from different parts of the nation may use regional variations, in theory all of the nation's people come to learn a standard language which enables them to communicate freely with each other. This issue of a 'standard language' is a particularly problematic one in countries with a history of colonialism and we will be exploring this issue when putting the nation in question in the next chapter. But for now, it is important that we hold on to the notion of a unitary national language. In addition, Anderson points out that the imagining of the nation displays specific features exemplified by two particular forms of writing: the realist novel and the daily newspaper. Anderson argues that 'these forms provided the technical means for "re-presenting" the *kind* of imagined community that is the nation' (*Imagined Communities*, p. 25). His point is that the assumptions about *time* and *space* common to these genres are duplicated in the ways nations are imagined.

Nations, like realist novels, tend to gather together a variety of people into one collective body, but it is highly unlikely that one person will ever meet all of his or her fellow nationals. Similarly, in realist novels rarely will *all* the characters meet together, unlike in a conventional detective novel where the suspects are frequently rounded up in one room at the end. However, the realist novel's multitude of characters are none the less united by *time* and *space*. They are connected by the same bounded, fixed landscape within which they all simultaneously exist. Also, the diverse activities of characters take place according to the same temporal scheme: the steady, onward movement of calendrical time epitomised by the ticking of the second hand on a clock. In reading the realist novel we sometimes notice different characters, unaware of each other's existence, performing separate activities *at the same time*. Think of how often you have read a sentence in a novel such as 'meanwhile, as Mr X was buying his lunch, across town Ms Y was catching her flight'. Although a realist novel's characters might lead separate lives, they ultimately share a common place and obey the same time schema.

These simultaneities of time and space are also implied by the form of the daily newspaper. Newspapers create communities from coincidence. They provide news of manifold events that have occurred at roughly the same time. These events are further linked by their occurrence in a location presumed to be common to readers – note how national newspapers will divide their contents into 'home affairs' (the nation) and 'foreign affairs' (all other nations). Anderson further argues that the *act of reading* a newspaper helps generate a sense of national community for the reader. When we read the paper at breakfast, or on the way home from college or work, we are aware that possibly thousands of others are doing exactly as we are, at precisely the same time.

The simultaneities of time and space exemplified in the form of the novel and the newspaper are at the heart of the ways by which we consider ourselves as part of a national community. Nations are narrated like novels and newspapers. Hence, individuals come to consider themselves belonging to a solid community moving steadily down (or up) history. An American will never meet, or even know the names of more than a handful of his ... fellow-Americans. He has no idea what they are up to at any one time. But he has complete confidence in their steady, anonymous, simultaneous activity. (p. 26)

Steady, anonymous, simultaneous – Anderson's vocabulary reflects the robust and orderly foundations upon which the myth of the nation rests. It promises structure, shelter and sequence for individuals, cementing a 'deep, horizontal comradeship' which unites the many into one imagined community through the function *of specific forms of narrative*.

There is one further important element that is often fundamental to nationalist representations: constructions of otherness. We encountered the creation of 'others' in our discussion of the Orientalist constructions of differences between the civilised Occident and the barbaric Orient. Every definition of identity is always defined *in relation* to something else. The placing of imaginative borders between nations is fundamental to their existence, not least because borders divide the nation's people from others outside. But as we shall see, particularly in the next chapter, the construction of the nation's borders is a process fraught with difficulties, and has all too often been its undoing.

Let us review the 'myth of the nation':

• Nations are imagined communities.
• Nations gather together many individuals who come to imagine their simultaneity with others. This unified collective is the nation's 'people'.
• Nations depend upon the invention and performance of histories, traditions and symbols which sustain the people's specific identity continuous between past and present.
• Nations evoke feelings of belonging, home and community for the people.
• Nations stimulate the people's sense that they are the rightful owners of a specific land.
• Nations standardise a unitary language accessible to all the people.
• Nations are often narrated through forms of representation which promote the unities of time and space.

- Nations place borders that separate the people 'within' from different peoples outside.

National liberation vs. imperialist domination

So far we have considered how, in Paul Gilroy's words, nations are created 'through elaborate cultural, ideological and political processes which culminate in [the individual's] feeling of connectedness to other national subjects and in the idea of a national interest that transcends the supposedly petty divisions of class, region, dialect or caste' (*Small Acts: Thoughts on the Politics of Black Cultures*, Serpent's Tail, 1993, p. 49). These feelings of connectedness have proved a valuable resource to many anti-colonial movements.

During several struggles against colonial rule in the twentieth century, the myth of the nation has proved highly potent and productive. It was popular with a variety of independence movements because it served many of their intellectuals and leaders as a valuable ideal behind which resistance to colonialism could unite. Speaking in 1970, Amilcar Cabral, a leading figure in the independence movement in Guinea-Bissau, described the contemporary conflict within several African colonies (as, indeed, it was in many other colonies in other parts of the world previously) specifically as one of 'national liberation in opposition to imperialist domination' (see Amilcar Cabral, 'National Liberation and Culture' in *Colonial Discourse and Post-Colonial Theory*, ed. Williams and Chrisman, pp. 54–5). The nation became mobilised as a powerful symbol which anti-colonial movements used to organise themselves against colonial rule. If colonialism had condemned millions to a life of subservience and dispossession, then anti-colonial nationalisms promised a new dawn of independence and political self-determination for colonised peoples. Many colonies were represented in this period as nations-in-chains, shackled by the forces of colonialism, whose peoples had been alienated from the land which was their rightful possession and which would be returned to them once independence dawned.

In making these kinds of claims, anti-colonial nationalist movements were often working with the national territorial borders that had not existed prior to colonialism and were often fixed by the colonising nations. For example, at the Berlin Conference of 1885 the Western powers divided up Africa between them by drawing arbitrary borders around various parts of the continent. The colonial borders of these new 'nations' ignored the Africans' own maps of the continent. In some cases they divided into two indigenous tribal lands; in others the new colonial boundaries circumscribed African peoples from different tribes with their own belief-systems and languages who collectively did not share a sense of comradeship. For example, the borders of colonial Nigeria established in 1914 circumscribed the lands of peoples who belonged variously to the Yoruba, Hausa, Kanuri and Igbo tribes. In identifying and fixing the borders of the colonised nations, many Western powers re-organised African political space. These borders were not ones that indigenous colonised peoples would have recognised.

So in calling for national liberation from colonialism, many anti-colonial nationalisms were working with the map of the world drawn by the colonisers. This was, on the one hand, an expedient and effective manoeuvre in the struggle for independence, but on the other it proved a potential source of problems in the post-independence period, as we shall explore in the next chapter. To complicate matters further, one of the most important results of Empire was the movement of peoples across the globe – of Africans and Indians to the Caribbean, of Europeans to America and Australasia. For these migrant peoples, their relationship with the land was complicated. How could they 'belong' to country to which they or their ancestors had arrived from elsewhere, a 'homeland' overseas? Which nation was 'truly' theirs?

So, the imagining of a sense of simultaneous national identity for often heterogeneous groups of people in the colonies has always had to face several challenges. How, then, did writers in the post-war period attempt to forge national consciousness during the period of decolonisation? There are two responses we will look at in this chapter in the context of Africa: the first is Negritude, the second emerges from Frantz Fanon's work on national culture.

Negritude

One of the most influential concepts used to forge 'deep, horizontal comradeship' for colonised peoples was *Negritude*. Negritude has been influential in Africa, the Caribbean and America. Today it is most often associated with the work of two writers and statesmen, Aimé Césaire and Léopold Senghor, although they in turn were influenced by the work of early twentieth-century writers such as Claude McKay and W. E. B. DuBois. As we shall see, Negritude works with many of the central tenets of the 'myth of the nation'. One of its aims was to unite peoples living in different nations through their shared ancestry and common origins. So, paradoxically, although we can think of Negritude as an important means by which anti-colonial national liberation in particular was furthered in certain nations, it always had aspirations to be a *pan-national* movement. Its significance as an important means of mounting anti-colonial resistance cannot be underestimated, even if it is today less sympathetically supported than it once was, as we shall discover.

Aimé Césaire was born in the French Caribbean colony of Martinique. He came to Paris in the 1930s to study, where he met fellow-student Léopold Senghor, from the French African colony of Senegal. Despite their very different backgrounds, Césaire and Senghor found themselves commonly identified by the French as *négres*, a derogatory insult that approximates to the racist term 'nigger' in English. Outraged at the Orientalist attitudes held by the French towards their colonised subjects, and energised by the heady intellectual and artistic environment of Paris, Césaire and Senghor fought back at derogatory views of black peoples by writing poetry and essays that represented being black as profoundly valuable. Whereas colonial discourses frequently represented black peoples as primitive and degenerate, having no culture of any real worth, these writers wrote in praise of the laudable qualities of black peoples and cultures.

In colonial discourses, blackness has been frequently evoked as the ultimate sign of the colonised's 'racial' degeneracy. In the nineteenth century, throughout Europe it was commonly believed that the world's population existed as a hierarchy of 'races' based upon colour, with white Europeans deemed the most civilised and black Africans as the most savage. The Hottentots of Southern Africa were often held to be the most 'primitive' of all (for an extended discussion of 'race' in colonial discourses, see Robert Young, *Colonial Desire: Hybridity in Theory, Culture and Race*, Routledge, 1995).

The legacy of this negative sense of blackness is still apparent in the English language today – think of how many expressions there are in which 'black' is used pejoratively (as in 'black market', 'black balled' or 'black magic'). 'Negritude', then, attempted to rescue blackness from its definition in negative terms. 'Blackness' was reconstructed as something positive and valuable, behind which black peoples throughout the world could unite as one body.

At the heart of Negritude was the celebration of 'blackness', but this was about much more than the colour of skin. 'Blackness' as it was addressed by the Negritude writers denoted a whole way of life grounded in perceived unique African qualities. For Senghor, Negritude was a project that attempted to return a sense of dignity and value to black peoples and their cultures. Whereas Western imperialism had dismissed African cultures as 'backwards' and 'primitive', in his prose and poetry Senghor celebrated their sophis-tication and special qualities. Black Africans, he argued, simply had a different relationship with the world than Europeans, and this influenced how they apprehended reality and represented it in their art. African art was just as aesthetically beautiful as the most trea-sured works from Europe – it was unjust of the West to consider African culture as 'primitive'.

In pursuing these arguments, Senghor made claims about the specific qualities to be found in all people of black African descent, whether they lived in Africa or had (been) moved to the Caribbean or America. For example, in 1962 he argued that Europeans studied reality from the coolly detached vantage of clinical scientific obser-vation. However, black Africans had a more intuitive relationship with the world:

> The African is as it were shut up in his black skin. He lives in primor-dial night. He does not begin by distinguishing himself from the object [of study], the tree or stone, the man or animal or social event. He does not keep it at a distance. He does not analyse it. Once he has come under its influence, he takes it like a blind man, still living, into his hands. He does not fix or kill it. He turns it over in his supple hands, he fingers it, he *feels* it. The African is one of the worms cre-ated on the Third Day ... a pure sensory field. (Léopold Senghor, *Prose and Poetry*, ed. and trans. John Reed and Clive Wake, Oxford University Press, 1965, pp. 29–30)

These intuitive qualities manifested themselves in things like 'emotional warmth' and a 'natural' sense of rhythm. '[W]hen I am watching a game of football', wrote Senghor, 'I take part in the game with my whole body. When I listen to jazz or to an African song, I have to make a violent effort of self-control (because I am a civilised man) to keep myself from singing and dancing' (p. 31). In this sentence, 'civilisation' stands for Senghor's Western education that has divided himself from himself, and made him suppress his instinctual responses because they are not deemed to be acceptably civil behaviour in France.

Senghor urged all those of black African descent to realign themselves with these special, unique qualities, to embrace their 'characteristics of the African soul' with pride and dignity. As he put it in 1956, 'the spirit of African civilisation animates, consciously or unconsciously, the best Negro artists of to-day, both in Africa and America' (p. 76). Like these artists, all blacks were compelled to restore their dignity 'by animating this world, here and now, with the values that come to us from our [African] past' (p. 78). Hence, as he defined it, Negritude

> is the awareness, defence and development of African cultural values. Negritude is a myth, I agree. And I agree that there are false myths, myths which breed division and hatred. Negritude as a true myth is the opposite of these. It is the awareness by a particular social group of people of its own situation in the world, and the expression of it by means of the concrete image. (p. 97)

So although Senghor argued fervently that Negritude was more than skin deep, drawing its resources from the cultural treasures of 'Mother Africa', the concrete image which forged a sense of unity was ultimately blackness itself.

Césaire's notion of Negritude was slightly different to Senghor's. Because of his birth in Martinique, Césaire grew up at a distance from Africa, both physically and imaginatively. On the one hand he was descended from the African slaves that had been brought to the Caribbean to work, but on the other he had never lived in Africa and could not know it like Senghor. His Africa was learned second-hand from his friends and his books, 'an Africa of the heart' as one critic has described it (A. James Arnold, *Modernism and Negritude*,

Harvard, 1981, p. 29). The recovery of an African past as a source of renewal was more problematic for black people in the Caribbean. Consequently, Césaire's version of Negritude was based much less on the perceived instinctual or essential differences between whites and blacks. He understood Negritude primarily as something to be measured 'with the compass of suffering'. This meant that black peoples were united more by their shared *experience* of oppression than by their essential qualities as 'Negroes'. That said, it is also fair to argue that Césaire's work is ambivalent towards the issue of the essential differences between white and black peoples and is marked by a tension between perceiving Negritude as grounded in instincts or in historical experiences.

Césaire's version of Negritude is best exemplified by his influential poem *Cahier d'un retour au pays natal* (*Notebook of a Return to My Native Land*), published in 1939 and revised several times in the proceeding decade. We will quote below from a first-class translation by Mireille Rosello and Annie Pritchard (published by Bloodaxe in 1995).

Combining Caribbean history with African myth and French surrealism, *Notebook of a Return to My Native Land* was inspired by Césaire's anticipation of, and reflections on, his return from France to Martinique in the late 1930s. A long, complex and inspiring poem, it is not easy to summarise. The 'native land' of the title is both Martinique and Africa, as Césaire muses upon the connections and disjunctions between these different yet historically linked locations. He reveals the investment that Martinique's black population has in African culture, but does *not* advocate a simple return to Africa as a salve to colonialism's ills. The narrator speaks out with memorable force against the sorry condition of Martinique's black peoples, subservient to the 'whip's corolla' of colonial order; he chastises blacks (and himself) for accepting too readily the white condemnation of blackness; but he also celebrates black people's perceived valuable aspects that have lain inert during their confinement by colonialism. He urges the black population of Martinique to unite as one and realise themselves specifically as a people within the Caribbean, with their own histories and predicaments. In forging a sense of collective identity they can join the fight with other oppressed peoples around the world against the colonial order. This sense of solidarity through suffering is captured in these famous lines:

> As there are hyena-men and panther-men, I shall be a Jew-man
> a kaffir-man
> a Hindu-from-Calcutta-man
> a man from-Harlem-who-does-not-vote (p. 85)

Oppressed peoples discover their unity in the simultaneity of their suffering, rather than with recourse to a common ancestral past (African or otherwise), although that past also remains a resource for the present. Only when this solidarity is struck can their imprisonment by white Europeans be challenged.

It is too quickly forgotten these days that Senghor and Césaire were passionate humanists, and that the long-term aim of Negritude was the emancipation of the entire human race, and not just black peoples, from its subjugation to colonial thought. To be sure, in the short term Negritude offered a way of uniting oppressed black peoples and defying their representation in colonial discourses, and it was pursued chiefly for this reason by its supporters. But both writers saw as the ultimate goal of Negritude the emancipation of *all* peoples from the sorry condition of colonialism. Although Senghor claimed that European and African cultures were fundamentally different, his ultimate aim was the dynamic synthesis of all cultures that would one day exist outside the invidious power relations of colonialism. Césaire too wrote with the purpose of promoting universal emancipation.

STOP and THINK

Constructions of Negritude have several sticking points that we need to consider in order to assess their strengths and weaknesses. Let us think critically about four:

1. *Negritude inverts the terms of colonial discourses.* It was a familiar trope of colonial discourses that black peoples were mysteriously 'closer to nature' than white Europeans – hence their tendency towards 'savagery'. The Negritude writers countered this view by accepting but *celebrating* their

'elemental' nature, as evidenced by Senghor's comments on intuition and rhythm quoted previously. However, his association of black peoples with 'primordial night' is problematic in that Senghor seems to accept the colonial stereotype of blackness and *work with it*, rather than reject it as arbitrary and specious. For many critics, Negritude did not *question* the negative associations of blackness, choosing instead to redeploy them as positives. Negritude is weakened as a revolutionary force because it continues to traffic in colonial stereotypes, not least the association between 'race' and skin colour. If colonial discourses make skin colour the ultimate sign of the degeneracy of the other, then how revolutionary is it to make 'blackness' the concrete image of cultural difference and political resistance?

2. *Negritude upholds separatist binary oppositions*. Negritude used the binary distinctions between white and black, African and European, common to many colonial discourses. Although Senghor and Césaire wanted universal synthesis between all people, their philosophies can lead to *separatism* by leaning dangerously upon the racialising conclusions that an individual's destiny is mystically connected to their colour.

3. *Negritude is nostalgic for a mythic African past*. Negritude often posited a 'golden age' of pre-colonial Africa from which black peoples had been separated by colonialism, and to which they must return. This was, to a degree, one of the great strengths of Negritude, in that it posited a denial of, and an affront to, colonial representations of African history and culture. Senghor argued for a return to an African spirit, while for Césaire 'return' meant the importance for Caribbean blacks to forge a connection with their ancestral home of Africa. However, less productively, these 'returns' depended upon the construction of a mythic pre-colonial African past before the time of colonialism which was free from the ills of the present. But did such a 'golden age' of perfection ever really exist?

4. *Negritude has very little to say about gender differences and inequalities*. In his celebration of African women, Senghor

argued that their primary roles were 'the source of the life-force and guardian of the house, that is to say, the depository of the clan's past and the guarantor of its future' (*Prose and Poetry*, p. 44). For this reason, 'the African woman does not need to be liberated. She has been free for many thousands of years' (p. 45). But many black women have challenged this view and fought to free themselves from their association with 'keeping house'. As some critics have argued, if Negritude makes a myth of Africa's past, it is very much a *male* myth. It united black peoples around a *masculinist* representation of blackness and cared little for the internal unequal relations of gender.

For these reasons, Negritude is today much less popular than it was. Although it did provide a means of inspiration in forging unity among oppressed peoples, and offered a different way of conceiving of African history and culture which refused colonial representations, in recent years Negritude has lost popularity as a revolutionary ideal primarily because it is seen to accept too uncritically many of the terms of colonial discourses, reversing rather than challenging them.

Frantz Fanon and national culture

As we noted in Chapter 1, Frantz Fanon is a hugely important figure in the field of postcolonialism and central to any discussion of anti-colonial resistance. As we observed previously, in 1953 he was appointed as head of the Blida-Joinville Hospital in Algeria at a time when the Algerians' struggle against France for national independence was mounting. Deeply affected by his experiences of racism in North Africa during the war, and politicised by his work with his Algerian patients who suffered mental torment as a consequence of their subjugation to a colonial power, Fanon eventually resigned his post to fight alongside the Algerians for independence and became a leading figure in their struggle. Hated in France, he survived numerous attempts on his life during the 1950s before falling ill with leukaemia. During this illness he worked on his important book *The*

Wretched of the Earth (trans. Constance Farrington, Penguin, [1961] 1967) moving first to Russia for treatment and then eventually to America where he died in December 1961. His body was shipped to Algeria and buried on the Algerian battlefield.

Fanon's writings cover a range of areas and have been influential in a number of fields, such as psychiatry, philosophy, politics and cultural studies. In a literary context, Fanon's work has been used as a means of conceptualising the construction of identity under colonialism (something we touched upon briefly in Chapter 1), and as a way of configuring the relationship between literary representations and the construction of national consciousness during the struggle against colonialism.

This latter theme forms part of *The Wretched of the Earth* in a chapter entitled 'On National Culture' (pp. 166–99 of the Penguin Classics (1967) translation). Originally a statement made at the Second Congress of Black Artists and Writers in Rome in 1959, Fanon stressed the urgent responsibility of writers and intellectuals to forge national consciousness in their work as part of the struggle for independence. However, he rejected the call for the nostalgic celebration of a mythic African past central to Negritude writings. He advocated a more dynamic and vacillating relationship between the past and the present than that made available by Negritude, although it must also be said that Fanon was sympathetic to the project of Negritude to a degree. None the less, Fanon's representation of the nation's 'people' was influenced primarily by Marx's writings on economics and social class, and his theorising of the resistance to colonialism ultimately refused an uncritical notion of an African past, the universal idea of the 'Negro', and the pan-national aspirations of Negritude.

Taking as his focus the operations of colonialism in a specifically African context, 'On National Culture' begins with Fanon's important critique of Negritude and the 'native intellectual'. The term 'native intellectual' refers to the writers and thinkers of the colonised nation who have often been educated under the auspices of the colonising power (think of Bhabha's 'mimic men' who we considered in the previous chapter). Consequently, the Western-educated native intellectual is in danger of identifying more with the middle-class bourgeoisie of the *colonising* nation rather than with the *indigenous* masses. This complicates the role the native intellectual plays in contributing to the people's anti-colonial nationalist struggle. Like the Negritude writers, the native intellectual at first refuses the view that colonised peoples had no meaningful culture prior to the arrival of the colonisers. Hence, '[t]he past is given back its value' (p. 170) by the native intellectual who comes to cherish all that colonialism dismisses as evidence of barbarism. However, Fanon is dissatisfied with the *pan-national* focus of this initial retort to colonialism. He notes how native intellectuals have, in the past, attempted to cherish a *generalised* pan-African culture in their resistance to colonial ways of seeing. But this tendency 'to speak more of African culture than of national culture will tend to lead them up a blind alley' (p. 172). This is because the historical circumstances of African peoples in different parts of the globe cannot be so readily unified. To create an abstract notion of a pan-African culture is to ignore the different conditions of African peoples in a variety of locations, such as America or the Caribbean. Negritude might promise unity, but it is a unity based on false premises. African peoples face different challenges in a variety of locations at any one moment in time:

> Negro-ism therefore finds its first limitation in the phenomena which take account of the formation of the historical character of men. Negro and African-Negro culture broke up into different entities because the men who wished to incarnate these cultures realised that every culture is first and foremost national, and that the problems which kept Richard Wright or Langston Hughes [in America] on the alert were fundamentally different from those which might confront Léopold Senghor [in Senegal] or Jomo Kenyatta [in Kenya]. (p. 174)

Fanon therefore asserts the idea of the nation as the focal point for anti-colonial resistance not least because it allows the native intellectual to address the *specific* historical circumstances and challenges of one *particular* colonised location. That said, he is not wholly critical of the desire to champion indigenous cultures in defiance of colonialism's derogatory representations of them. Although Negritude is described as a 'turn backwards' (p. 175), it is a necessary and painful step towards the creation of national consciousness.

The construction of a specifically national consciousness is

dependent upon important *cultural* activities. National consciousness and national culture are inseparable from each other; anti-
colonial resistance cannot succeed without them. Writers, artists
and intellectuals have a *vital* role to play in imagining the nation, and
they participate centrally to resisting colonialism. Fanon suggests
that the creation of a distinctly national culture moves through three
phases.

In the *first*, the native intellectual attempts what he calls 'unqual-
ified assimilation' (p. 179). For example, this means that he or she is
inspired by and attempts to copy the dominant trends in the literature of the colonising power. In so doing the cultural traditions of
the colonised nation are ignored as the native intellectual aspires to
reproduce the cultural fashions of the colonising power. Hence the
native intellectual is damagingly estranged from the indigenous
masses, identifying more with the colonising power rather than with
those suffering the effects of colonialism.

In the *second* phase, the native intellectual grows dissatisfied with
copying the coloniser and instead becomes immersed in the cultural
history of the people. In this phase he or she 'turns backwards' and
champions all things indigenous. Fanon calls this the literature of
'just-before-the-battle' when the native intellectual begins to reflect
upon the past of the people. However, he or she still stands apart
from the mass of the people and maintains 'exterior relations' (p.
179) with them only. That is to say, the cultural traditions of the
colonised people are lauded uncritically. By championing the cultural treasures of the colonised nation the native intellectual
becomes too concerned with cherishing the past and ignores the
struggles taking place in the present. The native intellectual is in
danger of fiddling while the country burns. Indigenous cultural traditions are venerated as if the very fact of their existence is enough
to challenge the derogation of the colonised people. But, as Fanon
points out, '[y]ou will never make colonialism blush for shame by
spreading out little-known cultural treasures under its eyes' (pp.
179–80). Glorifying the cultural treasures of the past is not enough.
Rather, a new way of mobilising inherited culture is required, one
that puts it *actively* to work rather than *passively* on display. In so
doing, the native intellectual becomes drawn into closer proximity
with the people.

This brings us to the *third* phase, or 'fighting phase' (p. 179), in which the native intellectual becomes directly involved in the people's struggle against colonialism. In this phase he or she becomes conscious of his or her previous estrangement from the people and realises that '[i]t is not enough to try to get back to the people in that past out of which they have already emerged' (p. 182). Rather than cherishing inert cultural traditions, a more *dynamic* relationship is attempted between the cultural inheritance of the past and the people's struggle against colonialism in the present. Traditional culture is mobilised as part of the people's fight against oppression and, consequently, *is transformed in the process*. If the native intellectual wishes to stay in step with the people, he or she must participate in the *reinterpretation* of traditional culture in the present with the aim of opening up the possibility of a new future. Fanon gives the example of oral storytellers who modify their work in order to participate in the forging of national consciousness:

> the oral tradition – stories, epics and songs of the people – which formerly were filed away as set pieces are now beginning to change. The storytellers who used to relate inert episodes now bring them alive and introduce into them modifications which are increasingly fundamental. There is a tendency to bring conflicts up to date and to modernise the kinds of struggle which the stories evoke, together with the names of heroes and types of weapons. (p. 193)

Through the *modification* of traditional culture the artist becomes a radical player in the people's struggle for independence, charged with the responsibility of both drawing inspiration from the people and compacting a sense of the people's national unity through their work. Rather than extracting from the past what is perceived to be their most valuable, timeless cultural treasures, the native intellectual learns from the people to *modify, reinterpret* and *reform* traditional culture at the service of forging a new national consciousness which places the struggle of the people at its heart. Hence *new, unusual forms of artistic expression* emerge in this phase that both contribute and bear witness to the dynamism of the people and their gathering energy for change. In these terms, traditional culture must undergo radical revision. Emphasising culture as first and foremost a vital, unstable activity that is always in the process of

being made and re-made, Fanon calls for 'the break-up of the old
strata of culture, a shattering which becomes increasingly fundamental' (p. 197). He concludes by underlining the central role culture has to play in creating the conditions for a national
consciousness that can resist the colonial power and lay the foundations for the newly independent nation. The struggle against colonialism 'in its development and in its internal progression sends
culture along different paths and traces out entirely new ones for it'
(p. 197). It is the responsibility of the native intellectual to forge and
to follow these new paths to the future and hence participate in the
burgeoning national culture, rather than retrace the steps back to an
ossified and inert past which takes him or her away from the
dynamism of the people's struggle.

Crucial to Fanon's understanding of national culture, then, is his
rendering of culture as dynamic and responsive to historical circumstances. There can be no return to an idealised notion of culture, as in Negritude, nor do the nation's masses take their cue from
Western-educated native intellectuals. Native intellectuals must
become attuned to the day-to-day struggle of the people if they are
to help forge national consciousness and culture. The result will be
unique to the moment of production rather than a repetition of pre-
existing cultural forms, and one which helps unite the intellectuals
and the masses. But the people's cultural inheritance remains a fundamental resource in forging national culture, one which is brought
into play with the necessities of the present. So, a sense of *collective
action* is fundamental to the sustenance of the nation; the nation is
the political manifestation of *all* the people.

Yet, like all prescriptive political programmes, Fanon's model of
national culture itself contains an element of idealism. One particular problem concerns the relations between the elite, Western-
educated native intellectual and the people. Can the native intellectual learn from the people, as Fanon demands, or will tensions
remain as a consequence of the divisions created by class and education? In his essay 'The Pitfalls of National Consciousness' (also in
The Wretched of the Earth, pp. 119–65), Fanon warns of the dangers
ahead for colonised nations if those that come to occupy positions of
power in the nation betray the people in the interests of the few. His
argument for the construction of a national consciousness that

reflects the needs of the people applies both *before* and *after* independence is achieved. The achievement of self-determination by the people's struggle is only a first step; the newly independent nation must conduct itself in the best interests of the people if all are to remain permanently free from colonial rule.

But Fanon warns that the newly independent nation is placed in jeopardy by the activities of what he terms the educated national middle class whose self-interests conflict with those of the people. In his view:

> In an under-developed country an authentic national middle class ought to consider as its bounden duty to betray the calling fate has marked out for it, and to put itself to school with the people: in other words to put at the people's disposal the intellectual and technical capital that it has snatched when going through the colonial universities. But unhappily we shall see that very often the national middle class does not follow this heroic, positive, fruitful and just path; rather, it disappears with its soul set at peace into the shocking ways – shocking because anti-national – of a traditional bourgeoisie, of a bourgeoisie which is stupidly, contemptibly, cynically bourgeois. (pp. 120–1)

Fanon is raising here the issue of *neo-colonialism*. He calls attention to the fact that the newly-independent nation can find itself administered by an indigenous middle class that uses its privileged education and position cheerfully to replicate the colonial administration of the nation for its own financial profit. This class is 'neo-colonial' in that it continues to exploit the people in a way not dissimilar to the colonialists. It is a situation when, in Fanon's words, 'the national bourgeoisie steps into the shoes of the former European settlement' (p. 122). The new administration does little to transform the nation economically. It does not set up new industries or alter marketing patterns. It does not govern in the interests of the people. Instead it makes the new nation economically subservient to the old colonial Western powers by allowing big foreign companies to establish themselves in the new nation, by continuing to send raw materials abroad for profit rather than feeding the people, by making the nation into a tourist centre for wealthy Westerners. The national middle class profit by these manoeuvres but those profits never reach the people who remain powerless and in poverty. A nation that remains economically dependent on the West, and that treats its people in this way, cannot call itself truly free from colonialism.

With some venom, Fanon condemns those he sees as betraying the people's struggle: 'because it lives to itself and cuts itself off from the people, undermined by its hereditary incapacity to think in terms of all the problems of the nation as seen from the point of view of the whole nation, the national middle class will have nothing better to do than to take on the role of manager for Western enterprise, and it will in practice set up its country as the brothel of Europe' (p. 123). Fanon warns that the achievement of independence is not an end but a new beginning, one that brings fresh challenges for the fledgling nation. A nationalism grounded in the collective interests of the people must continue to dictate the conduct of the nation *after* it gains the right to self-determination. The nation must not be hijacked by an indigenous middle class which acts like the previous colonial regime and does little to further the interests and conditions of the people. As with the construction of national consciousness before independence, writers have an important role to play in maintaining this vigilance after power has been seized.

Nationalism and literature

Without wishing to conflate theories of Negritude and Fanon's definition of anti-colonial nationalism, it is fair to say that each makes available to colonised peoples several important resources in their struggle against colonialism. We might recap these as follows:

- They assert the rights of colonised peoples to make their own *self-definitions*, rather than be defined by the colonisers.
- They offer the means through which divergent peoples within a colonised nation can construct *solidarity* across cultural and class differences.
- They *treasure* the cultural inheritance of the colonised people in defiance of colonial discourses, and can use it for revolutionary purposes.
- They offer the means to identify *alternative* histories, cultural traditions and knowledges which conflict with the representations of colonial discourses.

• With particular reference to Fanon, the advocacy of national consciousness creates an important mode of vigilance *after* independence and is concerned with the possibility of avoiding the pitfalls of *neo-colonialism*.

As Fanon's work intimates, literature could have (and indeed did have) an important role to play in the construction of a national consciousness. Césaire's *Notebook of a Return to My Native Land* is only one example of many literary texts from several countries with a history of colonialism during this period which were involved in creating and exploring national consciousness, as many critics of Commonwealth literature correctly noted at the time. As the Nigerian writer Chinua Achebe famously remarked in his 1964 lecture 'The Novelist as Teacher' (in *Commonwealth Literature*, ed. John Press, pp. 201–5), '[h]ere then is an adequate revolution for me to espouse – to help my society regain its belief in itself and put away the complexes of the years of denigration and self-denigration' (p. 204). Nationalist writing was one way of furthering this 'revolution'.

An excellent, highly-recommended comparative discussion of the relations between literature and nationalism is given by C. L. Innes in her essay '"Forging the Conscience of Their Race": Nationalist Writers' (in *New National and Post-Colonial Literatures: An Introduction*, ed. Bruce King, Clarendon Press, 1996, pp. 120–39). Innes looks at the work of nationalist writers such as W. B. Yeats in Ireland; Senghor, Chinua Achebe and Wole Soyinka in West Africa; and Joseph Furphy in Australia. She discovers a set of similar concerns in each, generated no doubt by the fact that different groups of nationalists 'were caught up in a similar dialectic, wherein the metropolitan imperial power categorises all "other" groups in opposition to its own self-image' (p. 122). Innes notes several characteristics in much nationalist writing which used European languages and literary forms (although she demonstrates at length the important differences which also exist between different nationalist literary texts). We can borrow her remarks to recap, and supplement, some of the observations we have made in this chapter.

First, nationalist writers asserted 'the existence of a culture which was the antithesis of the colonial one' (p. 123). This often meant celebrating the derogatory characteristics assigned to them in colonial discourses. Second, they emphasised the relationship between the people and the land in order to underline the illegitimate intrusion of the colonisers, asserting a 'unity between people and place' (p. 124). Third, there was a tendency in some nationalist writing to gender representations of colonial domination and nationalist resistance. Several nationalist texts featured plots which involved the conflicts of fathers and sons, through which is figured the patriarchal authority of the coloniser and resistances to it. This went hand in hand with a feminisation of the nation as a *motherland* (a problematic issue we will be addressing at length in the next chapter).

Innes's observations reveal the extent of the overlap between nationalist representations made in more overtly political discourses which we have looked at in this chapter, and the central concerns of much literary discourse in a variety of locations particularly during times of transition from colonial subservience to political independence. We are going to conclude this chapter by looking at how we might read closely *one* literary text as constructing a national consciousness, by using the concepts we have met in this chapter in our literary criticism. In addition, this will help anticipate our examination of several insoluble *problems* in nationalist representations which are the subject of the next chapter.

Constructing national consciousness: Ngugi's *A Grain of Wheat*

Ngugi wa Thiong'o's novel *A Grain of Wheat* (Heinemann, 1967) concerns the achievement of Kenyan independence ('Uhuru') on 12 December 1963. It explores several issues that have been raised in this chapter: how a writer contributes to the forging of national consciousness by narrating the people's struggle; the process of forging national symbols as well as the pitfalls; the challenge of independence; the danger of neo-colonialism.

Ngugi wa Thiong'o was born in Kamarithu, Kenya, in 1938. He studied at Makerere University College in Uganda in the early 1960s, and at the University of Leeds between 1964 and 1967 during which time he wrote *A Grain of Wheat*. He returned to Kenya to work in the Literature Department at the University of Nairobi. On 31 December 1977 he was arrested and detained without charge by the Kenyan police until 12 December 1978. On his release he was not allowed to continue in his academic post, and in 1982 he left Kenya to enter a self-imposed exile from his native land.

A Grain of Wheat is set during the four days leading up to Uhuru. Its central characters are members of the peasant community of Thabai Ridge, and through their memories Ngugi examines how the struggle for independence impacted on the ordinary lives of the peasant class. Much of the novel occurs in 'flashback' and bears witness to the 'Mau Mau' Rebellion to colonial rule. On 20 October 1952 a State of Emergency was declared in Kenya and several leading figures in the push for independence were arrested. As a consequence, many peasants left their homes and took to the hills where they waged a guerrilla war against the colonial powers. In Ngugi's novel we hear about the leading figures in the independence movement, such as Jomo Kenyatta, but only indirectly and as part of the wider memories of the central characters. This shows us that Ngugi's prime focus is on ordinary people, not their leaders.

So, Ngugi is following Fanon's lead in making the people the subject for his novel, and the fortunes of the Thabai community can be read as a mirror of the fledgling nation as a whole. As Ngugi writes in his essay 'Moving the Centre', the very choice of writing a novel in the 1960s that examined the lives of ordinary Kenyans was part of a wider 'struggle for the right to name the world for ourselves' (in *Moving the Centre*, James Currey, 1993, p. 3). His narrative constitutes a vital attempt to give voice to the people's collective identity and history. The novel's unnamed narrator specifically uses a 'collective' voice in the novel, often using such phrases as '[l]earned men will, no doubt, dig into the troubled times which we in Kenya underwent' (*A Grain of Wheat*, p. 131), and he locates himself as belonging to the people of Thabai in his comment that '[i]n our village and despite the drizzling rain, men and women and children, it seemed, had emptied themselves into the streets' (p. 203). In the following phrase the narrator characteristically speaks *for* the people and *to* the people: 'Most of us from Thabai first saw him at the New Rung'ei Market the day the heavy rain fell. You remember the Wednesday, just before Independence? Wind blew and the rain hit the ground at an angle' (p. 178). In terms of Fanon's work on national culture, the narrative voice of the text contributes to the construction of a national consciousness.

This sense of creating a narrative of the people is borne out by the novel's representation of the Thabai villagers. *A Grain of Wheat* gathers the stories of a series of interrelated characters, none of which is granted the position of its primary hero or heroine (although as we shall see their heroic status becomes an important issue in the novel). These characters each have their own chequered past which we learn through a series of flashbacks and memories. One of them, Kihika, has been killed by the time of Uhuru. Kihika is remembered as one of the heroes of the anti-colonial movement and had fought as a freedom fighter in the hills. He was betrayed to the colonial forces and subsequently murdered. Another key figure is Mugo. For much of the novel Mugo is believed to have sheltered Kihika while on the run. He is celebrated for this and for defending a female villager, Wambuku, from being beaten while digging a trench for the authorities, for which he is sent to a detention camp. He returns to Thabai a hero, but few suspect that he betrayed Kihika and caused his death.

Also sent to a detention camp was Gikonyo, a carpenter and hus-band of Mumbi, Kihika's sister. Initially a strong supporter of the anti-colonial struggle, Gikonyo freed himself from detention by confessing his oath of allegiance to the 'Movement'. His return to Thabai is marred by his discovery that Mumbi has borne a child to Karanja, his childhood rival and the colonialists' puppet Chief of Thabai during the State of Emergency. Karanja betrayed those fighting for independence, and is wrongly believed by many in Thabai to have been responsible for Kihika's death. Jealous of Gikonyo's marriage to Mumbi, during the Emergency Karanja attempted to use his office to seduce Mumbi, who steadfastly refused his advances and remained committed to her absent hus-band. Only when she learned from Karanja that Gikonyo had been freed did she lower her defences, which Karanja ruthlessly exploited.

Although *A Grain of Wheat* is not a conventionally realist novel due to its complex structure of memory and flashback, it does pro-mote the unities of time and space that Benedict Anderson identi-fied as crucial to the imagining of the nation. It focuses on a specific location common to all the characters, Thabai village, and in the characters' memories we gain a sense of what each was doing during the same period of time.

The novel raises all kinds of issues relevant to the myth of the nation and the coming of independence; we shall touch upon only a few. One issue is the construction of icons which anchor the people's feeling of a common national identity, a process that Ngugi both acknowledges and questions. Let us consider Kihika, the freedom fighter. In some respects, Kihika has similarities with Fanon's figure of the native intellectual. His resistance to the colonial authorities exemplifies Fanon's call for the *dynamic* use of past learning for present struggle. Kihika makes use both of ancestral learning and his colonial education to oppose colonial authority. We meet him early in the novel when Mugo remembers attending a rally in Rung'ei Market at which Kihika spoke. Kihika narrates to the crowd the story of the colonisation of the land by the British and early resistance to it, and calls for those at the rally to answer 'the call of a nation in turmoil' (p. 15). In mustering opposition he uses the resources of a Biblical quotation and an old proverb: '"Watch ye and pray," Kihika said, calling on his audience to remember the great Swahili proverb: *Kikulacho Kimo nguoni mwako*' (p.15). The incident is typical of how Kihika inspires the people by drawing upon *both* ancestral learning and the knowledge gained from his colonial schooling.

As a boy Kihika attended a Church of Scotland school where he received a Christian education and became obsessed with the story of Moses and the children of Israel. Kihika's knowledge of the Bible is used to resist the colonial teaching he is exposed to. The Bible was one of the chief resources that Christian missions used to condemn indigenous African religious practices and was often cited to legitimate the presence of the British in Africa, spreading Christian enlightenment in 'heathen' lands. Yet Kihika finds inspiration in the Biblical story of Moses which provides him with a way of rationalising and justifying Kenyan resistance. In effect he transforms the tool of the oppressors into the weapon of the oppressed. His sense of and support of his 'people' is derived from a mixture of Biblical education and ancestral knowledge. This interlacing of different kinds of knowledges gained from ancestral and colonial sources has affinities with Fanon's claim that the native intellectual should reinterpret, reform and modify cultural resources if they further a sense of the people's national unity.

Kihika preaches the importance of collective action rather than individual endeavour in his advocacy of anti-colonial resistance. Yet, problematically, his support for the movement does give him the aura of an extraordinary figure who soon acquires mythic status among the villagers. Throughout the novel there remains a tension between individual and collective action that is never fully resolved (this might prompt us to reconsider the idealism in Fanon's argument that the elite and the masses become united through a common nationalist cause.) The anti-colonial struggle requires leadership and inspiration, but those responsible must not become remote from the people. Ngugi recognises the necessity for figures around which collective action can be instigated and organised, but remains suspicious of the cult of personality that is often created in their wake. He carefully problematises our view of Kihika by referring to 'his immense arrogance' (p. 89) and his egotistical 'visions of himself [as] a saint, leading Kenyan people to freedom and power' (p. 83). There is a sense that the valuing of extraordinary individual heroes detracts from the attention to ordinary and daily acts of courage by the people.

Ngugi also uses Mugo to question the iconic, extraordinary status afforded to some individuals in the freedom struggle by pointing out the disjuncture between the heroic myth-making and the truths that myths may conceal. In the absence of the murdered Kihika, Mugo becomes the village's celebrated war hero and inherits some of the aura that had surrounded the man he betrayed. He is invited by members of the movement to lead a rally in Thabai on independence day that will honour the sacrifices of those that died fighting for independence. He also learns that Karanja will be wrongly accused at the rally as responsible for Kihika's death, with chilling consequences. For much of the novel Mugo lives under unbearable pressure, wracked with feelings of guilt made all the more uncomfortable by the praise of those around him. The women of the village often sing songs about his bravery when he passes by. His confession at the rally of his betrayal of Kihika travesties these myths. It is an act that bears witness to Ngugi's ambiguous attitude towards individual

actions in the novel. In his fatal public confession Mugo proves himself to be both a villain and a hero; not everyone would admit to a
crime that secures their execution. In this courageous act he at once
proves to be 'no ordinary man' (p. 180) but also no different from
Karanja and Gikonyo, who were also guilty of betraying the people
during the State of Emergency.

The occasion of Mugo's confession also questions the nature of
the moment of independence. Uhuru is on the one hand an occasion
for national joy and celebration, but on the other it is also a disquieting day of judgement. How should the people reckon with those
who committed crimes against the nation during the struggle? Who
is in a position to judge? In *A Grain of Wheat* it is difficult to separate the heroes from the villains as virtually every character could be
accused of committing a potentially shameful act during the colonial
period. The alternatives are set out early in the novel during a discussion concerning Kihika's death. One of the freedom fighters,
Koina, suggests that perhaps they should 'forget the whole thing' (p.
27). His colleague, General R., takes the opposite view by arguing
that '[t]raitors and collaborators must not escape revolutionary justice' (p. 27). It is an argument that Mugo's execution does not
resolve either way. Through Mugo's fate, Ngugi raises questions
about the conduct of the new nation after independence and the difficult challenges it faces.

The disquieting aspects of independence also emerge in Ngugi's
depiction of those who are assuming the vacated seats of power in
newly independent Kenya. In so doing he echoes Fanon's warning
concerning the neo–colonial exploitation of the people by the native
middle class. As Kenya approaches Uhuru many of the British settlers and administrators prepare to leave the country for good. One
settler, Richard Burton, puts his farm up for sale. Gikonyo and five
others decide they want to buy it. Gikonyo makes a trip to Nairobi
to see if his local MP can help him secure a government loan to buy
the farm. Gikonyo is made to wait with several others at the MP's
office. When he eventually arrives late we are told he 'greeted all the
people like a father or a headmaster his children' (p. 62). The MP
promises Gikonyo that he is confident he can secure the necessary
loan soon. But Gikonyo's trust in the MP is betrayed. Later in the
novel Gikonyo discovers that Burton's farm has been bought, and

'the new landowner was their own MP' (p. 169). The implication is
that the possessions of the colonialists are passing into the hands of
a new indigenous ruling class and not to the people of the movement. Ngugi suggests that even on the day of independence the
people's struggle is being betrayed by a new ruling class that has
little concern for the people:

> General R. recalled Lt Koina's recent misgivings. Koina talked of
> seeing the ghosts of the colonial past still haunting Independent
> Kenya. And it was true that those now marching in the streets of
> Nairobi were not the soldiers of the Kenya Land and Freedom Army
> but of the King's African Rifles, the … colonial forces. (p. 220)

In one sense, the occasion of independence itself stands on trail at
the end of the novel. Will Uhuru bring new opportunities for the
inhabitants of Thabai? How will an independent Kenya differ from
its days as a British colony? In this passage Ngugi holds a mirror up
to the nation and is not pleased with the conditions it reflects.

It might seem, then, that Ngugi takes a sombre view of newly-
independent Kenya, the tenor of which recalls Fanon's misgivings in
his essay 'The Pitfalls of National Consciousness'. But there is hope
in the novel too for a better future for the nation, and this is figured
through the relationship of Mumbi and Gikonyo. In order to make
this reading we need to recall C. L. Innes's point about the *gendering* of the nation in some nationalist literature, and notice that
Mumbi is presented as an allegorical mother-figure of the Kenyan
nation. Her name recalls the celebrated mother of the Gikuyu, one
of the main tribes in Kenya. The fact that she becomes a mother
during the State of Emergency is also significant, especially when we
remember that her brother Kihika often describes Kenya as 'our
mother' (p. 89). While in detention, Gikonyo's dreams of freedom
are focused upon his desire to return to Mumbi. His fantasy of the
movement's defeat of the British becomes intertwined with his
being reunited with Mumbi: 'His reunion with Mumbi would see
the birth of a new Kenya (p. 105). In *A Grain of Wheat*, Mumbi is
clearly represented as a mother-figure of the nation central to the
revolutionary vocabulary of Kihika and the people's struggle.

The reunion of Gikonyo and Mumbi is not the glorious affair of
which Gikonyo dreams, due to his discovering that Mumbi has

borne a child to Karanja. Gikonyo imagines that she has been having an affair during the time of his detention (the reality is of course very different) and his treatment of her eventually makes her leave him. But in the last chapter of the novel a potential reunion is hinted at, which might be read as a nationalist representation. As Gikonyo lies in hospital with a broken arm he is visited by Mumbi. The atmosphere between them is strained, but Gikonyo surprises Mumbi by asking for the first time about her child, who is ill. If Mumbi is the mother of the nation, it follows that her child symbolises the new Kenya. Her child was born as a result of the union between Mumbi and the collaborator Karanja, suggesting that the new Kenya inherits both the people's struggle against colonialism and their complicity with it. Significantly, the child is sick. The new Kenya is not free from the ills of the old, it seems, and those Kenyans who have survived the struggle must find ways of dealing with their painful past. Mumbi's response to Gikonyo's suggestion of their reconciliation suggests at a wider level how difficult and lengthy this process may be:

> People try to rub out things, but they cannot. Things are not so easy. What has passed between us is too much to be passed over in a sentence. We need to talk, to open our hearts to one another, examine them, and then together plan the future we want. (p. 247)

The happy future of the nation remains to be secured. Mumbi's comments emphasise the need for further collective action in her stress on 'planning together' that furthers the process of healing. This is not the quick forgetting of the past favoured by Lt. Koina nor the ugly one-sided mob-rule of General R. that took Mugo's life so swiftly after his confession. The novel's final image, a carving of a woman big with child, emphasises how Ngugi concludes by stressing the possibility of rebirth, growth and redemption.

In our examination of *A Grain of Wheat* we have witnessed the fundamental importance of the idea of the nation as central to much of the literature written at the time of decolonisation, and discovered how an attention to the nation can illuminate our reading of a text. However, Ngugi's use of Mumbi as a maternal icon of the nation is a questionable manoeuvre; also, his use of the English language and the literary form of the novel as the means to create a distinctly *national* representation also require comment. These gesture towards a wider series of problems concerning representations of the nation which have been raised in more recent years. This is the subject of our next chapter.

Selected reading

Achebe, Chinua, 'The Novelist as Teacher' in John Press (ed.), *Commonwealth Literature: Unity and Diversity in a Common Culture*, (Heinemann, 1965), pp. 201–5.

An oft-quoted and important essay in which Achebe discusses the importance of literature in the regeneration of the colonised.

Anderson, Benedict, *Imagined Communities: Reflections on the Origins and Spread of Nationalism* (Verso, 1983).

A highly influential text which has become a touch-stone in much postcolonial criticism concerned with nationalist representations.

Arnold, A. James, *Modernism and Negritude* (Harvard, 1981).

A wide-ranging, clear and sophisticated study of the origins and influence of Negritude aesthetics.

Boehmer, Elleke, *Colonial and Postcolonial Literature* (Oxford University Press, 1995).

Chapter 3, 'The Stirrings of New Nationalism', offers a critical and illuminating literary history of postcolonial nationalist writing.

Caute, David, *Fanon* (Fontana, 1970).

An excellent, short introductory guide to Fanon.

Eagleton, Terry, Fredric Jameson and Edward W. Said, *Nationalism, Colonialism and Literature* (University of Minnesota Press, 1990).

Includes an important essay by each critic and an excellent introduction by Seamus Deane.

Fanon, Frantz, *The Wretched of the Earth*, trans. Constance Farrington (Penguin, 1967 [1961]).

Collecting together several of Fanon's salient essays, this is recommended reading for any study of nationalist representations, Negritude and anti-colonial resistance.

Gellner, Ernest, *Nations and Nationalism* (Blackwell, 1983).

A useful if conservative study of the Western origins of the ideas of nation and nationalism.

Gordon, Lewis, T. Denean Sharpley-Whiting and Renée T. White (eds),

Fanon: A Critical Reader (Blackwell, 1996).

A sophisticated and up-to-date collection of critical essays about Fanon which trace the enduring influence of his work. For the more advanced reader.

Hawley, John C. (ed.), *Writing the Nation: Self and Country in the Post-Colonial Imagination* (Editions Rodopi, 1996).

A lively collection of essays which explore nationalist representations across a range of postcolonial literary texts.

Hutchinson, John and Anthony D. Smith (eds), *Nationalism* (Oxford University Press, 1994).

An excellent anthology of some of the most influential writing on nationalism in a variety of contexts.

Innes, C. L., '"Forging the Conscience of Their Race": Nationalist Writers' in Bruce King (ed.), *New National and Post-Colonial Literatures: An Introduction* (Clarendon Press, 1996), pp. 120–39.

An excellent and highly informative comparative study of nationalist representations in postcolonial literatures, highly recommended for new readers in the field.

Renan, Ernest, 'What is a Nation?', trans. Martin Thom in Homi K. Bhabha (ed.), *Nation and Narration* (Routledge, 1990), pp. 8–22.

An influential statement on the idea of the nation, first delivered in 1882.

4

The nation in question

The disenchantment with nationalism

Simon Gikandi has argued in his book *Maps of Englishness: Writing Identity in the Culture of Colonialism* (Columbia University Press, 1996) that 'nationalism cannot seriously be considered to be the alternative to imperialism that it was once thought to be' (p. 7). Although debatable, this comment none the less bears witness to the fact that in the years since the busy period of decolonisation there has emerged a disenchantment with the ideas of nation and nationalism. This is in many ways a consequence of the *historical experience* of decolonisation when several national liberation movements, particularly in Africa and the Caribbean, confronted a series of often insoluble problems once formal independence was achieved. As Bruce King argues,

> [w]here the end of the Second World War brought a demand for national political independence to the forefront as a solution to the problems of the colonies, this was soon found to be an unrealistic hope as many new nations became divided by civil war and micro-nationalisms ... or failed to develop economically or to offer social justice to those outside the government and its supporters. (*West Indian Literature*, second edition, Macmillan, 1995, p. 3)

This chapter concerns the divisions within the nation which threaten the realisation of its ideals. We shall consider how nationalist representations might contribute to the continued *oppression* of some groups within the national population who have *not* experienced liberation in the period of formal independence. From their points of view, 'national liberation' seems almost a contradictory term. Do myths of the nation unify all of the people living within the nation's territorial boundaries, or can they stimulate division and conflict? We will be looking in this chapter primarily at the relationship between the imagined community of the nation and its internal divisions, and exploring in particular how the contradictions of nationalism impact upon both reading and writing nationalist representations, with specific reference to Chinua Achebe's novel *Anthills of the Savannah* (1987).

In the previous chapter we noted how many advocates of nationalism often faced two problems: the complicity of national liberation movements in Western myth-making, and the complications caused by the fact that many occupants of colonial lands did not possess a sense of (to use Benedict Anderson's phrase) 'deep, horizontal comradeship' prior to the advent of colonial government. The production of a unified imaginary community can be both nationalism's greatest strength and its ultimate weakness. Although the myth of the nation might function as a valuable resource in uniting a people in opposition to colonialism, it often does so by ignoring the diversity of those individuals it seeks to homogenise – created out of gender, racial, religious and cultural differences, as we shall explore below. Many once-colonised nations have struggled with the internal differences that threaten the production of national unity. As we shall see, this does not simply reflect a political failure on the part of the newly independent nations, but perhaps reveals a problem *inherent* in the concept of the nation itself. These historical changes have impacted upon the ways in which the nation is theorised, and we shall be looking at some of these in a specifically postcolonial context. As Etienne Balibar puts it in his essay 'Racism and Nationalism', many decolonised nations have undergone the painful experience of 'seeing nationalisms of liberation turned into nationalisms of domination' (in Balibar and Wallerstein, *Race, Nation, Class*, Verso, 1991, p. 46).

However, we do not want to begin this chapter by simply accepting Gikandi's view that nations and nationalisms are today old-fashioned ideas discredited by failure. It is true to say that for many commentators the idea of the nation is rapidly becoming outdated. In a world of instant mass communications, multinational capitalism and global travel, the ideas of nation, nationalism and national identity seem increasingly anachronistic in an increasingly *international* world. Yet critics of the myth of the nation can often disregard too quickly some of the valuable resources it makes available to anti-colonial resistance. Ultimately, by examining nationalist representations and their problems across this chapter and the last, I am inviting you to make up your own minds about the myth of the nation as a productive concept.

So, let us begin to work through some of the salient criticisms which have been made about both the form and the content of anti-colonial nationalist representations.

Nationalism: a derivative discourse?

As we noted previously, the nation is first and foremost a Western idea, one which emerged at a certain moment in Western history due to specific economic circumstances. How enabling is it, then, for anti-colonial nationalist movements who are attempting to challenge their subservience to Western views of the world? As Partha Chatterjee explains in his influential book *Nationalist Thought and the Colonial World* (Zed, 1986), the origins of the nation in the West have much to do with the pursuit of a set of human ideals often identified as the European 'Enlightenment'. From this vantage, European forms of nationalism are 'part of the same historical process which saw the rise of industrialism and democracy' and 'nationalism represents the attempt to actualise in political terms the universal urge for liberty and progress' (p. 2). However, this 'liberal' view of the nation repeatedly comes up against a dilemma: how can nationalism *also* facilitate illiberal movements and regimes which create internecine violence, political crises and civil war? Chatterjee points out that there is a conflict right at the heart of nationalism which he calls the 'liberal dilemma': nationalism may *promise* liberty and universal suffrage, but is *complicit* in undemocratic forms of government and domination. The sense of the Western nations as representing the very best in human progress and civilisation, firmly committed to a project of modernisation, becomes all too quickly a way of legitimating colonial expansion in moral terms. That is to say, colonialism can be justified with recourse to nationalism as a liberal, morally just, crusade to conquer the perceived ignorance and savagery *of others*.

The 'liberal dilemma' of nationalism becomes particularly problematic in colonial contexts. In using nationalism, many anti-colonial movements attempted to *appropriate* the liberal aspects of Western nationalism which promised the moral and political rights of liberty and political self-determination for the people. But as Chatterjee argues, they could not avoid also perpetuating nationalism's 'illiberal' and colonial aspects too:

> Nationalism sought to demonstrate the falsity of the colonial claim that the backward peoples were culturally incapable of ruling themselves in the conditions of the modern world. Nationalism denied the alleged inferiority of the colonised people; it also asserted that a backward nation could 'modernise' itself while retaining its cultural identity. It thus produced a discourse in which, even as it challenged the colonial claim to political domination, it also accepted the very intellectual premises of 'modernity' on which colonial domination was based. (p. 30)

Chatterjee argues that anti-colonial nationalisms inevitably have to use one of the chief tools of the colonialists, and this makes them culpable in continuing to traffic in colonial ideas. Not only have many once-colonised nations derived their national borders from the map-making of the colonial powers (as we saw with Nigeria), the nation *as a concept* is also derived from European colonial thinking.

This critique of the nation and nationalism on the grounds that they are derivative of Western colonial discourses raises some important questions. To what extent do anti-colonial nationalisms significantly differ from Western nationalisms? Do they perpetuate problematic colonial assumptions about the necessity to 'modernise' seemingly 'backward' communities? Do colonial and anti-colonial nationalisms regard the colonised nation in the same way?

The answers to these questions will differ from nation to nation, but to dismiss the ideas of nation and nationalism on the grounds that they have Western colonial origins seems rather naive, not least because it denies the fact that old ideas can be put to new purposes.

As Neil Lazarus argues in his essay 'National Consciousness and the Specificity of (Post) Colonial Intellectualism' (in *Colonial Discourse/Postcolonial Theory*, ed. Barker, Hulme and Iversen, pp. 197–220), 'we should be willing to concede that "the people" could or would not have spoken the language of nationalism without transforming it at least to some degree into a discourse capable of expressing their own aspirations' (p. 217). This is something that Partha Chatterjee explores in relation to anti-colonial nationalism in India, although he claims that the innovations he finds in an Indian context are by no means confined to this location.

Echoing perhaps Fanon's three stages of Algerian nationalism (which we explored in Chapter 3), Chatterjee's narrative of Indian nationalism in *Nationalist Thought and the Colonial World* also focuses on three important phases in which nationalism is derived from Western thought – but is *transformed* as it is turned to new, anti-colonial purposes. In the first phase, the **moment of departure**, anti-colonial nationalist movements emerge which *accept* that modern European culture 'possesses attributes which make the European culturally equipped for power and progress, while such attributes are lacking in "traditional" cultures of the East, thus dooming these countries to poverty and subjection' (*Nationalist Thought and the Colonial World*, p. 50). In addition, although European culture may be technologically advanced, the cultures of the East are posited as possessing a heightened 'spiritual' aspect. Anti-colonial nationalism in the first phase aims to marry the technological greatness of the West with the spiritual greatness of the East. Importantly, this aim is pursued chiefly by members of the colonised elites, in whose refined intellects such a plan has been hatched. Fanon had argued that the colonised belonging to the Western-educated, economically elite classes must put themselves 'to school with the people', in an attempt to close the gap between the elite and the masses and co-ordinate their different positions within a shared plan. But Chatterjee argues that historically, and at least in an Indian context, something different happened. The elite attempted to mobilise the masses in their nationalist aims, but also made sure that the masses *remained distant* from the trappings of power and continually subject to the whims and rule of the colonised elite.

This is the second phase, the **moment of manoeuvre**. Often this involves seeming to embrace popular, 'anti-modern' ways as a means of upbraiding the modernising violence of the colonial nation; yet, ultimately such manoeuvres enable anti-colonial nationalist movements to move closer to establishing and administering 'modern' institutions in the colonised nation. The elite appropriates the forms and functions of popular or folk culture, *not* in order to discover alternative, indigenous forms of knowledge that refute Western 'modernity', but as a way of gaining mass support for the elite's attempts to take over control of 'modern' forms of technological, political and economic power from the colonisers. Chatterjee cites the work of Mahatma Gandhi as an example of this 'manoeuvre'.

In the third phase, the **moment of arrival**, the ambitions of the second phase are realised and nationalist thought in the colonial world emerges as a unified, coherent and rational discourse. The nationalist elite claim that their 'modern' attitudes are coterminous with 'popular consciousness' and enjoy the support of the people, deemed to be a unified and singular entity sharing the same political aims. But that co-ordination of the elite with the masses masks an unequal, neo-colonial power relation of the kind which Fanon warned against in 'The Pitfalls of National Consciousness'.

STOP and THINK

Chatterjee's argument raises two main areas of debate which we can bring into focus in a different context by revisiting our exploration of *A Grain of Wheat* conducted in the previous chapter.

First, does the appropriation of nationalism by the colonised eliminate sufficiently its colonial attitudes? Do the various manoeuvres of anti-colonial nationalisms ever dissolve the illiberal tendencies of Western nationalism? As we saw, in Ngugi's novel there are characters (such as General R.) keen to distinguish between who can and cannot belong to the newly independent nation.

Second, how do the relations between the colonised elite and

the masses problematise anti-colonial nationalisms? How 'popular' can they be? Can they claim to represent faithfully the
aims, objectives and attitudes of the masses or does anti-colonial nationalism coerce the masses into following an elite project? Who benefits the most from 'national liberation', and
what are these benefits? For example, in *A Grain of Wheat* the
MP who buys the farm that Gikonyo wanted does not seem to
be supporting the initiatives of the poorer people of the region.

As always, we must remember that the answers to such
questions may differ according to national context, and it is
dangerous to presuppose that all anti-colonial nationalisms,
and the problems they encounter and create, are the same.
But sometimes it is useful to pose general questions *as a
means of beginning* your explorations of anti-colonial nationalist representations – just as Chatterjee's work on Indian
nationalism enabled us to understand better some of the issues
at stake in Ngugi's novel of Kenya.

Nationalism, representation and the elite

Chatterjee's attention to the problematic relations between nationalist elites and the masses requires further attention, not least because
this impacts upon the ways in which the nation is represented.
Interrogations of anti-colonial nationalisms on the grounds of their
alleged elitism make two important points. First, following Fanon,
anti-colonial nationalism can result in the replacement of a Western,
colonial ruling class with a Western-educated, 'indigenous' ruling
class who seem to speak on behalf of the people but function to keep
the people disempowered. Second, representations of nationalist
struggle tend to celebrate the inspirational activities of *individual
members of the elite* and do not recognise the role played by less privileged individuals or groups in resisting colonial rule.

This latter issue has been one of the key areas of concern for a
number of scholars known collectively as the *Subaltern Studies*
group. Influenced variously by the writings of Karl Marx, Antonio
Gramsci and Michel Foucault, these critics have explored the ways
in which representations of Indian nationalism either ignore the

contributions made to anti-colonial struggles by the masses, or explain their activities in such a way that the particular and local forms of 'subaltern consciousness' are not represented adequately. As Ranajit Guha explains in his essay 'On Some Aspects of the His-toriography of Colonial India' (in *Selected Subaltern Studies*, ed. Ranajit Guha and Gayatri Chakravorty Spivak, Oxford University Press, 1988), the term 'subaltern' (borrowed from the work of Gramsci) is used to signify the many different peoples who did not comprise the colonial elite. These might include 'the lesser rural gentry, impoverished landlords, rich peasants and upper-middle-class peasants' (p. 44), although members of the subaltern classes could work either for or against the interests of the elite depending on the situation. Guha's essay calls attention to the ways that con-temporary representations of Indian anti-colonial nationalism tend to place the subaltern classes as subject to the whims of the elite. Hence, Indian nationalism often reads as 'primarily an idealist ven-ture in which the indigenous elite led the people from subjugation to freedom ... The history of Indian nationalism is thus written up as a sort of spiritual biography of the Indian elite' (p. 38). Guha ren-ders these representations suspect on the grounds that they are locked inside a certain way of thinking about Indian nationalism that privileges elite consciousness over subaltern consciousness. The activities, efforts and decisions made by members of the subaltern classes are rarely regarded; and when they are, Guha argues that little attention is paid to the specific forms and functions of their insurgency. Nor is the conflictual relationship between elite and subaltern groups explored. As Guha puts it elsewhere in *Selected Subaltern Studies*, the rebellious subaltern too often 'is excluded as the conscious subject of his [*sic*] own history' (p. 77).

Guha's argument raises a particularly important question: how can we recover 'subaltern consciousness' when it is either ignored in historical representations or rendered in such as way as to ignore its specificity? This has proved an insoluble issue which we shall be returning to in more detail when we consider Gayatri Chakravorty Spivak's important essay 'Can the Subaltern Speak?' in Chapter 6. But it is clear in the present context that nationalist representations, in Guha's view, support elitism and fail to bear witness to the (often different) activities and arguments of the people.

Nationalism, 'race' and ethnicity

In her book *The Politics of Home: Postcolonial Relocations and Twentieth-Century Fiction* (Cambridge University Press, 1996), Rosemary Marangoly George makes the succinct and highly useful remark that 'nationalism leads to the interpretation of diverse phenomenon through one glossary, thus erasing specificities, setting norms and limits, lopping off tangentials' (p. 14). It is here that the 'illiberal' aspects of nationalism most starkly appear. Historically, particularly divisive criteria have been used in some countries with a history of colonialism as ways of manufacturing national unity – criteria based upon ideas of racial, ethnic or religious exclusivity. While this has rewarded some with the trappings of power, others have found themselves restricted from positions of authority and condemned as second-class citizens.

Let us consider the ways in which 'race' and ethnicity have been used to set the 'norms and limits' of the nation's imagined community. The first thing to note is that these terms do *not* mean the same thing, although they have some similarities. Taking 'race' first, it is important to realise that all constructions of racial difference are based upon human invention and not biological fact. There exist no objective criteria by which human beings can be neatly grouped into separate 'races', each fundamentally different from the other. Racial differences are best thought of as *political constructions* which serve the interests of certain groups of people. Theories of racial difference are often highly selective in choosing certain biological 'facts' in making distinctions. Skin colour has often been the primary sign of racial difference and a frequent target of racialising discourses, often taken as evidence of some form of 'natural' difference between, say, white and black Africans. We tend not to think of people with different eye colours as fundamentally different, yet this is just as much a biological 'fact' as skin colour.

In short, we are proposing that our perceptions of racial difference are constructed socially for particular political purposes, and are, of course, open to contestation and change. 'Race' as a category is the result of this social and historical process which we can call *racialisation*. Racism is the ideology that upholds the discrimination against certain people on the grounds of perceived racial difference and claims these constructions of racial identity are true or natural. Thus, throughout this book we will place 'race' within quotation marks as a way of continually emphasising its existence as a *historical construct* and not a biological given.

Both 'race' and ethnicity are concepts used to posit a common bond or identity between individuals. But whereas 'race' tends to prioritise physiological features as evidence of similarity between individuals, the parameters of 'ethnicity' tend to be more wide. As Floya Anthias and Nira Yuval-Davis helpfully explain:

> Ethnic groups involve the positing of boundaries in relation to who can and cannot belong according to certain parameters which are extremely heterogeneous, ranging from the credentials of birth to being born in the right place, conforming to cultural or other symbolic practices, language, and very centrally behaving in sexually appropriate ways.
> (Anthias and Yuval-Davis, *Racialised Boundaries: Race, Nation, Gender, Colour and Class and the Anti-racist Struggle*, Routledge, 1992, p. 4)

Ethnicity tends to involve a variety of social practices, rituals and traditions in identifying different collective groups. Although 'race' and ethnicity are *not* synonymous, both can be used as the grounds for discrimination. Members of particular ethnic groups or 'races' might find themselves disqualified from certain positions of power.

However, without wishing at all to diminish the potential divisiveness of these constructions, ethnic and racial identities can also be used by marginalised peoples as valuable resources (think, for example, of the work of the Negritude writers we considered in the previous chapter). In particular, an individual's ethnicity can provide an invaluable sense of belonging to a particular group in the present, and also to a tradition or inheritance of cultural and historical treasures. The potential uses of ethnicity and racial difference are variable over time and space, and need not always be divisive.

In the context of nationalism, 'race' and ethnicity have been used to further certain illiberal aims. Etienne Balibar's essay 'Racism and Nationalism' (cited earlier) explores the ways in which nationalism can become complicit with racism by privileging one racialised group above another as the nation's most legitimate or 'true' people. The perception of 'race' can function as a primary strategy in constructing myths of national unity and in deciding who may or may not belong to the rightful people. As part of his argument Balibar makes a useful distinction between *external* and *internal* racism (see pp. 38–40). *External racism* is a form of xenophobia, when groups of people who are located outside the borders of the nation are discriminated against on the grounds of their 'race'. *Internal racism* is directed at those who live within the nation but are not deemed to belong to the imagined community of the national people due to their perceived 'race'. Internal racism can result in its most extreme and violent form in the *extermination* of racialised individuals (as in the destruction of Aboriginal communities in Tazmania in the nineteenth century, for example) or the *oppression* of racialised groups who are awarded a low position in the social hierarchy (we might think about indigenous or 'First Nations' peoples in Canada as evidence of this point). In these terms, perceptions of 'race' can structure the nation's 'norms and limits'.

One of the effects of racist ideologies is to produce a sense of national identity gained through the exclusion and denigration of others, as Balibar points out:

> racism always tends to operate in an inverted fashion ... the racial-cultural identity of 'true nationals' remains invisible, but it can be inferred (and is ensured) *a contrario* by the alleged, quasi-hallucinatory visibility of 'false nationals': the Jews, 'wogs', immigrants, 'Pakis', natives, Blacks. (p. 60)

This leads Balibar to posit that nationalism always has a *reciprocal* relation with racism (although the nature of that relation can take many different forms): where one is found, the other is never far away. Therefore, in using nationalism, it is claimed that decolonising peoples are in danger of perpetuating a concept which tends to support divisive processes of racialisation. It is no surprise to Balibar that in the process of decolonisation, illiberal racist tendencies have been 'reproduced, expanded and re-activated' (p. 43).

So, if nationalism is derived from the West, then attempts to construct a unifying myth of the nation can exacerbate existing conflicts between groups in some once-colonised nations or between different 'races' or ethnicities. Let us consider one example of this, post-independence Nigeria. Inheriting its borders from British colonialism, Nigeria is an intersection of many different African peoples. Its population consists of peoples from a variety of ethnic groups, such as Hausa, Fulani, Yoruba, Igbo, Kanuri, Tiv and Ijaw (which are all also internally multifarious). In addition to the many different beliefs held by these peoples, a large percentage of Nigerians are Muslims or Christians. Manufacturing a sense of national unity between them within the territorial borders inherited from colonialism has proven a difficult task, and has led to bloody conflict in recent years. In 1966, six years after formal independence there occurred two military coups. The first was led by Igbo army officers in the North, the second by members of the Hausa people. The result was bloodshed and enforced migrations; many Igbos in the north fled to the Eastern region of the country in fear for their lives. In 1967 the Eastern region declared itself the republic of Biafra, and civil war ensued until 1970 when the Biafran forces surrendered. One million people were killed during the war. Two more military coups followed, in 1975 and 1976. An elected government ruled Nigeria between 1979 and 1983, but since then military rule has returned. At the time of writing, a return to civil government is pending.

STOP and THINK

There is not enough room to deal with the complexity of recent Nigerian history here. But even this thumbnail sketch of Nigeria's fortunes gives some sense of the internal divisions and struggles between ethnic groups who feel that their interests are being threatened by others. Manufacturing a sense of unity in this context has become too often a bloody affair with one ethnicity seeking to become the ruling group, or attempting to secede from the nation entirely as in the case of Biafra.

These experiences also enable us to consider the fact that, for some peoples, the imagined community of the nation *need not* be the primary mode of collectivity: forms of group-identity based on ethnicity can be deemed far more important. We are led to ponder the following question: how productive is the myth of the nation in the decolonised world? It may well have provided a valuable resource in organising anti-colonial resistance movements during colonial rule, but is it as valuable after the colonial period where conditions are different? National borders were, after all, often invented during colonialism. How much sense does it make to use them in a changed and changing world?

Nationalism, gender and sexuality

In our discussion of Ngugi's *A Grain of Wheat*, we considered the character of Mumbi as an iconic mother-figure of the newly independent Kenya. The metaphorical association between woman, mother and nation is familiar to many nationalist discourses, as C. L. Innes suggests in her essay '"Forging the Conscience of Their Race": Nationalist Writers'. In both literary and popular representations, the nation has frequently been depicted iconically as a female. In a British context we might think about the female figure of Britannia that appears in variety of representations, from paintings to poetry to banknotes. Nationalism is very frequently a *gendered* discourse; it traffics in representations of men and women which serve to reinforce patriarchal inequalities between them. Nationalist representations have been in danger of perpetuating disempowering representations of women.

Several feminist critics have pointed out a tendency towards *male chauvinism* in many forms of nationalism. In using women as icons of the nation, nationalist representations reinforce images of the passive female who depends upon active males to defend her honour. They also assert the chief agents of decolonisation as men; thus the process of national liberation is constructed as an exclusively male endeavour which ignores the contributions made by millions of women to countless independence struggles around the globe. Many anti-colonial nationalisms have represented the nation in gendered terms. This has had important implications for women's relationship with the nation in many different contexts. As Carole Boyce Davies puts it in her book *Black Women, Writing and Identity* (Routledge, 1994), 'nationalism thus far seems to exist primarily as a male activity with women distinctly left out or peripheralised in the various national constructs. Thus, the feminine was deployed at the symbolic level, as in "Mother Africa" or "Mother India"' (p. 12).

Additionally, gendered representations of the nation also inter-sect with issues of sexuality and thus re-enact some of the manoeu-vres of Orientalism. As the editors of *Nationalisms and Sexualities* (ed. Andrew Parker et al., Routledge, 1992) remind us, representa-tions of the nation as a mother threatened by foreign aggression often appear specifically in terms of *sexual* violation: 'how deeply ingrained has been the depiction of the homeland as a female body whose violation by foreigners requires its citizens and allies to rush to her defence' (p. 6).

The extent to which nationalism often traffics in patriarchal rep-resentations of women, and the ways in which female agency in anti-colonial struggles has been frequently ignored in nationalist representations, have led some to reject nationalism on the grounds that it has done little to challenge female subordination to patriar-chal norms in many once-colonised countries. Historically, it seems, men and women experience national liberation differently: women do not reap equal benefits from decolonisation for reasons of gender inequality. Women's contributions to the nationalist struggle are too quickly forgotten after independence is achieved and do not appear in nationalist representations. The editors of *Nationalisms and Sex-ualities* point out that women have effected the overthrow of colonial power in many times and places but have found the decolonised nation is hardly interested in female liberation: 'In anti-colonial struggles … feminist programmes have been sacrificed to the cause of national liberation and, in the aftermath of independence, women have been reconsigned to their formerly "domestic" roles' (*Nation-alisms and Sexualities*, p. 7). According to these views, the construc-tion of a national people has tended to privilege men as the active agents in national liberation and the chief beneficiaries of political and economic power gained through the nationalist struggle.

The feminist critique of nationalism has been helpfully sum-marised by Floya Anthias and Nira Yuval-Davis in their intro-duction to *Woman-Nation-State* (ed. Anthias and Yuval-Davis, Macmillan, 1989), a collection of essays that explores the relation-ship between women, the nation, and state policy in a variety of loca-tions which include Australia, South Africa and Uganda. Of course, any summary always runs the risk of ignoring historical specificity. None the less, it is worth quoting here insofar as it equips us with a useful series of contexts which we can apply in our readings of nationalist representations. Furthermore, it also indicates how gender and sexual issues often become inseparably bound up with ethnicity. We have separated above the issues of ethnicity and gender/sexuality for the purposes of clarity, but we must note that nationalist representations often bind ethnicity, gender and sexuality together in complex ways.

According to Anthias and Yuval-Davis, there are 'five major (although not exclusive) ways' in which women historically have been positioned within nationalist discourses (p. 7):

1. as biological reproducers of members of ethnic collectivities;
2. as reproducers of the boundaries of ethnic/national groups;
3. as participating centrally in the ideological reproduction of the collectivity and as transmitters of its culture;
4. as signifiers of ethnic/national differences – as a focus and symbol in ideological discourses used in the construction, reproduction and transformation of ethnic categories;
5. as participants in national, economic, political and military struggles.

Let us take briefly each of these categories:

1. First, as *biological reproducers of members of ethnic collectivities*, women are encouraged by the state to believe that it is their duty to produce children to replenish the numbers of those who 'rightfully' belong to the nation for reasons of ethnicity. Contrariwise, women who are not deemed to belong to the 'proper' ethnic group can find themselves subject to forced sterilisation.
2. As *reproducers of the boundaries of ethnic groups*, women are charged with ensuring that the act of reproduction does not threaten group identity at a symbolic level. To take one example, in some cases it is taboo for women to have sex with men of a different ethnic group or social class. Such borders must not be crossed. Hence the act of biological reproduction is organised in such a way as to support social reproduction.
3. As *transmitters of culture*, women are deemed to be the primary educators of children and responsible for introducing them to

the heritage and traditions of the nation's culture. Women's role as reproducers is at once biological and cultural.

4. As *signifiers of ethnic/national differences*, women are used as icons, such as the mother-figures of the nation which we explored earlier. These iconic representations offer no means by which women's manifold experiences of and contributions to anti-colonial nationalism can become the subject of nationalist representations.

5. Finally, we are reminded that women are *participants in national, economic, political and military struggles*, contrary to many nationalist representations which depict women 'in a supportive and nurturing relation to men' (p. 10).

This last point is especially important. In making their list, Anthias and Yuval-Davis point out that nationalist discourses attempt to position women in particular ways which serve patriarchal, sexual and ethnic interests. But we must not let these representations distract us from the fact that women actively contributed to nationalist struggles and, after decolonisation, have resisted the operations of forms of patriarchy.

The nation and its margins

One of the most influential and challenging interventions in the debate concerning nationalist representations is Homi K. Bhabha's essay 'DissemiNation: Time, Narrative and the Margins of the Modern Nation'. Bhabha's essay first appeared in a collection of essays *Nation and Narration* (ed. Homi K. Bhabha, Routledge, 1990) and is reprinted in *The Location of Culture* (Routledge, 1994), pp. 139–70 – we shall use the latter in our discussion. Bhabha's essay reveals nationalist representations as highly unstable and fragile constructions which cannot ever produce the unity they promise. This is because, in Bhabha's argument, they become split by similar kinds of ambivalence to those that threaten the coherence of colonial discourses. In making this argument, the essay might make us think about the worrying *similarities* between colonial discourses and nationalist representations.

As we have seen, it is the aim of nationalist discourses to create community out of difference, to convert the 'many' into 'one'. In so doing, Bhabha argues, they engage with two contradictory modes of representation, which he calls the *pedagogic* and the *performative*, each possessing its own relationship with time (or 'temporality'). Nationalist discourses are split by a disruptive 'double narrative movement' (*The Location of Culture*, p. 145). On the one hand, nationalism is a 'pedagogic' discourse. It claims a fixed origin for the nation and asserts a sense of a *continuous* history which links the nation's people in the present to previous generations of national subjects. It is 'pedagogical' because it warrants the authority, legitimacy and primacy of the nation as the central political and social unit which collects the population into a 'people'. The people are the *object* of pedagogical discourse; they are the body which nationalism constructs and upon which it acts. Pedagogical narratives are shaped by a 'continuist, accumulative temporality' (p. 145) which gives the impression of the steady, linear movement of time from past to present to future – as in the narrative of the nation's history, for example, the 'story of the tribe' which offers a genealogical account of the people's common fortunes.

But on the other hand, Bhabha argues that nationalist discourses are *simultaneously* 'performative'. This term refers to the ways in which nationalist icons and popular signs (all those representations which help fix its 'norms and limits') must be *continually rehearsed* by the people in order to keep secure the sense of 'deep, horizontal comradeship'. A national culture must be *endlessly* performed; the arbitrary range of symbols which it uses to forge unity require *repeated* inscription as the stuff of national significance. 'The scraps, patches and rags of daily life must be repeatedly turned into the signs of a coherent national culture' writes Bhabha (p. 145). In these terms, the people are also the *subjects* of nationalist discourses, actively involved in the (re)production of its signs and traditions: they must repeatedly tell their history, perform the nation's rituals, celebrate its great figures and commemorate its anniversaries. Hence, nationalist discourses in their performative aspects function under a *different* temporality, the 'repetitious' and 'recursive' (p. 145).

As a consequence of this 'double' narrative movement, the nation is split by what Bhabha terms the 'conceptual ambivalence' (p. 146) at the heart of its discursive strategies. The nation is always being pulled between two incompatible opposites: the nation as a fixed, originary essence (continuist and pedagogic), and the nation as socially manufactured and devoid of a fixed origin (repetitive and performative). Between these two positions, out of this 'disjunctive temporality' (p. 148), a sense of the nation's homogeneous 'people' begins to fragment. The pedagogical representation of the people as 'object' constructs an idealised image of unity and coherence in the past. But because of the necessity for the performance of the nation's signs by the people as 'subject', the pedagogical ideal of the homogeneous people can never be realised. This is because the performative necessity of nationalist representations enables all those placed on the margins of its norms and limits – such as women, migrants, the working class, the peasantry, those of a different 'race' or ethnicity – to *intervene* in the signifying process and *challenge* the dominant representations with narratives of their own. A plural population can never be converted into a singular people because plurality and difference can never be entirely banished:

> We are [hence] confronted with the nation split within itself, articulating the heterogeneity of its population. The barred Nation *It/Self*, alienated from its eternal self-generation, becomes a liminal signifying space that is *internally* marked by the discourse of minorities, the heterogeneous histories of contending peoples, antagonistic authorities and tense locations of cultural difference. (p. 148)

So, the necessity for the perpetual regeneration of the nation via the performance of its signs cannot help but expose it to the interventions of those which are placed on the margins of its 'norms and limits'. It is through the performative aspects of nationalist discourses that difference returns *from within* to challenge the homogeneous nation with its unified people and myths of origin, as the marginalised people of the population are granted an opportunity to intervene in the production of the nation's representation of itself to itself. Bhabha fixes upon these counter-narratives of the nation which 'disturb those ideological manoeuvres through which "imagined communities" are given essentialist identities' (p. 149). Nationalist discourses require essence, origin, unity and coherence, and need to *forget* the presence and the narratives of certain peoples within its imaginary boundaries in order to function. But the ideal of coherence remains forever out of reach due to the disjunctive temporality – continuist *and* repetitive – which splits the nation. Counter-narratives interrupt the nation's smooth self-generation at the level of the performative, revealing *different* experiences, histories and representations which nationalist discourses depend on excluding. Hence, 'the national memory is always the site of the hybridity of histories and the displacement of narratives' (p. 169).

Bhabha's argument is compelling not least because it represents the nation in its more illiberal guises, while also revealing that its propensity to marginalise certain peoples can never fully realise itself. Nationalist discourses are frustrated in their aims due to the necessity of the performative which renders the nation ambivalent. For those considered marginal to the nation's 'proper' people, this is, perhaps, a valuable and positive argument to pursue. Bhabha represents nationalist discourses as fragile, split and contradictory, rather than benevolent and inclusive.

Yet problems remain with his essay. First, it is not entirely clear where the agency for counter-narratives of the nation exists. Does the agency for resistance derive from the acts of representation by those from the nation's margins, or is it found mystically within nationalism itself? If it is the latter, then why have nationalist discourses been so powerful? Just as Bhabha's critique of 'the discourse of colonialism' fails to account for its continued political authority, so too does his critique of nationalism leave a similar question unanswered. Second, although Bhabha is more culturally specific here than in his work on the ambivalence of colonial discourse, there is still a tendency to universalise his model of the ambivalence of nationalist representations despite the fact that he claims to be making 'no general theory' (p. 170).

Ultimately, Bhabha's essay asserts that there can never be any one, coherent, common narrative through which a nation and its people can be adequately captured. The nation remains a site of heterogeneity and difference. Narratives which claim otherwise can do so only through the marginalisation of certain groups, yet even this claim will be undone by the disjunctive temporalities which they cannot help but create. In Bhabha's work, nationalist discourses are *ultimately* illiberal and must *always* be challenged.

STOP and THINK

In examining the problems with nationalist representations in this chapter so far, we might be tempted to dismiss the ideas of nation and nationalism on the grounds that, ultimately, they cannot ever be free from marginalising, illiberal tendencies. But should nationalism be so readily dismissed?

Benita Parry's recent essay, 'Resistance Theory/Theorising Resistance, or Two Cheers for Nativism', (in *Colonial Discourse/ Postcolonial Theory*, ed. Barker, Hulme and Iversen, pp. 172–96) invites us to think more flexibly than this. Parry reminds us of the efficacy and value of national discourses in the decolonised world. In looking again at the Negritude writers and the work of Frantz Fanon, often criticised today for accepting too readily colonial forms of knowledge, she argues that 'it is surely necessary to refrain from a sanctimonious reproof of modes of writing resistance which do not conform to contemporary theoretical rules about discursive radicalism' (p. 179). Although Parry acknowledges the ways in which much anti-colonial nationalist writing in North and West Africa during the 1950s and 1960s repeated some of the prescriptive tendencies and chauvinism of nationalism, dismissing this writing today as ideologically corrupt avoids thinking about nationalist representations in their historical contexts. This manifold archive of anti-colonial writing may well have had its ideological limitations, such as the essentialising of 'blackness' by the Negritude writers. Yet in claiming agency and authority for black subjects, these writers released important 'revolutionary energies' and contributed much to anti-colonial resistance in 'valorising the cultures denigrated by colonialism' (p. 179).

In your view, should the conceptual failings of nationalism as revealed by Bhabha and others detract from its productivity as a revolutionary anti-colonial strategy of resistance? To what extent would you condemn nationalism because it ultimately failed, in Parry's terms, 'to contest the conventions of that system of knowledge it supposedly challenges' (p. 172)?

The problems of using English

So far we have examined some of the *conceptual* problems of nation-alist representations. Let us turn next to problems of specific lan-guage-use, and address the thorny debates about the role of English as a national language in once-colonised countries.

In many parts of the British Empire, English was the primary lan-guage of government and administration, and used in the education of colonised subjects (we will be exploring this latter issue in detail in the next chapter). After independence, many colonial nations inherited economic, governmental and educational institutions, sev-eral of which were often administered in English. The English lan-guage is a part of this colonial 'inheritance'. Its existence as the language of colonial power has complicated its status as the language of the independent nation, and there are conflicting attitudes towards English as the national language of once-colonised coun-tries. Can it ever function as the national language of the nation after colonialism? The answer to this question varies from location to location; but let us consider just a couple of brief examples.

English in the settler nations

The English language is one of the several European languages (like French, Spanish, Portuguese and Dutch) which has become a national language in once-colonised countries. Yet many writers and critics in the settler nations have been keen to differentiate their usage of English from its standard form which evolved in Britain. There is a sense that the terms of reference and conceptual vocabu-lary of English, as well as the cultural values it carried, are not easily suited to describing the experiences of a different place. The Aus-tralian poet Judith Wright remarked in 1965 that the European set-tler was faced with a problem on arrival in Australia, as their sense of European 'tradition' and 'inheritance' soon began to weaken: 'the older culture which had given [the settler's] life a meaning beyond the personal, by linking him [*sic*] with the past, began to lose its power over him. It had authority still, but his real share in it drib-bled away; for the true function of an art and a culture is to interpret us to ourselves, and to relate us to the country and the society in which we live' (*Preoccupations in Australian Poetry*, Oxford University Press, 1965, p. xviii). In other words, the English language as it had been previously used was not capable of bearing witness to the particular sights, sounds and experiences of this new, Australian environment. For Wright, European-descended Australian writers were faced with a question: what kind of relationship were they to have with a language they had inherited but was not readily suited to the task of 'making Australia into our real spiritual home' (Wright, p. xviii)?

Managing the relationship with English in the settler colonies has remained a problematic issue. One solution to Wright's question has been the *reworking* of English under its new conditions, forcing it to change from its standard version into something new and more suited to the new surroundings. Bill Ashcroft has theorised this process in his essay 'Constitutive Graphonomy: A Post-Colonial Theory of Literary Writing' (in *After Europe: Critical Theory and Post-Colonial Writing*, ed. Stephen Slemon and Helen Tiffin, Dangaroo, 1989, pp. 58–73). Ashcroft explores how all language-utterances (let's call them 'texts' for short) are produced and received in specific contexts and emerge from unique situations. Meaning depends upon the *moment* of textual production and the *place* where texts are produced. Each limits and determines the range of meanings available to a text. So, when English is used in a once-colonised location, the specifics of the site of textual production will necessarily force its meanings to *change*. The new forms of 'english' which result are deliberately proclaimed to be *distant* from the received norm, and offer a means for English speakers in the settler colonies to conceive of their difference through their language:

> But even in the most monoglossic settler cultures the sub-cultural distancing which generates the evolution of variant language shows that the linguistic cultures encompassed by the term 'English' are vastly heterogeneous. Most importantly, post-colonial literatures provide … a writing which actually *installs* distance and absence in the interstices of the text. (p. 61)

Although the new differentiated 'english' can be recognised by standard English speakers – it has a degree of sameness that enables comprehension outside of its specific site of enunciation – it may contain elements that remain distant to the standard English reader and defy their powers of comprehension.

Ashcroft's ideas are central to *The Empire Writes Back* (Routledge, 1989) which we discussed in Chapter 1, and many of the criticisms of that book apply to his essay. Although admirable in its attempt to address the specific *situatedness* of all language usage, the argument becomes rather detached from the specifics of place and is rather generalising, both in terms of postcolonial 'english' usage and standard English. But he does provide us with a useful model for explaining how English is adapted in new contexts, a process that has been crucial to the construction of images of national and cultural identity in the settler colonies.

However, English-language representations of the nation in the settler colonies are problematised by the presence of native or Aboriginal peoples descended from communities which existed before Europeans arrived. What status is afforded to the languages of native or Aboriginal peoples? What relationship do these peoples have with English? Do national representations include these peoples too? More often than not, native or Aboriginal peoples have had a conflictual relationship with the English language. In the preface to Jeanne Perrault and Sylvia Vance's edited collection *Writing the Circle: Native Women of Western Canada* (University of Oklahoma Press, 1993), Emma LaRocque shows how Aboriginal voices have been silenced in Canada due to the primacy of English, particularly in its written forms. Native languages, frequently oral rather than written, have been marginalised or dismissed in educational and other institutions along with the cultural values and traditions to which they testify. In addition, native peoples who have written in English have found it difficult to be heard, or have even had their critical representations of Canada dismissed as 'parochial'. LaRocque describes specifically the relationship between the 'Native woman writer' and the English language with these memorable words which are worth quoting at length:

> To a Native woman, English is like an ideological onion whose stinging layers of racism and sexism must be peeled away before it can be fully enjoyed ... Native readers and writers do not look at English words the same way as non-Natives may, for we have certain associations with a host of them. It is difficult to accept the following terms

as neutral: savage, primitive, pagan, medicine man, shaman, warrior, squaw, redskin, hostile, civilisation, developed, progress, the national interest, bitter, angry, happy hunting grounds, brave, buck, redman, chief, tribe, or even Indian. These are just a few of the string of epithets that have been pejoratively used to *specifically* indicate the ranking of Indian peoples as inferior to Europeans, thus to perpetuate their dehumanisation. (p. xx)

LaRocque forcefully asks us to question the extent to which English functions as a national language in settler countries facilitating a 'deep, horizontal comradeship' for all. In her view, native peoples have been left out of conventional representations of Canada. Ashcroft's argument that English is changed into 'english' through its use in new environs may be true, but the newly created 'english' may remain a mode of *internal colonialism* for native peoples, whose language, representations and values are dismissed as parochial to the nation defined largely in the white settlers' terms. However, this does *not* lead LaRocque to dismiss or reject English, due to the fact of its establishment for better or worse in Canada. English does not solely belong to those of European descent. 'To read, speak and write in English is the birthright of contemporary Native peoples', she argues. 'I have sought to master this language so that it would no longer master me' (p. xxvi).

English in the settled nations

India's languages are various, including Hindi, Urdu, English, Punjabi, and Bengali, to name a few. Yet there has developed an exciting body of Indian literature in English, produced by such figures as R. K. Narayan, Nayantara Sahgal, Anita Desai, Salman Rushdie and Amitav Ghosh. Can we read this literature as a national literature? The dangers of doing so are pointed out by the Marxist critic Aijaz Ahmad in his book *In Theory: Classes, Nations, Literatures* (Verso, 1992). Ahmad is contemptuous of the ways in which Indian literature in English is often read as a national literature particularly in Western universities, despite the fact that it is produced in the main by an English-speaking minority drawn from the more wealthy cosmopolitan classes. Ahmad complains that this creates a situation where 'only the literary document produced in English is a *national* document; all else is regional, hence minor and forgettable, so that English emerges in this imagination not as *one* of the Indian languages, which undoubtedly it is, but as *the* language of national integration and bourgeois civility' (p. 75). This state of affairs is unacceptable to Ahmad. There are a multitude of different languages in India with their own narratives, opinions and values, but these remain marginalised if only English texts are deemed to be constitutive of the 'norms and limits' of Indian national culture. Ahmad claims that the continuing predominance of English in India at administrative and cultural levels is best described as 'neo-colonial', in that it continues to exclude many millions of Indians who are not literate in English. In his view the English language continues to serve the interests of the educated elite and not the people as a whole.

Forceful as it is, Ahmad's argument seems rigidly mechanical. He can offer no account of how English might have been changed by its use in a new context (as Ashcroft does in his essay). Nor does he think about how writers from the 'privileged elite' might use English in subversive ways.

Ngugi wa Thiong'o has also come to adopt a hostile attitude to English. Since 1980 he has stopped writing in English and now writes in his native tongue, Gikuyu. In his book *Decolonising the Mind: The Politics of Language in African Literature* (James Currey, 1981), Ngugi gives his reasons for rejecting English. As a child Gikuyu was the language spoken in Ngugi's home and by the workers in the fields. His early schooling was also conducted in Gikuyu, but when the State of Emergency was declared in 1952, Gikuyu was replaced at school by English. Children found speaking Gikuyu in school were punished and the language was suppressed. For Ngugi the silencing of Gikuyu was a violent and destructive act of colonialism. To dismiss a language is to dismiss a whole culture:

> Culture embodies those moral, ethical and aesthetic values, the set of spiritual eyeglasses, through which [a people] come to view themselves and their place in the universe. Values are the basis of a people's identity, their sense of particularity as members of the human race. All this is carried by language. Language as culture is the collective memory bank of a people's experience in history. (pp. 14–15)

Ngugi reasons that if he continues to write in English, he remains split off from the 'memory bank' of his community, a split caused by colonialism which he wishes to heal. To write in English is to deal in the values of the oppressor, to see the world through colonial lenses and not through inherited 'spiritual eyeglasses'. Therefore Ngugi declares his determination to 'restore the Kenyan child to his environment' (p. 28) by writing in his mother tongue. He calls on other African writers to renounce English so that, through the use of indigenous language, they might 'reconnect themselves to the revolutionary traditions of an organised peasantry and working class in Africa in their struggle to defeat imperialism' (p. 29). In these terms, English *interrupts* the creation of a national consciousness after independence, and its continuing use must be opposed.

Of course, Ngugi's relationship with English is different to those of European descent in the settler colonies. He cannot make the same kind of claims which Judith Wright made about English. Still, there is more than a touch of nostalgia in Ngugi's argument, as if he is keen to recover an idealised community experienced in childhood relatively unravished by the effects of colonialism. Can things be so easily reversed? Also, the representation of language here tends to be rather homogenising and tidy. Nevertheless, his stinging attack on English as a major weapon of colonialism asks us to question once again the extent to which English can be freed from the colonial values it supported and articulated.

These rejections of English have by no means proven popular, as the vast body of postcolonial literature in English testifies. In tackling the issue of English we must never forget to take into account the *specific linguistic conditions* of different locations. In the Caribbean for example, English cannot be so easily censured. Along with other European languages such as Dutch or Spanish, English became one of the dominant languages in the region during the colonial period. Indigenous languages perished with the indigenous peoples, while the languages of the African slaves shipped across the Atlantic to work on the plantations were discouraged by the colonial authorities. Today, English remains one of the predominant languages of education and power. Consequently, it is more widely spoken among the population than English in India and is less easy to reject. In contrast to the situation Ngugi describes in Kenya, it is also difficult to recover an 'indigenous' language in the Caribbean to which one 'belongs' when the native languages have been destroyed and the most frequently spoken languages were brought from overseas, from Europe, Africa and India.

English remains widely spoken in parts of the Caribbean, but its form has been radically changed by its users. Edward Kamau Brathwaite explores these changes in his work on 'nation language'. This is a term used in his influential lecture *History of the Voice* (New Beacon Books, 1984), which is an exploration of the innovative uses of English in Caribbean poetry. Brathwaite celebrates Anglophone Caribbean poets who are attempting to articulate their unique historical and cultural situation through their deployment of 'nation language'. Brathwaite shows how various poets are inflecting the English language with different kinds of rhythms, sounds, syntax and forms of expression which can be traced back to African speech patterns. This is 'nation language', and one of its main functions is the articulation of an appropriate register, or 'voice' in which Caribbean experiences can be fully represented. Standard English is transformed in 'nation language' due to the different syncopations and patterns of spoken English in the Caribbean. Indeed, 'nation language' is the language of the people – crucially, it is *not* an elite language – who are finding different ways of giving voice to their experiences which refuse the inherited European models and break out of their confines. These everyday voices become the inspiration for new ways of using English literary and linguistic forms in poetry.

In their turn, the 'nation language' poets of the Caribbean perform a vital social function in their work which Brathwaite explains as follows: 'for the needs of the kind of emerging society that I am defending – for the people who have to recite "The boy/stood on/the burn/ing deck" for so long, who are unable to express the power of the hurricane in the way that they write their words – at last, our poets, today, are recognising that it is essential that they use the resources which have always been there, but which have been denied to them' (p. 42). Through 'nation language', poets find their own unique 'voice' that is particular and appropriate to the Caribbean; and not solely derived from, nor obedient to, its European sources.

Brathwaite's essay is a wonderful exercise in claiming artistic dignity and aesthetic sophistication for a use of English which might be seen by some as sub-standard or bastardised. However, his term 'nation language' is more figurative than literal and can be a little misleading. Primarily it is a concept used to describe language-use in poetry from many Caribbean nations; 'nation language' is not really specific to any one of these nations in particular. It does not advocate a *strict* sense of Caribbean collectivity: the variety of 'nation language' poetry celebrates innovation and heterogeneity. There are no definitive 'norms and limits' set for the use of English. Paradoxically, 'nation language' does not constitute a rigorous nationalist discourse although Brathwaite does demonstrate how poets can stimulate a sense of a unique, valuable culture particular to the region and enable Caribbeans to reconsider their alleged inferior position in relation to European culture. This is an approach to English which contrasts with Ngugi's dismissal.

However, granted that 'nation language' is a fairly elastic term, we are left with little sense of how language-use might differ from place to place, and why. Also, Brathwaite's focus is exclusively on African-descended Caribbeans and thus cannot claim to represent all the peoples in the Carribean, who may have Indian or European ancestry (or more than one). Although he writes equally enthusiastically about male and female poets, the issue of gender difference is not broached. 'Nation language' is not free from some of the problems with more methodical nationalist representations which we explored earlier. None the less, Brathwaite's *History of the Voice* invites us to think that the concept of the nation may continue to perform vital cultural and political work in certain contexts, despite the many theoretical shortcomings which we have been exploring.

STOP and THINK

When you pursue the forms and functions of English in different locations, ask yourself the following questions: how was English introduced to this particular region? What functions (administrative, educational, cultural) did it serve? Who spoke it, and how did they learn it? What role does English play there today? Is it a common or minority language? Is it a popular language or the language of the privileged? English as a national language is never free from problems in all once-colonised countries. We must not assume that postcolonial literary texts in English offer us representative or typical illustrations of the nation as a whole.

The nation in question: Chinua Achebe's *Anthills of the Savannah*

Let us conclude by considering *Anthills of the Savannah* by Chinua Achebe. Achebe was born in 1930 in Ogidi, Nigeria. He was educated at University College, Ibadan and received a BA from London University in 1953. His first novel, *Things Fall Apart* (1958) is often hailed as one of the founding texts of postcolonial literature. *Anthills of the Savannah* is his most recent novel, written at a time of growing disenchantment with the revolutionary ideals of anti-colonial nationalism. It is a complex, thought-provoking text, and we will approach it in the light of the issues we have raised in this chapter.

Written some time after the end of colonialism in West Africa, *Anthills of the Savannah* is Achebe's sober examination of the fortunes of West African nations such as Nigeria since formal independence was achieved. Set in the fictional country of Kangan, the novel's plot depicts the mixed fortunes of the military government and its eventual defeat in a *coup d'état*. Many of its central characters are well-educated members from the upper reaches of Kangan society, each involved with the government at various levels. The male figures – Sam, Christopher Oriko and Ikem Osodi – have known each other from childhood, and each has spent time being educated in Britain. Sam received military training at Sandhurst and, as the novel opens, has assumed control of Kangan after a military coup. Re-naming himself 'His Excellency' and firmly ensconced in the Presidential Palace in Bassa, he has suffered humiliation in a recent referendum in which he hoped to establish himself as president for life. One province in the north-west, Abazon, failed to support him, thus making us question the extent to which the Kangan people share a 'deep, horizontal comradeship'. Throughout the novel Abazon is reported to be suffering a severe drought, and it is hinted that His Excellency has played a part in reducing the water supply to the region as retribution for its lack of support.

His Excellency's cabinet includes Chris as the Minister of Information. Previously, Chris had been editor of the *National Gazette*. This role is now filled by Ikem, an Abazonian by birth and an aspiring poet. Then there is Beatrice Okoh, who works as a Senior Assistant Secretary for the government's Finance department. Like the others, Beatrice knows Sam from their younger days and is having a relationship with Chris.

His Excellency is keen to control the flow of information circulating both inside Kangan and to the world at large, and appoints Chris partly to ensure that only those representations supportive of his government are published. However Ikem, as the editor of the *National Gazette*, holds such control in contempt and has been less than sympathetic to the government in some of his editorials. When Ikem meets with a delegation of Abazonians who visit the Presidential Palace to petition His Excellency to visit the region to see the damage wrought by the drought, His Excellency uses this as an excuse to deal with the unruly editor. Ikem is declared an anti-government agitator and dismissed from his post for allegedly helping organise the Abazonians' petition. Undaunted, Ikem gives a lecture at the University of Bassa in which he condemns the government's actions and urges the students to begin mending the corruption that has damaged Kangan. Almost immediately he is arrested and shot in police custody. His death is officially reported as the result of Ikem's foolish attempt to wrestle a gun from a guard.

Appalled at this cover-up of his friend's murder, Chris arranges to meet with members of the international press and tells them the truth, putting him on a collision course with His Excellency. Soon Chris is a wanted man. Ikem's and Chris's supporters decide that Chris should leave Bassa and head for the safety of Abazon. At the edge of Abazon province, the bus on which he is travelling incognito stops beside a group celebrating the news of His Excellency's downfall in a coup. During the revelry a drunken police officer begins to drag a young girl away, with sinister intentions. When Chris confronts him he is shot dead.

These events do *not* constitute the whole story, and the novel does not end there. The fortunes of the elite, male characters are placed among other voices and stories, particularly those of women. A crucial figure is Beatrice. Like the others she received a Western-style education in Kangan as a girl and later completed a degree in English at a London university. As a child she suffers the strict discipline of her patriarchal father, and this sensitises her to inequalities of gender. 'That every woman wants a man to complete her is a piece of male chauvinist bullshit I had completely rejected before I knew there was anything like Women's Lib', she remarks. 'You often hear our people say: But that's something you picked up in England. Absolute rubbish! There was enough male chauvinism in my father's house to last me seven reincarnations!' (p. 88).

Through the character of Beatrice, Achebe draws attention to the chauvinism of the powerful male characters and points out that their fortunes do not constitute an adequate representation of the nation's history. This is a point which Beatrice explicitly makes to Chris: 'Well, you fellows, all three of you, are incredibly conceited. The story of this country, as far as you are concerned, is the story of the three of you' (p. 66). This 'conceited' story could be described in Ranajit Guha's terms as an 'elite historiography' in which 'subaltern' voices remain silenced. Although focusing in the main on the Kangan elite, Achebe is keen to point that their story can never provide the complete narrative of the nation. Beatrice is one of several characters who disturb the elite male characters' autonomy over the narrative of Kangan's fortunes and enable issues such as gender difference to be raised.

Chauvinism appears at several parts of the text. In an early scene, His Excellency displays chauvinism by inviting Beatrice to a drinks party in order to provide the 'woman's angle' (p. 80) on Kangan for an American journalist. Chris is not free from chauvinism either; prior to the party he hints obliquely that she should keep all her 'options open' when dealing with His Excellency. The sexual connotations of this suggestion anger Beatrice, and she makes her feelings known to Chris after the party. She also criticises Ikem's radical political views on the grounds that he can imagine 'no clear role for women' (p. 91).

Gender relations are further complicated by other factors. Beatrice's well-educated background and social privilege are underlined in her dealings with her maid Agatha, to whom she talks in 'pidgin'

English. As Dennis Walder explains, 'it is important to distinguish between pidgins, which have small vocabularies, restricted structures, lack expressive potential and are usually not a first language, and *creoles*, which are distinct varieties of English spoken as their mother tongue by "native speakers"' (*Post-Colonial Literatures in English*, Blackwell, 1998, p. 47). Beatrice must adopt a different language in order to communicate with her maid. This begs the questions: How representative is Beatrice of women like Agatha? How do differences in women's economic status affect female collectivity? It is difficult to assert a 'deep, horizontal comradeship' amongst the Kangan women when their potential sisterhood is complicated by 'vertical' social differences.

Another important character in a similar position to Agatha is the market woman Elewa, Ikem's lover, whom bears a child after Ikem's death. Like Agatha, Elewa speaks the same form of pidgin English. The Western-educated characters certainly know this language – Chris speaks pidgin on his travels to Abazon – but do not use it when they speak with each other. These different uses of English bear witness to gender and class positions which are not elite, and their presence raises important questions. First, the reader is asked to question the kind of relationship that the ruling, Western-educated characters have with those from other classes. Are their world-views similar if they speak different languages? The differences in register suggest that the English-speaking elite might not be in step with the masses. Second, it raises issues concerning national languages. Can the nation's language be the received English which is used in government and by the educated elite, but not necessarily at large? These differences of language reveal the difficulties concerning imagining communities through a shared language, while pointing out the distance between the elite and the masses in Kangan.

Thus, *Anthills of the Savannah* gathers a variety of voices from different members of the nation without attempting to homogenise them into one collective voice. This is reflected in the novel's structure, which switches between the first-person narratives of Chris, Ikem and Beatrice, as well as third-person narration. The story is passed from one voice to the other, and in so doing the strengths and limits of each character's views are underscored. We are also made aware of those voices that the novel does *not* gather, but still acknowledges. In his lecture to the students, Ikem points out that those keen to fight the government in the name of a workers' or peasants' revolution should look around the lecture theatre and notice the absence of people from both groups. In a similar fashion, *Anthills of the Savannah* calls attention to the fact that its narrative of the nation cannot depict the nation's people as a whole, just as His Excellency's attempt to represent the nation as its leader is undermined by the unruly province of Abazon. There are always other voices missing. The novel's view, like that of its characters, must remain selective and limited.

In these terms, *Anthills of the Savannah* offers an important critique of the nation after independence. On the one hand it suggests in a West African context that the fortunes of the nation have been damaged by a chauvinistic educated elite separated from the bulk of the people by education, class, power and privilege. But the nation as an ideal is not completely rejected. Achebe considers if solutions exist to the nation's ills which do not fall back on familiar nationalist representations. Is it possible to build a nation where all voices count, not just those of the English-speaking privileged males? Can relationships be built between different peoples which do not smother difference, nor set 'norms and limits' which result in marginalisation? Will the nation ever be free of illiberal tendencies?

These issues are raised in the novel's important final chapter, which depicts the naming of Elewa's baby daughter. Whereas the opening chapter of the novel depicted the machinations of His Excellency's male cabinet, the closing chapter is female-centred with Beatrice and Elewa playing important roles. Invited to the ceremony are many characters from outside the elite who have featured in the novel, and whose gathering constitutes an image of a diverse yet interrelated community. This heterogeneous congregation suggests an *alternative* image of nationhood in Kangan which challenges the exclusivity of His Excellency's elite chauvinist cabinet.

Borrowing some terms from Homi Bhabha, we could describe the naming ceremony as a moment when the performative interrupts the pedagogical. The baby-naming ceremony has solemn and fixed protocols, yet in the final scene at Beatrice's flat a different kind of ceremony is performed. Although it takes place on the seventh market day, as tradition dictates, other rules are broken. A male

should perform the naming, but instead Beatrice decides to 'impro-
vise a ritual' (p. 222) and conduct the naming herself. The name that
is chosen, Amaechina ('The-remnant-shall-return'), is a boy's
name, but Elewa dismisses this incongruity: 'Girl fit answer am also'
(p. 222). The naming of Amaechina depicts a *reconfiguration* of conventional gender roles so that the mapping of the future can be the
result of the efforts of both men and women. As the daughter of the
subversive writer Ikem and the market girl Elewa, Amaechina is perhaps symbolic of a new egalitarian life for the nation that repudiates
the chauvinism and exclusivity of the Western-educated elite. As
Elewa's uncle puts it, Kangan has been a troubled nation since independence 'because those who make plans make plans for themselves
only and their families (p. 228). But Amaechina is 'the daughter of
all of us' (p. 228): she is a symbol of diversity in collectivity.

In Ikem's writings, His Excellency had been compared to an
angry sun whose 'crimson torches fire the furnaces of heaven and
the roaring holocaust of your vengeance fills the skies' (p. 30). Significantly, Beatrice is also linked to the sun through the comparisons
made between her and the goddess Idemili:

> In the beginning Power rampaged through our world, naked. So the
> Almighty, looking at his creation through the round undying eye of
> the Sun, saw and pondered and finally decided to send his daughter,
> Idemili, to bear witness to the moral nature of authority by wrapping
> around Power's rude waist a loincloth of peace and modesty. (p. 102)

Idemili ascends to earth in a pillar of water which quenches the fam-
ished earth. The myth recalls the situation in Abazon, where the
drought-stricken region is suffering under His Excellency's rule.
Later in the novel, when Chris and Beatrice make love, Chris calls
her a priestess or goddess. By the final chapter, Beatrice has been
constructed via the myth of Idemili almost as a new goddess of hope,
who has questioned the moral authority of the Kangan elite to
govern the nation and introduced peace and modesty into the novel.
Although she is an elite character, she challenges and subverts its
primacy. She survives the destructive days of His Excellency's government and heralds a new age in the final chapter as she presides
over a new form of naming ceremony – just like the anthills of the
savannah in Ikem's Hymn to the Sun, 'surviving to tell the new grass

of the savannah about last year's brush fires' (p. 31). In these terms, *Anthills of the Savannah* depicts the destructive activities of the Western-educated elite and urges a new kind of nation-building which includes those often left out of conventional nationalist representations. Yet the *idea* of the nation is not rejected outright.

STOP AND THINK

In using Beatrice as a means of articulating new hopes and possibilities for Kangan, Achebe perhaps remains guilty of using women primarily as redemptive, mythic icons of the nation. Is Beatrice's role in the novel significantly different to that of Mumbi in Ngugi's *A Grain of Wheat*? In her essay 'Of Goddesses and Stories: Gender and a New Politics in Achebe's *Anthills of The Savannah*' (in *Chinua Achebe: A Celebration*, ed. Kirsten Holst Petersen and Anna Rutherford, Dangaroo/Heinemann, 1990, pp. 102-112), Elleke Boehmer persuasively argues that 'the way in which Achebe privileges woman continues to bear familiar markings for gender ... this must to a certain extent compromise his re-imagined hope' (p. 108). Do you agree? Is Achebe's representation of women free from the charges made by Anthias and Yuval-Davis concerning women in chauvinistic nationalist representations? Does *Anthills of the Savannah* successfully resist the problems in nationalist representations which we have explored in this chapter, despite its best intentions?

Selected reading

Ahmad, Aijaz, *In Theory: Classes, Nations, Literatures* (Verso, 1992).
    Offers at times a fierce defence of nationalism in the light of recent innovations in postcolonial theory.

Ashcroft, W. D., 'Constitutive Graphonomy: A Post-Colonial Theory of Writing' in Stephen Slemon and Helen Tiffin (eds), *After Europe* (Dangaroo, 1989), pp. 58–73.
    A theoretically ambitious and influential (if problematic) attempt to account for different language uses that can be deemed 'postcolonial'.

Bhabha, Homi K. (ed.), *Nation and Narration* (Routledge, 1990).

Required reading for 'the nation in question'. Has several essays which critique nationalist representations in colonial, postcolonial and other contexts, as well as an earlier version of Bhabha's 'DissemiNation: Time, Narrative and the Margins of the Modern Nation' (in Homi K. Bhabha, *The Location of Culture*, Routledge, 1994).

Chatterjee, Partha, *Nationalist Thought and the Colonial World: A Derivative Discourse?* (Zed, 1986).

Has an excellent overview of critiques of nationalism in relation to colonialism in the opening chapter.

Gikandi, Simon, *Maps of Englishness: Writing Identity in the Culture of Colonialism* (Columbia University Press, 1996).

The opening chapter to this challenging text maps out the disenchantment with nationalism in the latter decades of the twentieth century.

Jayawardena, Kumari, *Feminism and Nationalism in the Third World* (Zed, 1986).

For the more advanced reader, this text examines the troubled fortunes of women's movements in relation to forms of Asian nationalism.

Lazarus, Neil, 'National Consciousness and the Specificity of (Post) Colonial Intellectualism' in Barker, Hulme and Iversen (eds), *Colonial Discourse/Postcolonial Theory* (Manchester University Press, 1994), pp. 197–220).

An essay which seeks to account for 'the continuing indispensability of national consciousness to the decolonising project' (p. 198).

Lazarus, Neil, *Nationalism and Cultural Practice in the Postcolonial World* (Cambridge University Press, 1999).

Murray, Stuart (ed.), *Not on any Map: Essays on Postcoloniality and Cultural Nationalism* (Exeter University Press, 1997).

Ngugi wa Thiong'o, *Decolonising the Mind: The Politics of Language in African Literature* (James Currey, 1981).

Chapter 1, 'The Language of African Literature', contains Ngugi's argument concerning his decision no longer to write in English.

Parker, Andrew, Mary Russo, Doris Sommer and Patricia Yaeger (eds), *Nationalisms and Sexualities* (Routledge, 1992).

Includes several useful essays which critique nationalist representations for their questionable gender and sexual politics.

Parry, Benita, 'Resistance Theory/Theorising Resistance, or Two Cheers for Nativism' in Barker, Hulme and Iversen (eds), *Colonial Discourse/*

Postcolonial Theory (Manchester University Press, 1994), pp. 172–96.
A critical essay on Negritude, Fanon and nationalism which takes issue with the recent disparagement of nationalist representations.

Yuval-Davis, Nira and Flora Anthias (eds), *Woman–Nation–State* (Macmillan, 1989).
Includes a variety of essays which deal with the problematic relations of women and nationalism in several contexts, as well as an excellent theoretical introduction.

5

Re-reading and re-writing English literature

Introduction

Writing about her experience of the study of English Literature in India, Meenakshi Mukherjee has defended postcolonialism as an emancipatory concept on the grounds that 'it makes us interrogate many aspects of the study of literature that we were made to take for granted, enabling us ... to re-interpret some of the old canonical texts from Europe from the perspective of our specific historical and geographical location' (*Interrogating Post-Colonialism: Theory, Text and Context*, eds. Harish Trivedi and Meenakshi Mukherjee, Indian Institute of Advanced Study, 1996, pp. 3-4). The re-interpretation of 'classic' English literary works has become an important area of postcolonialism and has impacted upon all kinds of literary debates, in particular the ongoing disputes about which texts can be considered as possessing 'literary value' and the criteria we use to measure it.

This chapter will introduce these issues by taking as points of orientation two inter-related themes: the *re-reading* of literary 'classics' in the light of postcolonial scholarship and experience, and the *re-writing* of received literary texts by postcolonial writers. In so doing we shall be looking at two novels: Charlotte Brontë's *Jane Eyre* (1847), and Jean Rhys's *Wide Sargasso Sea* (1966) which engages with Brontë's text.

Colonialism and the teaching of English literature

Mukherjee's phrase 'old canonical texts' refers to the 'canon' of English literature: the writers and their work which are believed to be of particular, rare value for reasons of aesthetic beauty and moral sense. I shall be using the term 'classic' to refer to this kind of text. The inverted commas will be kept to signal that it is a matter for debate whether or not texts are *inherently* valuable or worthy; for some, the status of 'classic' is ultimately awarded by readers. Hence, the literary value of a text is open to disagreement and change.

Many postcolonial writers and critics were taught the 'classics' of English literature in once-colonised locations, where English literature has been an important subject on the curriculum. For example, the Antiguan writer Jamaica Kincaid recalls studying 'the Brontës, Hardy, Shakespeare, Milton, Keats … They were read to us while we sat under a tree' (in *Caribbean Women Writers*, ed. Selwyn Cudjoe, Calaloux, 1990). The teaching of English literature in the colonies must be understood as part of the many ways in which Western colonial powers such as Britain asserted their cultural and moral superiority while at the same time devaluing indigenous cultural products. The image of Jamaica Kincaid sitting under her tree in Antigua reading a series of texts that ostensibly concern British locations, culture and history is a striking example of the ways in which many of those in the colonies were asked to perceive of Western nations as places where the very best in art and learning were produced, the lasting value of which could survive in locations far removed from the texts' point of origin. However, the *responses* to English literature by people in similar positions to Kincaid are particularly interesting and varied, and we shall be considering their character in this chapter.

Education is arguably a crucial ideological apparatus of the state by which certain values are asserted as the best or most true. Colonialism uses educational institutions to augment the perceived legitimacy and propriety of itself, as well as providing the means by which colonial power can be maintained. This is the argument of Gauri Viswanathan's book *Masks of Conquest: Literary Study and British Rule in India* (Faber, 1989). Viswanathan's study concerns the emergence of English literature as a subject in educational

establishments in India during the early nineteenth century specifically to serve colonial interests. Many administrators were keen to
build an English–speaking Indian workforce that would help carry
out the work of the colonial authorities. Lord Macaulay, president of
the Council on Education in India, put it thus in his now infamous
'Minute on Indian Education' of 1835:

> It is impossible for us, with our limited means, to attempt to educate
> the body of the people. We must at present do our best to form a class
> who may be interpreters between us and the millions whom we
> govern; a class of persons, Indian in blood and colour, but English in
> taste, in opinions, in morals, and in intellect. To that class we may
> leave it to refine the vernacular dialects of the country, to enrich those
> dialects with terms of science borrowed from Western nomenclature,
> and to render them by degrees fit vehicles for conveying knowledge
> to the great mass of the population. (reprinted in *The Post-Colonial
> Studies Reader*, p. 430)

Macaulay's pronouncement rests upon several assumptions.
Knowledge is deemed the enriching possession of the 'scientific'
West and must be taught to those in India, but the process is not reciprocal. An Orientalist hierarchy is asserted between a knowledge-
able, civilised West and an ignorant, savage East. Thus, the
education of Indians is part of a civilising process that involves a certain *moral* improvement – it is not just a process that will heighten
intellect and opinion. The education of Indians for the purposes of
consolidating power is legitimised by seeming morally just and
improving.

This was also the concern of many evangelicals in India at the
time who were keen that Indians converted to Christianity. However,
it became clear during the early nineteenth century that many Indians objected to the denigration of their own religions by missionaries and the teaching of biblical scripture in schools. Viswanathan
argues that evangelicals coped with this problem by trying to pro-
mote Christian morality indirectly through the teaching of English
literature. Rather than studying issues such as grammar or diction,
English literary texts were presented in profoundly moral terms,
with students invited to consider how texts conveyed 'truths' at once
universal and timeless, yet entirely correspondent with Christian

morality. 'The importance of English literature for this process could not be exaggerated', argues Viswanathan; 'as the source of moral values for correct behaviour and action, it represented a convenient replacement for direct religious instruction' (*Masks of Conquest*, p. 93). The study of English literature became the study of models of moral worth to the extent that English literature seemed first and foremost *about* morality. This weaving together of morality with a specifically *English* literature had important ideological consequences. Literature implied that moral behaviour and English behaviour were synonymous, so that the English literary text functioned 'as a surrogate Englishman in his highest and most perfect state' (p. 20). In reading English literature in moral terms, then, Indian students were being exposed to a code of values deemed Christian and universal, yet also specifically identified with the colonising nation.

So, in an Indian context Viswanathan reveals that the teaching of English literature in the colonies was complicit with the maintenance of colonial power. And although it is never wise to generalise, it is fair to say that writers from other colonised locations have often pointed out this relationship. For many in countries with a history of colonialism, English literary texts have become considered *not* as timeless works of art remote from history but as complicit in the colonising enterprise itself. So, when Meenakshi Mukherjee argues that postcolonialism 'makes us interrogate many aspects of the study of literature that we were made to take for granted', we understand that the ability to read literary texts in ways *different to* those which have been laid down, can contribute to resisting the assumptions of colonial discourses which may still circulate today.

It is important to realise this 'interrogation' can take several forms. On the one hand it can lead to the questioning of the value of specific literary texts. In 1975 Chinua Achebe controversially denounced Joseph Conrad's *Heart of Darkness* (1899) on the grounds that it proved how Conrad was a thoroughgoing racist (see Chinua Achebe, 'An Image of Africa: Racism in Conrad's *Heart of Darkness*' reprinted in Joseph Conrad, *Heart of Darkness*, ed. Robert Kimbrough, Norton Critical Edition, 1988, pp. 251–62). Achebe objected to Conrad's derogatory and dehumanising representation of Africa and Africans, and pointed out that it remained one of the most commonly taught books in English departments in American universities as part of the canon of 'great' literature. In continuing to teach this novel as 'great', Conrad's alleged late-Victorian racism was being perpetuated in the present day as this supposedly racist text was falsely presented to students as of exceptional literary value.

But Achebe's dismissal of this 'classic' text is not definitive. Although many object to the 'classics' either because they proffer colonialist views of the world, or because they first encountered them as part of a colonial education, several writers have emphasised that the relationship between literary 'classics' and themselves has also been a *productive* one. Writers have *put literary 'classics' to new uses* for which they were scarcely originally intended.

For example, consider Shakespeare's *The Tempest*, which is set on an un-named magical island and frequently depicts the magician Prospero in command of his unruly subjects Ariel and (especially) Caliban. Some postcolonial writers, such as George Lamming and Aimé Césaire from the Caribbean, have re-read the relationship between Prospero and Caliban as exemplifying the relationship between coloniser and colonised, and have used this response to the play in structuring their own writings (see Lamming's use of Prospero and Caliban in his book of essays *The Pleasures of Exile*, Michael Joseph, 1960) This is *not* the same as claiming that Shakespeare wrote a play about colonialism; although there has been much debate about the extent to which the play takes colonialism as its subject, as in Peter Hulme's excellent book *Colonial Encounters: Europe and the Native Caribbean 1492–1797*, (Routledge, 1986). Rather, we need to consider how the received literary 'classics' can become *resources* for those writing to articulate postcolonial positions who use them as *points of departure*. Many writers enter into a *productive critical dialogue* with literary 'classics'. Although they reveal how a 'classic' can be culpable with colonialism, they also make available new ways of dealing with the 'classics' which make new meanings possible. We shall explore this 'productive critical dialogue' further at the end of the chapter when considering Jean Rhys's *Wide Sargasso Sea*.

Colonial contexts

Let us concentrate first on looking at how literary 'classics' have
been re-read. Postcolonial literary criticism has affinities with other
kinds of study in recent years concerned with reading literary texts
in relation to their historical, social and cultural contexts, rather
than timeless expressions of universally acknowledged moral
values. 'Context' refers to something more dynamic and less unified than 'historical background'; it is used to suggest the many
dominant issues, debates and knowledges in circulation at the time
a text was written, the various and competing ways in which people
conceived of their reality in the past. All societies labour under certain assumptions about how the world is ordered. As we have seen
previously, colonialism operates in part *discursively* by asserting
knowledge about such things as 'race', gender, differences in culture and nation, and so on. Colonial representations will tend to
support a view of the world which justifies the continuing legitimacy of colonialism.

Reading a text in relation to its contexts involves doing two things
simultaneously: first, identifying how such contexts are made present or absent in a text, and second, exploring how the text itself may
intervene in the debates of its day and applaud or resist dominant
views of the world. We must not forget that literary texts are always
mediations: they do not passively reflect the world but actively interrogate it, take up various positions in relation to prevailing views,
resist or critique dominant ways of seeing. To read a text in its historical, social and cultural contexts is to attend to the ways it *dynamically* deals with the issues it raises. And in a colonial context, it is
also perhaps to refute the dominant way of teaching literature as
expressing lasting moral truths contradictorily deemed at once
timeless yet specifically characteristic of the colonising nation.

For many postcolonial critics, reading an established 'classic' of
literature written at the time of colonialism often involves exploring its relationship with many of the issues and assumptions that
were fundamental to colonial discourses. In Chapter 2 we thought
about how Kipling's 'The Overland Mail' could be read in relation
to theories of colonial discourses. The reasons for this were reasonably straightforward: Kipling lived in India as a young man and

his poem is set in colonial India, so it would seem appropriate to read the poem in the manner we explored. However, postcolonial re-readings of literary works have in some instances focused upon texts that might seem hardly to deal with colonialism. Just because a literary text is *not* set in a colonial location, nor makes colonialism the predominant theme to be explored, it does not follow that such texts are free from the realities of the British Empire. In recent years, several literary 'classics' have been re-read to reveal, sometimes controversially, their hitherto unseen investment in colonialism.

STOP and THINK

How many 'classic' works of literature can you think of in which the existence and influence of Britain's relationship with colonial lands overseas plays a part? What role do the colonies, or characters from the colonies, play in these texts? To what extent do these texts support or problematise some of the assumptions in colonial discourses which we have met in previous chapters? For example, you might like to consider the importance of the colony of Virginia in Daniel Defoe's *Moll Flanders* (1722) or Australia in Charles Dickens's *Great Expectations* (1861).

Reading literature 'contrapuntally'

Two 'classic' English novels that have been re-read in their colonial contexts are Jane Austen's *Mansfield Park* (1814) and – as we will explore at some length – Charlotte Brontë's *Jane Eyre* (1847). *Mansfield Park*'s relations with colonial contexts have been discussed at some length by Edward W. Said in his book *Culture and Imperialism* (Vintage, 1993). As part of his lucid and convincing argument that Western culture cannot be understood without recognising its fundamental investment in imperialism, Said explores the relations between Austen's *Mansfield Park* and Britain's colonisation of the Caribbean island of Antigua. Said provocatively argues that the Antiguan material in the novel is not marginal but central to the novel's meaning, and the connections between the locations of Mansfield Park and Antigua are vital.

Mansfield Park is the property of Sir Thomas and Lady Bertram. As Said argues, Sir Thomas's economic interests in the Caribbean provide the material wealth upon which the comfortable middle-class lifestyle of Mansfield Park depends. The seemingly domestic, interior world of this English country house cannot exist independent from the world outside, no matter how remote it might seem from the plantations of Antigua. Indeed, the inseparability of the world 'inside' and 'outside' the house is reflected in other ways. Throughout much of the novel Sir Thomas is absent from Mansfield Park, tending to some problems that have arisen on his plantation in Antigua. In his absence, the younger characters at Mansfield Park become unruly. On his return, Sir Thomas instantly puts a stop to their disorderly conduct and re-establishes decorum. Said suggests that Sir Thomas's ability to set his house in order on his return is reflective of his role as a colonial landlord:

> There is nothing in *Mansfield Park* that would contradict us, however, were we to assume that Sir Thomas does exactly the same things – on a larger scale – in his Antigua 'plantations'. Whatever was wrong there … Sir Thomas was able to fix, thereby maintaining his control over his colonial domain. More clearly than anywhere else in her fiction, Austen here synchronises domestic with international authority, making it plain that the values associated with such higher things as ordination, law, and propriety must be grounded firmly in actual rule over and possession of territory. She sees clearly that to hold and rule Mansfield Park is to hold and rule an imperial estate in close, not to say inevitable association with it. What assures the domestic tranquillity and attractive harmony of one is the productivity and regulated discipline of the other. (*Culture and Imperialism*, p. 104)

The parallels Said detects between these locations supports his argument that the borders between inside and outside, domestic and international, England and Empire are permeable. The interior world of Mansfield Park is not static or enclosed, but dynamic and dependent upon being resourced from the outside. Fanny's movement from her poor Portsmouth beginnings to the eventual heir of Mansfield Park secures its future, just as Sir Thomas's movements between England and Antigua safeguard its economic health. Indeed, Said believes Fanny's journey corresponds at a small-scale level to Sir Thomas's transatlantic ventures: both bring resources from the outside into Mansfield Park, upon which its subsequent security depends.

There are three consequences of re-reading *Mansfield Park* in its colonial contexts. First, such a reading bears witness to what Said calls the *worldliness* of culture. This term reminds us that literary texts emerge from and have complex engagements with the historical, social and political conditions of their time, amongst which colonialism is fundamental in the nineteenth century. Second, this approach both exemplifies and encourages *contrapuntal readings* of literary texts. Said defines a contrapuntal reading as one which remains simultaneously aware 'both of the metropolitan history that is narrated and of those other histories against which (and together with which) the dominating discourse acts' (p. 59). For example, in order to read *Mansfield Park* contrapuntally we must recognise that the dominant world-view offered by the novel is grounded in various presumptions. The novel bears witness to the existence of the slave plantations in Antigua but assumes that there is nothing very objectionable in this fact. Reading *Mansfield Park* contrapuntally not only involves spotting moments when the colonies are represented; it is also to bring to the novel a knowledge of the history of the Caribbean which the novel is not necessarily writing but upon which it ultimately depends. The history which helps to shape *Mansfield Park* is not just limited to the social changes occurring in Britain at the beginning of the nineteenth century, but is also the history of colonisation and its resistance (one wonders why Sir Bertram's Antiguan estate is in such disarray in the first place). Ultimately, contrapuntal readings 'must take account of both processes, that of imperialism and that of resistance to it' (p. 79).

The third point concerns literary value. Reading texts contrapuntally, Said argues, often reminds the critic of the continuing value of the literary work being studied. *Mansfield Park* may have 'affiliations with a sordid history' of slavery (p. 114) but in Said's view there is no need to devalue the novel as a consequence. The brilliance of Austen's work depends upon the complex and subtle ways she configures the relations between Mansfield Park and Antigua. A lesser work 'wears its historical affiliation more plainly; its worldliness is simple and direct, the way a jingoistic ditty … connects directly to the situation and constituency that coined it' (p. 116).

STOP and THINK

Said's comments about literary value are questionable. Why shouldn't a text's affiliations with a 'sordid history' prompt us to question how and why we value that particular text? And why is a subtle and complex text more valuable than one that is 'simple and direct'? From one position it could be argued that Said's line of thought inevitably takes him to the brink of asking large questions about literary evaluation, yet at the last moment he shrinks from the consequences of his own argument by defending rather too adamantly the unshakeable value of the many literary 'classics' he cites.

Yet, an alternative response might suggest that Said is trying to read the literary 'classics' with more subtlety than someone like Chinua Achebe, whose critique of Conrad's *Heart of Darkness* led it to be condemned because it did not pass a certain ideological test. Said's reinstatement in *Culture and Imperialism* of the value of *Mansfield Park* suggests that literary value need not be entirely dependent upon a text's ideological moorings. In so doing, Said perhaps keeps open a debate on literary value which Achebe's reading of Conrad forecloses.

We shall be returning to the problematic area of literary value in our exploration of *Jane Eyre*. But it is worth giving some thought throughout this chapter to whether, in your view, re-reading texts in their colonial contexts alters how *you* value them, and why.

Re-reading Charlotte Brontë's *Jane Eyre*

Let us now turn to reading a literary 'classic' in the light of some of the ideas we have gathered so far. In what follows we aim to emphasise some of the purposes, methods, and the difficult questions raised by reading Charlotte Brontë's *Jane Eyre* in relation to its colonial contexts. We shall be using the current Penguin Classics (1985) edition of the novel edited by Q. D. Leavis.

Jane Eyre follows the life of a young girl from her childhood into the first years of adulthood. At the beginning of the novel Jane is a lonely orphan living miserably at Gateshead Hall in the company of her Aunt Reed and three cousins. The subject of much cruelty and little love from the Reeds, she is sent away to the strict regime of Lowood school where, after some initial unpleasantness instigated by the puritanical Mr Brocklehurst, she enjoys a more supportive environment and begins to flourish. She eventually works as a teacher in the School, and as an eighteen-year-old is employed as a governess to a young French child, Adèle, at Thornfield Hall.

At Thornfield she meets Edward Rochester, the wealthy owner of the Hall, and the pair gradually fall in love. Thornfield is a place both of happiness and disquiet for Jane. She enjoys her role as governess but struggles to control her strong feelings for Rochester. She settles into the house and makes good relationships with many of the staff, but is occasionally disturbed at night by a strange laughter coming from the room above hers. Several mysterious incidents also occur; in one, Jane is forced to pull a sleeping Rochester from his chamber which inexplicably has been set on fire.

Eventually Rochester and Jane confess their feelings of love for each other and agree to marry. During the night before the wedding, Jane wakes to see reflected in her mirror a strange dark figure ripping her wedding-veil in two. The next day, the wedding service is interrupted by John Mason, previously a guest at Thornfield, who claims to Jane's horror that her marriage cannot take place as Rochester already has a wife. Rochester is forced to admit that he is indeed married, to Mr Mason's sister, Bertha. Bertha is the figure that Jane saw the previous night, whom Rochester has kept locked up in the room above Jane's. Rochester explains that his marriage to Bertha was the result of his father's financial dealings. His father had intended that the Rochester family fortune should pass to the eldest son, Rowland. In order to provide an income for his second son Edward, he secured Edward's marriage to Bertha, the daughter of a planter and merchant living in Jamaica. Bertha's mother was a Jamaican Creole (a term which Brontë uses to signify 'racially

mixed' parentage) believed to be dead, but after the marriage
Rochester learned that she was locked in a lunatic asylum. Once
married, Bertha also sinks swiftly into lunacy. Rochester decides to
quit Jamaica and return to Thornfield with his wife, whom he has
since kept secretly imprisoned in the attic.

Appalled and upset at these revelations, Jane leaves Thornfield
secretly soon after the failed wedding. After wandering lonely, des-
olate and hungry, she is taken in by a parson, St. John Rivers, and his
two sisters, Diana and Mary, at Moor House. Calling herself Jane
Elliott, she recuperates and soon takes charge of the local village
school. By chance St. John Rivers discovers Jane's true identity and
reveals that she is the cousin of himself, Diana and Mary. In a further twist, Jane learns that she is to inherit the fortune of twenty
thousand pounds from her uncle John Eyre, a wine merchant from
Madeira (a Portuguese-governed island off the Moroccan coast).
Jane shares this inheritance equally between the cousins and then
faces another challenge: an offer of marriage from St. John Rivers.
St. John is keen to travel to India to work as a missionary; he has
been teaching Jane Hindustani, and wishes her to accompany him.
Jane turns down the offer and decides instead to return to Thornfield to be reunited with her beloved Rochester. She finds only ruins.
Soon after Jane's departure from Thornfield Hall, Bertha had
escaped her confines and set the house ablaze. The fire claimed her
life and left Rochester blind and missing a hand – but also a widower.
Jane finds Rochester, is lovingly reunited with him, and as she
famously announces in the last chapter, 'Reader, I married him'
(p. 474). The novel ends with the news that Rochester has regained
some sight, that the now-wealthy Diana and Mary have both happily
married, and with the image of St. John braving the dangers of India
as he pursues his pioneering missionary work, although Jane anticipates she will soon learn of his death abroad.

Such a scant summary of *Jane Eyre* does little justice to the intri-
cate twists and turns of Brontë's narrative, but it should be notice-
able even in a brief account like this the extent to which colonialism
and colonial locations are crucial to the events of the novel. Two particular colonial scenarios are conjured: via the Masons we are
exposed to the plantation-owning community in Jamaica, while St.
John Rivers connects the novel with British missionary work in

India. In addition, elements from colonial locations also emerge in the novel *figuratively*; that is, they supply Jane with a series of images and metaphors which she uses to articulate her own position on several occasions. The economic relationships between the novel's characters are particularly vital to the plot. Edward Rochester's first marriage to Jamaican-born Bertha gains him a fortune of thirty thousand pounds which makes possible his affluent lifestyle at Thornfield. And as Susan Meyer reminds us in her excellent essay '"Indian Ink": Colonialism and the Figurative Strategy of *Jane Eyre*', Jane's inheritance of twenty thousand pounds also has a colonial source:

> It comes from her uncle in Madeira, who is an agent for a Jamaican wine manufacturer, Bertha's brother. The location of Jane's uncle John [Eyre] in Madeira, off Morocco, on the West African coast, where Richard Mason stops on his way home from England, also indirectly suggests, through Mason's itinerary, the triangular route of the British slave traders, and suggests that John Eyre's wealth is implicated in the slave trade. (Susan Meyer, *Imperialism at Home: Race and Victorian Women's Fiction*, Cornell, 1996, p. 93)

Put bluntly, without the money made from colonialism, Rochester could not enjoy the luxuries of Thornfield Hall, nor could Jane secure a life with Rochester and facilitate the happy and respectable marriages of her cousins Diana and Mary, who were otherwise destined to live as humble governesses for wealthy families in the southeast of England. So, as Judie Newman puts it, at the end of the novel 'Jane and Rochester settle down to a happy married life on the proceeds of the Empire' (*The Ballistic Bard: Postcolonial Fictions*, Edward Arnold, 1995, p. 14).

Yet despite the novel's use of the economics of colonialism, rereadings of *Jane Eyre* in its colonial contexts have emerged only in recent years. One of the most important is Gayatri Chakravorty Spivak's ground-breaking if cryptic essay 'Three Women's Texts and A Critique of Imperialism', first published in 1985 (in *'Race', Writing and Difference*, ed. Henry Louis Gates jr., University of Chicago Press, pp. 262–80). This essay is especially important as it reveals how *Jane Eyre* is implicated in colonialism not just in terms of economic wealth, but *at the levels of narrative and representation*.

In order to explore this claim, we first need to place Spivak's essay in its own context. 'Three Women's Texts and A Critique of Imperialism' is ostensibly a response to Anglo-American feminist literary criticism of the late 1970s, in which *Jane Eyre* had become a celebrated or 'cult' text. Sandra M. Gilbert and Susan Gubar in their ground-breaking book *The Madwoman in the Attic: The Woman Writer and the Nineteenth-Century Literary Imagination* (Yale University Press, 1979) celebrate Jane as a proto-feminist heroine who struggles successfully to achieve female self-determination in an otherwise patriarchal and oppressive world. Spivak suggests that celebratory readings of the novel as politically subversive are flawed in their lack of attention to the fact that 'imperialism, understood as England's social mission, was a crucial part of the cultural representation of England to the English' ('Three Women's Texts and A Critique of Imperialism', p. 262). Jane's journey from subservience to female self-determination, economic security and marriage on her terms could not occur without the oppression of Bertha Mason, Rochester's Creole wife from Jamaica. Spivak points out that Gilbert and Gubar read Bertha always *in relation* to Jane, never as an individual self in her own right. In their words, Bertha is Jane's 'truest and darkest double: she is the angry aspect of the orphan child, the ferocious secret self that Jane has been trying to repress ever since her days at Gateshead' (*Madwoman in the Attic*, p. 360). Thus conceived, Bertha's lunacy represents the anger that Jane represses in order to be deemed an acceptable woman in a patriarchal world. This reading of Bertha purely in relation to Jane's self leaves out the colonial context of Bertha's imprisonment and fails to examine some of the assumptions concerning Bertha's lunacy and her representation in terms of 'race'.

For example, consider the moment when Rochester takes Jane to see Bertha just after the wedding has been disrupted by Mr Mason. Jane describes seeing a figure 'whether beast or human being, one could not at first sight tell' (*Jane Eyre*, p. 321). Bertha's ambiguous bestiality, her wild and violent nature dovetail with her 'mixed' Creole lineage and Jamaican birthplace. This slippage repeats a frequent assumption in colonial discourses that those born of parents not from the same 'race' are degenerate beings, perhaps not fully human, closer to animals. Bertha is robbed of human selfhood; she has no voice in the novel other than the demoniac laughter and the discomforting noises that Jane reports. Her animalistic character disqualifies her from the journey of human self-determination for which Jane is celebrated by Anglo–American feminist critics.

Bertha's half-human Creole 'savagery' leaves its mark most memorably in the novel when she sets fire to Thornfield Hall and jumps to her death in an apparent act of suicide, rather than allow Rochester to save her from the burning building. But note that this act is of fundamental consequence to the plot: Bertha is the major impediment to Jane's process of movement from the position of misbegotten orphan to one of legitimacy, fortune and especially marriage. Jane can only clinch this position as a consequence of Bertha's death in the blaze. By attending to the ways in which Bertha is derogatively characterised, and the fact that her suicide acts as a crucial cog in the 'structural motors' ('Three Women's Texts', p. 263) of the narrative, Spivak reveals how Jane's journey towards legitimacy, fulfilment and agency cannot occur without the persistent subservience of Bertha Mason to the requirements of the plot. Bertha is always connected to Jane as an 'other'; she never achieves any self of her own. Jane's journey to self-fulfilment and her happy marriage are achieved at the cost of Bertha's human selfhood and, ultimately, her life. As Spivak memorably puts it, Bertha 'must play out her role, act out the transformation of her "self" into that fictive Other, set fire to the house and kill herself, so that Jane Eyre can become the feminist individualist heroine of British fiction' (p. 270).

Spivak's reading of *Jane Eyre* underlines the novel's investment in colonial realities and thus complicates the ease with which it might be read as a politically subversive feminist text. According to Spivak, a reading which does not take colonialism into account 'reproduces the axioms of imperialism' (p. 262). By reading Bertha Mason *metaphorically* as the repressed side of Jane's psyche, at most an expression of the 'secret self' of the main character, Gilbert and Gubar stand accused of this charge. Spivak's reading of the novel returns it to its colonial contexts, and ultimately urges new strategies of reading which take colonialism into account when approaching not only this novel, but nineteenth-century literature in general.

One (perhaps unintentional) result of Spivak's essay is the

impression that *Jane Eyre* is entirely complicit with many of the assumptions in colonial discourses. A examination of other passages in the novel might seem to support this reading, although as we shall see later it is not the only conclusion that can be made. The first passage is taken from Rochester's narrative of his marriage to Bertha which occurs in Chapter 27. Rochester is describing a 'fiery West Indian night' (*Jane Eyre*, p. 335) during which he contemplated committing suicide rather than having to endure the future with his lunatic wife:

> Being unable to sleep in bed, I got up and opened the window. The air was like sulphur-streams – I could find no refreshment anywhere. Mosquitoes came buzzing in and hummed sullenly round the room; the sea, which I could hear from thence, rumbled dull like an earthquake – black clouds were casting up over it; the moon was setting in the waves, broad and red, like a hot cannon-ball – she threw her last bloody glance over a world quivering with the ferment of tempest. I was physically influenced by the atmosphere and scene, and my ears were filled with the curses the maniac [Bertha] still shrieked out. (p. 335)

This passage seems to perpetuate many colonial assumptions. Rochester's terms of reference depict Jamaica as a satanic and apocalyptic location. The references to the 'sulphur-streams' of air, the ominous noise of the sea, and the 'hot cannon-ball' of the moon give the impression of Jamaica as a hell-on-earth. His senses are assaulted and disturbed: he sees a blood-red landscape under black clouds; he hears rumblings like an earthquake and the screams of his wife from another room of the house; the intense heat denies him sleep or comfort. It is as if the very demoniac nature of the landscape gets into the being of those unfortunate enough to live there, as Rochester admits. The crazed world outside is responsible for driving Rochester wild, and his decision to shoot himself shows how much his mind has been deranged by the stormy environment. Consequently, the tumultuous conditions of Jamaica seem to have affected Bertha, who similarly displays fiery, tempestuous and turbulent behaviour. Bertha represents what Rochester could become – indeed, perhaps *has* become – by staying in Jamaica: lunatic and useless, at the mercy of demoniac forces that will turn his life into a living hell.

What saves him from madness and suicide? The answer is particularly revealing. As Rochester describes it, a wind 'fresh from
Europe' (p. 335) breaks the storm and offers relief from the crazed
conditions of the night. By the morning he, like the weather, has had
a change of heart; and the landscape too has also changed:

> The sweet wind from Europe was still whispering in the refreshed
> leaves, and the Atlantic was thundering in glorious liberty; my heart,
> dried up and scorched for a long time, swelled to the tone, and filled
> with living blood – my being longed for renewal – my soul thirsted
> for a pure draught. I saw hope revive – and felt regeneration possi-
> ble. From a flowery arch at the bottom of my garden I gazed over the
> sea – bluer than the sky: the old world was beyond; clear prospects
> opened. (p. 336)

This passage depicts a different Jamaica, one of growth and beauty,
as suggested by the references to the clear blue sea, the refreshed
leaves, the flowery arch where Rochester looks again at the world.
Note that although this passage acknowledges the beauty of the
landscape, one that contrasts sharply with the bleak, mosquito-
infested environment of the night before, 'regeneration' has been
produced by the 'sweet' wind from Europe that 'whispers' in the
leaves, as opposed to the fiery 'West Indian night' when it seemed
the world was in the midst of an earthquake. This series of contrasts
– sulphurous/sweet, rumble/whisper, thirst/refreshment – also
connects with other contrasts between the scenes, such as the black
fiery night and the blue regenerative morning.

In comparing these two scenes we notice how Brontë constructs
her fictional world in terms of what we might term *manichean*
oppositions. This is a term popularised by Abdul JanMohamed in
his book *Manichean Aesthetics: The Politics of Literature in Colonial
Africa* (University of Massachusetts Press, 1983), which we can
borrow for our example. 'Manichean aesthetics' refers to a system
of representations which conceives of the world in terms of
opposed categories, from which comes a chain of associations.
Reality is constructed as a series of polarities which derive from the
opposition posited between light and darkness, and good and evil.
This provides a structure of both meaning and morality. So, in a
system of manichean aesthetics, all that is light is orderly, tractable,

rational, angelic and ultimately good; whereas all that is dark is degenerate, chaotic, transgressive, lunatic, satanic and hence evil. In *Jane Eyre*, the blue light of the morning reveals that the 'old world beyond' has magically broken through the tempestuous night of the new world and saved Rochester's life from self-destruction. The relationship between Jamaica and Europe is both contrasting and unequal, the latter having more power than the former despite the spectacular apocalyptic storm of the night before.

These passages would suggest that *Jane Eyre* can be read as reproducing some of the assumptions of colonial discourses. The representation of Bertha and of Jamaica, as well as the economic relations of the novel, bear witness to the relationship between *Jane Eyre* and the contexts of colonialism. They remind us that the canonical 'classical' works of English literature did not emerge, and do not exist, remote from history, culture and politics.

STOP and THINK

There remains a problem in re-reading literary 'classics' as colonial discourses. Are we to conclude that Charlotte Brontë is somehow a colonialist in the light of our reading so far? If so, what purpose does this conclusion serve? If, as Patrick Brantlinger points out, in British literature of the mid-nineteenth century there was an 'easy confidence that rarely saw anything problematic' about imperialism (*Rule of Darkness*, Cornell, 1988, p. 29), should we be surprised that aspects of Brontë's work conform to colonialist views? It might be mistaken to think of Brontë as a typically British colonialist in her outlook, not least because she was the daughter of a Cornish mother and an Irish-born Church of England clergyman (who, incidentally, changed the Irish family name 'Brunty' to the more Germanic-sounding 'Brontë' with its famous umlaut).

To return to an issue we raised earlier: does the novel's investment in colonialism threaten its status as a work of artistic value? Should *Jane Eyre* be stripped of its status as a 'classic'? These have proven difficult questions to answer, and it is worth spending some time thinking about the answers you would give, and why.

Jane Eyre: a postcolonial text?

In the light of Spivak's essay, several critics have pursued relations between *Jane Eyre* and its colonial contexts, but have been more speculative as to the extent to which the novel is complicit with nineteenth-century British colonialism. To re-read *Jane Eyre* as merely reflective of the assumptions of colonial discourses only takes us so far. Re-reading literary 'classics' in relation to their colonial contexts is perhaps not particularly productive if all we do is label and dismiss those texts once and for all as ideologically corrupt or 'colonialist'. We are in danger of imposing upon the literature from the past the concerns of the present, and in one sense we cannot claim to be reading historically at all. Said would describe this critical response as a 'rhetoric of blame' (*Culture and Imperialism*, p. 115) used by some critics to denounce retrospectively literary works which seem to support a colonial view of the world.

Furthermore, it is not perhaps wise to assume that the manichean view of the world articulated by Edward Rochester in his descriptions of Jamaica is also the view of Charlotte Brontë. Few, I suspect, would assume that Shakespeare was anti-Scottish after watching a performance of *Macbeth*. But perhaps most importantly, this kind of labelling fails to consider conceiving of texts as potentially *questioning* colonial views. Indeed, for some critics, the point of re-reading these texts is not just to show how they confirm dominant perspectives, but how they might be read as *challenging* these views.

In these terms, 'classic' texts are re-read to uncover emergent, counter-colonialist positions that they may, perhaps unwittingly, make available to the reader. In so doing, by identifying how colonialism was brought to *crisis* in the literature from the past, this critical enterprise lends support to the continued challenge to colonialism in the present by underlining the ways in which colonialism has been subverted. Many literary texts can be re-read to discover the hitherto hidden history of *resistance* to colonialism that they also articulate, often inadvertently. Although this approach also involves reading a past text in the light of present concerns, as all readings unavoidably do, perhaps this reading strategy enables a more dynamic and potentially resourceful relationship between literature from the past and present concerns. In re-reading the 'classic' text readers can *put that text to work*, rather than either placing it on a pedestal or tossing it to one side as a consequence of whether or not it is deemed free from ideological taint. Furthermore, an attention to the counter-colonial properties of the literary 'classic' might also enable a way of challenging the kind of generalising view of literary history that Brantlinger risks in the description of mid-nineteenth-century literature we encountered a moment ago.

In *Jane Eyre*, we can find the possibility of subversion in, perhaps surprisingly, Bertha Mason. As we have seen, Bertha is described as degenerate, half-animal; a figure whose behaviour both reflects and seems created by the tempestuous, chaotic and fiery environs of the West Indies. How can this figure be subversive? Bertha's incendiary character is of particular importance when we recall that Brontë was writing *Jane Eyre* in the 1840s. Many of the slaves working on the plantations in Jamaica were originally Africans who had been captured, shipped in appalling conditions across the Atlantic Ocean and sold to the plantation-owners. (This horrific journey, often referred to as the 'Middle Passage', has been an important subject in postcolonial literature from the Caribbean). Britain abolished the slave trade in 1808 but it still permitted the use of slaves as hard labour on the plantations. Full slave emancipation in the British Caribbean possessions was achieved between 1834 and 1838, the period which Susan Meyer argues roughly corresponds to Jane's time at Thornfield Hall and her eventual marriage to Rochester. During the 1830s, resistance by the slaves to their conditions was widespread. In western Jamaica between December 1831 and early 1832 there occurred what historians call the 'Baptist War', when over sixty thousand slaves rose against the British. Fires were started which served as beacons to let other slaves know that an uprising had begun, and the burning of the plantations was an important part of the slaves' resistance (see Peter Fryer, *Black People in the British Empire: An Introduction*, Pluto, 1988, pp. 92–7). It could be argued that Bertha's attempt to set fire to Rochester's chamber while he is asleep, and her eventual razing of Thornfield Hall to the ground, recall the fiery resistant activities of slaves in Jamaica.

Susan Meyer argues that '[t]he story of Bertha, however finally unsympathetic to her as a human being, nonetheless does make an indictment of British imperialism in the West Indies and the stained wealth that came from its oppressive rule' (*Imperialism at Home*, p. 71). Although the novel never allows Bertha to tell her own story (rather than have it narrated by Rochester), it does bear witness to resistance to colonial rule occurring at the time. Firdous Azim reads Bertha's unruly temperament as evidence of the ultimate failure of colonialism to control those from whom it commanded obedience. As she persuasively puts it, '[t]he figure of Bertha Mason is significant, as she represents the failure of the pedagogical, colonising enterprise. Recalcitrant and uneducatable, she escapes the dominating and hegemonising imperialist and educational processes' (*The Colonial Rise of the Novel*, Routledge, 1993, p. 183). Following Said's model, Bertha's unruly presence can be read *contrapuntally* as resistant to the rule of those who deem her less than fully human, and paradigmatic of the plantation slaves who rose against the oppressive rule of the Jamaican slave-owners.

Bertha also might be seen to resist the authoritative eye of our narrator, Jane Eyre. Let us briefly recall the dehumanising description of Bertha that interested Spivak:

> In the deep shade, at the farther end of the room, a figure ran backwards and forwards. What it was, whether beast or human, one could not, at first sight tell: it grovelled, seemingly, on all fours; it snatched and growled like some strange wild animal: but it was covered with clothing, and a quantity of dark, grizzled hair, wild as a mane, hid its head and face. (*Jane Eyre*, p. 321)

This is a remarkable moment in the novel. Prior to this passage the reader has been teased by the enigmatic noises and strange figures that disrupt Jane's nights. The revelation of Bertha promises to solve the mystery by allowing Jane to look upon that which has been hitherto concealed. But notice how, in a series of vague phrases, Jane struggles to render what she sees. Bertha is not clearly visible to Jane's eye; she remains in shade, *seeming* to grovel, looking like *some* strange animal. Her head and face remain hidden from view. We could read this passage as evidence of the extent to which colonial discourses (if we take the passage as an example of such) often disqualify the colonised subject from being adequately represented. But from another position we might notice how the presence of Bertha *problematises* Jane's position as an omniscient narrator. Jane's authority as a narrator is challenged as Bertha will not be readily captured within Jane's narrative. She is beyond easy rendering in language. Is Bertha's hiding of her face and head a purposeful act, an attempt to escape representation?

If Bertha exists to make possible Jane's proto-feminist journey from orphanhood to money and marriage, perhaps in this crucial passage she threatens to bring Jane's fictional world to crisis by threatening to escape containment within its descriptive confines. In this imprecise description the omniscient narrative of the nineteenth-century realist novel is pushed to its limits by the presence of an unruly colonised subject who threatens to escape that which sentences her. Maybe at this moment *Jane Eyre* is more a postcolonial than a colonial text.

STOP and THINK

As we noted above, *Jane Eyre* connects with colonialism in at least two locations: Jamaica and India. Think about how India is represented in the text. At one point, at the climax to Chapter 24, Jane compares herself to Indian Hindu women who ascend their husbands' funeral pyres and perform the act of *sati*, or widow burning. How would you read this passage? What is at stake in Jane's appropriation of this position?

Also, how might the final chapter of the novel, including details of St. John Rivers's life in India as a missionary, influence the extent to which this novel supports or critiques British colonialism?

Postcolonial re-writings: Jean Rhys, *Wide Sargasso Sea*

Earlier we noted that many writers have entered into a productive critical dialogue with literary 'classics', where the 'classic' text is interrogated but also can function as an important imaginative resource. Let us conclude this chapter by exploring how Jean Rhys rewrites *Jane Eyre* in her novel *Wide Sargasso Sea* (1966). We shall use the latest Penguin Classics (1997) edition of the novel, edited and introduced by Angela Smith.

Jean Rhys was born in the Caribbean island of Dominica in 1890 and moved to Britain as a sixteen-year-old. Her Welsh father had come to the island as a young man while her mother's family had been based there throughout the nineteenth century and had once owned slaves. Rhys had a significant relationship with the Caribbean and Britain, yet her sense of belonging to both was complicated by the circumstances of her birth. As a descendent of the white slave-owning class, her relations with black Caribbeans descended from slavery could not be unaffected by the historical circumstances of the region, and as a Dominican-born white woman she could not consider herself first and foremost British. As Helen Carr summarises, 'Rhys was a colonial in terms of her history, even though she can be considered a postcolonial in her attitude to the Empire and in her employment of many postcolonial strategies (*Jean Rhys*, Northcote House, 1996, p. 18).

Perhaps because of her Caribbean background, Rhys became preoccupied with Brontë's Bertha Mason with whom in some respects she occupied a similar position. Bertha's father is Jonas Mason, a planter and merchant, and thus a member of the colonising community in Jamaica. Both Bertha's mother and Rhys's mother were Creoles; both Bertha and Rhys left the Caribbean for England as young women. We might describe *Wide Sargasso Sea* as a novel in which Rhys takes as her point of inspiration the figure of Bertha Mason and places her centre-stage, allowing her the possibility to achieve selfhood and granting her the opportunity of telling things from her point of view (although, as we shall see, there are problems in making this statement). This is not done for the purposes of 'completing' *Jane Eyre*, adding the story that is missing from the novel like a missing piece from a jigsaw. Instead, the relationship between the two novels is much more dynamic and dialogic, enabling an *interrogation* of the agency of the 'classic' text to fix meaning. Furthermore, the extent to which *Wide Sargasso Sea* can be (or should be) read squarely in terms of *Jane Eyre* is also open to debate. As we shall see, Rhys's novel both *engages with* and *refuses Jane Eyre* as an author-itative source. We can regard this refusal as part of the postcolonial strategies which Carr claims for Rhys's writing.

Wide Sargasso Sea proceeds through three parts. The first is nar-rated by Antoinette Cosway, who records her childhood with her widowed mother Annette in a large house, Coulibri, in Jamaica just after the Emancipation Act which formally ended slavery. She remembers her childhood as a time of both beauty and danger. With the power of the plantation-owning class in decline, the relationship between the black and white communities becomes increasingly tense. Antoinette's mother marries Mr Mason, who attempts to reinvest Coulibri with some of its previous grandeur and authority. But Coulibri is set on fire and Antoinette's brother Pierre is killed. The incident drives Annette to distraction, and Antoinette is sent away to a convent school during which time her mother dies. Later, as a seventeen-year-old she is visited by her step-father Mr Mason who invites her to live with him in Jamaica.

In Part 2 the narrative shifts unexpectedly to an un-named male character who, it quickly transpires, has married Antoinette. The couple are on their honeymoon at Granbois. Although this figure is never named, the reader familiar with *Jane Eyre* might assume that this character is analogous to Brontë's Rochester. At first it seems their relationship is benign, but it soon becomes fraught with ten-sion. The un-named narrator takes to calling his wife 'Bertha', a name to which she objects. Antoinette's husband is uncomfortable with the island and its inhabitants, especially his wife's black servant Christophine. Eventually he is contacted by one Daniel Cosway who claims to be Antoinette's half-brother. He informs the narrator about the madness of the Cosway family and links Christophine to the practice of obeah (or voodoo). Choosing to believe Daniel, the narrator convinces himself that he has been tricked into marriage, and his relationship with Antoinette deteriorates. Antoinette inter-rupts the narrative and tells briefly of how she pleads with Christophine to give her a potion that will make her husband love her again. Instead, her husband has a sexual encounter with a black servant, Amélie, and decides to return to England with the wealth he has inherited through his marriage. Antoinette will come too, although under duress.

The third part of the novel is set in England, in a large house. The opening paragraphs are narrated by Grace Poole but the rest is delivered by Antoinette. She contrasts her memories of Caribbean life with the grey surroundings of her attic cell, and tells of her wanderings through the house at night. In a remarkable climax to the novel she dreams of setting the house on fire and jumping from the rooftop. On waking she resolves 'what I have to do' (*Wide Sargasso Sea*, p. 124). She takes a candle and the keys from the slumbering Grace Poole and leaves the room. The novel ends with Antoinette walking with the candle along a dark passage.

There are two elements of the text upon which we shall particularly focus: the novel's curious narrative structure and the importance of naming. As might be clear from our summary, one of the novel's complexities concerns narrative voice. The text has two major first-person narrators, Antoinette and her husband, as well as other contributors such as Grace Poole and Daniel Cosway. This beckons questions concerning the overall control of the narrative in *Wide Sargasso Sea*. Antoinette's representation of events comes into competition with her husband's. On several occasions in the text our attention is drawn to the incompatibility of each other's vista, as they both compete for the control of meaning. For example, at one point in the husband's narrative he argues with Antoinette about the appearance and manner of Christophine:

> 'Her coffee is delicious [I said] but her language is horrible and she might hold her dress up. It must get very dirty, yards of it trailing on the floor.'
>
> 'When they don't hold their dress up it's for respect,' said Antoinette. 'Or for feast days or going to Mass.'
>
> 'And is this feast day?'
>
> 'She wanted it to be a feast day.'
>
> 'Whatever the reason it is not a clean habit.'
>
> 'It is. You don't understand at all. They don't care about getting a dress dirty because it shows it isn't the only dress they have.' (*Wide Sargasso Sea*, pp. 52–3)

In this exchange, Antoinette's husband lacks knowledge of local custom. His interpretation of events is not allowed to stand unchallenged. The incident is in stark contrast to Rochester's position in

Jane Eyre, where his version of life in the Caribbean is the only one the reader has, while Bertha is reduced to shrieks and unintelligible noises. In the quotation above the husband is confronted with his own ignorance of cultural specificity. But he refuses to learn and dismisses Antoinette's view ('Whatever the reason it is not a clean habit'). In this clash of perspectives we can trace a contest of power which is simultaneously colonial and patriarchal. In this exchange we might also find figured the relationship between *Jane Eyre* and *Wide Sargasso Sea*, with the latter *answering back* and critically challenging the views of Caribbean people and places in the former.

Antoinette's husband wishes to be the arbiter rather than the recipient of knowledge, and he aims to assert his control over his wife by contesting her views. This is reflected in the novel's structure by the fact that (apart from one hiatus) he is the narrator of their married life in the Caribbean which constitutes Part 2. In marrying Antoinette, he also lays claim to the authority over her *representation*. Antoinette's debasement takes place entirely within his first-person narrative. He chooses to believe Daniel Cosway's slander that 'there is madness in that family' (p. 59) and that she has had intimate relations with her cousin Sandi, preferring these allegations to Antoinette's version of her family history. By the end of Part 2 he has *made for himself* his own version of events in which he believes that his father and eldest brother have married him off to Antoinette so as to be rid of him, situating her as the focal point for his anger:

> They bought me, *me* with your paltry money. You helped them do it. You deceived me, betrayed me, and you'll do worse if you get the chance ... (*That girl she look you straight in the eye and talk sweet talk – and it's lies she tell you. Lies. Her mother was so. They say she worse than her mother.*) (p. 110)

In this quotation the un-named narrator's interior monologue slips into the voice of Daniel Cosway. The italicised sentences are a quotation of a speech made by Daniel to Antoinette's husband earlier in the novel. It is these *masculine* voices which attempt to define and confine Antoinette, (re)constructing her character and passing judgement on her behaviour. Hence, Rhys exposes the ways in which colonial discourses create their own images of alterity rather than reflect an existent reality, while undercutting this process by highlighting the extent to which the husband's knowledge is based on the flimsiest of evidence. This passage also exposes the complicity between colonialism and patriarchy which we will pursue in Chapter 6.

Significantly, Antoinette's husband makes a drawing which anticipates both her fate and that of Bertha Mason in *Jane Eyre*:

> I drew a house surrounded by trees. A large house. I divided the third floor into rooms and in one room I drew a standing woman – a child's scribble, a dot for a head, a larger one for the body, a triangle for a skirt, slanting lines for arms and feet. But it was an English house. (pp. 105–6)

This quotation is crucial on two counts. First, it represents the extent to which Antoinette's husband lays claim to the power of representing her on his own terms. She becomes what he makes of her. Second, the 'child's scribble' of Antoinette as a crude line drawing hardly approximates to the complex character we have met in the first section of *Wide Sargasso Sea* and reminds us that, both in this novel and in *Jane Eyre*, Antoinette and Bertha are *not* the crude definitions given by their husbands. No matter how much others try to define Antoinette's identity, we know she is not what her husband represents in his narrative. His power of representation is not secure, not complete in this text.

In these terms, Antoinette is both *confined by* and *escapes* her representation by other characters in *Wide Sargasso Sea*. This is reflected in the novel's structure. Her husband may relate the longest section of the narrative, reflecting his desire to control meaning, but Antoinette's voice interrupts his at the novel's central point in Part 2. She is also the novel's first and last narrator, making her husband's narratives contained inside hers. Neither character is fully in control. Meaning and definition are continually contested in this narrative, and it is difficult to fix meaning in the ways that Antoinette's husband would like. Significantly, unruly voices are *always* deemed threatening to authority in the novel. Antoinette's husband fears that if he stays in the Caribbean 'I'd be gossiped about, sung about (but they make up songs about everything, everybody. You should hear the one about the Governor's wife)' (p. 105). According to Grace Poole, there are complaints about the gossip concerning Antoinette in the attic: '*there were hints about the woman he brought back to England with him. Next day Mrs Eff wanted to see me and she complained about gossip. I don't allow gossip*' (p. 115). Rhys draws attention to the presence of unruly voices of people in sub-servient positions which challenge and unnerve those in positions of power. In so doing the novel explores the ways by which those made subject to others can resist the attempts by authority figures to fix meaning and establish their voices as the dominant and controlling ones. This contest, I would argue, is epitomised in the relationship between Antoinette and her husband.

Attending to how some characters attempt to fix meaning while others resist being fixed through voicing their own perspectives helps us consider the important intertextual relationship between *Jane Eyre* and *Wide Sargasso Sea*. As we have seen, Rhys's novel does much more than 'fill in' the gaps missing in Brontë's work. Yet in tethering *Wide Sargasso Sea* to *Jane Eyre*, Rhys might be in danger of constructing an unequal power relationship between the two by positioning *Jane Eyre* as an authoritative source-text from which the meanings of Rhys's novel are derived. In making *Jane Eyre* the point of authoritative reference, it could be argued that *Wide Sargasso Sea* remains dependent upon Brontë's novel in a way that mirrors Antoinette's subservience to her husband's design. Indeed, one might go so far as to say that the dependent relationship between two texts echoes the colonial relationship between Britain and its Caribbean colonies, with Rhys's novel 'governed' by the dictates of *Jane Eyre*.

However, *Wide Sargasso Sea* complicates its relationship with *Jane Eyre* in several ways which make it difficult to draw these con-clusions. To take but two: first, consider how *Wide Sargasso Sea* is set during the 1830s and 1840s, specifically *after* much of the action of *Jane Eyre* takes place. Yet, if the novel is meant to be the life of Bertha Mason *before* her transportation to England as the first Mrs Rochester then this cannot be right: the action must have occurred much earlier in time. This oddity has led the novel to be called a 'post-dated prequel' of *Jane Eyre*. The temporal anomaly makes *Wide Sargasso Sea* seem to pre-date *Jane Eyre*, and position Rhys's novel as that which anticipates the action of Brontë's text (as opposed to the other way round). As Judie Newman succinctly puts it, '[b]y commandeering *Jane Eyre* as *her* sequel, therefore, Rhys enjoins future readers to envisage Victorian Britain as dependent upon her colonies, just as Brontë's heroine depends upon a colonial inheritance to gain her own independence' (*The Ballistic Bard*, p. 15). So, in complicating the potentially dependent relationship between the texts, Rhys attempts to resist her novel being fully contained by Brontë's. Indeed, Antoinette's challenge to the narrative authority of her husband reflects the novel's relationship as a whole with *Jane Eyre*. *Wide Sargasso Sea* stands in a similar relationship to *Jane Eyre*, engaging with Brontë's novel in order to challenge its meaning by criticising its representations. This activity of 'putting meaning on the move' is an important postcolonial strategy which motivates the re-writing of 'classic' texts. *Wide Sargasso Sea* is in part engendered by *Jane Eyre*, but its meanings are not fully determined by it. Instead, Rhys's novel turns to challenge the meanings made available in Brontë's work by entering into critical dialogue with it.

Which leads us, finally, to the naming of characters in *Wide Sargasso Sea*. Names are often central to our sense of identity. Note how Antoinette's name is constantly changing in the novel as her family circumstances alter (some critics refer to her as Bertha Antoinette Cosway Mason Rochester!). Such a long convoluted name calls attention to the extent to which Antoinette's identity is always being defined in relation both *to* men and *by* men. To what extent is Antoinette ever really free of others' definitions of her identity and in control of her self? In addition, why is her husband never named as Rochester?

It is tempting perhaps to fix 'Bertha Antoinette Cosway Mason Rochester' as simply 'Bertha' and her husband as 'Rochester', but in so doing we perhaps re-enact something not too dissimilar from Antoinette's husband's 'child's scribble' of a woman in a house in England: we trap these characters inside representations made by somebody else which only *approximate* to the individuals we have met. If we identify Brontë's novel as the source of meaning which can explain and resolve the ambiguities of naming in Rhys's text, we perhaps do what Rhys does not do: we as readers construct that hierarchical relationship in which *Wide Sargasso Sea* is contained and determined by *Jane Eyre*. We no longer think of Antoinette and her

husband as fictional creations of Rhys independent from semantic
determination by another text.

Through the complications surrounding naming, Rhys reminds
us that *we as readers always have an active role to play* in the creation
and questioning of meaning. *Wide Sargasso Sea* demands that we
think carefully about our attempts to fix meaning and resolve ambiguity, to discover one authoritative voice amongst the clamour of
many voices. It invites us to consider that such attempts might not
be too remote from colonial and patriarchal impulses to fix representations of others whose voices are consequently silenced. Ultimately, the extent to which *Wide Sargasso Sea* confirms or resists the
authority of *Jane Eyre* is the responsibility of the reader, who may or
may not choose to treat *Jane Eyre* as an authoritive source and settle
the nature of the relationship between the two. Rhys may well
deploy postcolonial narrative strategies, as Helen Carr claimed; but
we need to think also about our agency and responsibility as readers
if we are not to erase the subversive potential of *Wide Sargasso Sea*.

'Re-writing': possibilities and problems

In the light of our discussion, let us recap what can be involved in
the 're-writing' of a literary 'classic':

- A re-writing does much more than merely 'fill in' the gaps perceived in the source-text. Rather, it enters into a *productive critical dialogue* with the source-text.
- A re-writing takes the source-text as a point of inspiration and
  departure, but its meanings are not fully determined by it.
- A re-writing often exists to *resist* or *challenge* colonialist representations of colonised peoples and cultures perceived in the
  source-text and popular readings of it. In this way we might consider a re-writing of a 'classic' text as 'postcolonial'.
- A re-writing often implicates the reader as an *active agent* in
  determining the meanings made possible by the dialogue
  between the source-text and its re-writing.

But for some, re-writings of literary 'classics' are not without their
problems which must also be faced when exploring the interface
between the source-text and the re-writing.

First, a re-writing often imagines that the reader will be familiar with the source-text it utilises, and thus is addressed first and foremost to an educated reader versed in the literary works of the colonising culture. For some this makes re-writings directed at a small privileged and educated elite. Those of us who have not had access to the source-text will be in a relatively deficient position. Second, a re-writing will always remain tethered in some degree to its antecedent. This problematises the extent to which postcolonial re-writings of literary 'classics' ever can be really independent of colonial culture. The re-writing will always invest value in the source-text as a point of reference, no matter how much it is challenged as a consequence. For this reason, some critics believe that re-writings can never fully challenge the authority of the 'classic' text; indeed, re-writings continue to invest literary 'classics' with value by making them a point of reference for postcolonial texts.

STOP and THINK

In this chapter we have looked at *Jane Eyre* as containing both colonial *and* postcolonial moments, and it is worth concluding by thinking about the tethering of *Wide Sargasso Sea* to *Jane Eyre*. Can Rhys's text fully eradicate its dependence on Brontë's work? In reading *Wide Sargasso Sea* as a postcolonial text we must also recognise the possible perpetuation of a colonial relationship between the source-text and its re-writing. If *Jane Eyre* is not simply a colonial text, then *Wide Sargasso Sea* is perhaps not readily regarded as postcolonial. As we are discovering in this book as a whole, these categories are by no means mutually exclusive or absolute.

Selected reading

Azim, Firdous, *The Colonial Rise of the Novel* (Routledge, 1993).
    An excellent study of nineteenth-century fiction in its colonial contexts.
Brantlinger, Patrick, *Rule of Darkness: British Literature and Imperialism 1830–1914* (Cornell University Press, 1988).

A wide-ranging examination of mostly nineteenth-century English literature which plots changing attitudes to colonialism and their manifestation in the writing of the period. The chapter on Conrad's *Heart of Darkness* is especially useful.

Carr, Helen, *Jean Rhys* (Northcote House, 1996).

A recent, short and compelling study of Jean Rhys which accounts for Rhys's particular kinds of modernist, feminist and postcolonial writing. Chapter 2, 'Feminist and Postcolonial Approaches to Jean Rhys', is particularly useful.

Childs, Peter (ed.), *Post-Colonial Theory and English Literature: A Reader* (Edinburgh University Press, 1999).

A useful collection of salient essays which deal in the main with the re-reading of the 'classics', including Shakespeare's *The Tempest*, Daniel Defoe's *Robinson Crusoe* (1719), Brontë's *Jane Eyre*, Conrad's *Heart of Darkness* and James Joyce's *Ulysses* (1922).

Fryer, Peter, *Black People in the British Empire: An Introduction* (Pluto, 1988).

An excellent historical work which depicts the rule and resistance of black peoples during colonialism.

Hulme, Peter, *Colonial Encounters: Europe and the Native Caribbean 1492–1797* (Routledge, 1986).

Includes a long, scholarly study of Shakespeare's *The Tempest* in its colonial contexts, highly recommended.

James, Selma, *The Ladies and the Mammies: Jane Austen and Jean Rhys* (Falling Wall Press, 1983).

Meyer, Susan, '"Indian Ink": Colonialism and the Figurative Strategy in *Jane Eyre*' in *Imperialism at Home: Race and Victorian Women's Fiction* (Cornell, 1996).

In my view the best essay on *Jane Eyre* and its colonial contexts, and a good example of 'contrapuntal' reading. Witty, erudite and highly pursuasive. Reprinted in Peter Childs's collection cited above.

Newman, Judie, *The Ballistic Bard: Postcolonial Fictions* (Edward Arnold, 1995).

A stimulating, lively and challenging text which looks at several different postcolonial re-writings of 'classic' texts and offers a series of imaginative readings. The first chapter, 'I Walked With a Zombie', is a wonderful reading of the intertextual relationship between *Jane Eyre* and *Wide Sargasso Sea*. The introduction is also highly recommended.

Said, Edward W., *Culture and Imperialism* (Vintage, 1993).

A major work in postcolonialism in which Said traces the relations between Western culture and Western imperialism in a variety of genres and looks at the work of Conrad, Austen, Yeats and others. The second half of the book deals with the resistance to Western culture and imperialism by colonised peoples.

Southam, Brian, 'The Silence of the Bertrams: Slavery and the Chronology of *Mansfield Park*', *Times Literary Supplement*, 17 February 1995.

A highly informative essay which looks in detail at the historical contexts of Austen's novel.

Spivak, Gayatri Chakravorty, 'Three Women's Texts and A Critique of Imperialism' in Henry Louis Gates, jr. (ed.), *'Race', Writing and Difference* (University of Chicago Press, 1985), pp. 262–80.

This is Spivak's influential reading of *Jane Eyre*, *Wide Sargasso Sea* and Mary Shelley's *Frankenstein*, and required reading when thinking about re-reading and re-writing 'classic' texts. This essay features moments of some difficulty and can be hard to follow in places, so proceed through it slowly.

Viswanathan, Gauri, *Masks of Conquest: Literary Study and British Rule in India* (Faber, 1989).

A prolonged and detailed study of the teaching of English in India which has proven highly influential for postcolonial critics and writers.

Zonana, Joyce, 'The Sultan and the Slave: Feminist Orientalism and the Structure of *Jane Eyre*', *Signs: Journal for Women in Culture and Society*, 18 (3), 1993, pp. 592–617.

An examination of Brontë's problematic use of Orientalism for her own feminist purposes. (Reprinted in Peter Childs's collection cited above.)

Postcolonialism and feminism

Some definitions

Postcolonial feminist criticism is extensive and variable. Its analyses range across representations of women in once-colonised countries and in Western locations. Some critics have concentrated on the constructions of gender difference during the colonial period, in both colonial and anti-colonial discourses; while others have concerned themselves with the representations of women in postcolonial discourses, with particular reference to the work of women writers. At the level of theory, postcolonial feminist critics have raised a number of conceptual, methodological and political problems involved in the study of representations of gender, some of which we will be looking at in detail in this chapter. These problems are at once specific to feminist concerns, such as the possibility of finding an international, cross-cultural sisterhood between 'First World' and 'Third World' women, as well as more general problems concerning who has the right to speak for whom, and the relationship between the critic and their object of analysis. Indeed, it would be fair to say that some of the most groundbreaking, thought-provoking and influential work within postcolonialism has come from debates concerning representations of gender difference in postcolonial contexts.

In calling this chapter 'postcolonialism *and* feminism', it might seem that feminism is something which is anterior to postcolonialism. This would be grossly incorrect. We should be clear that feminist work is a constitutive part of the field of postcolonialism, and we have seen in previous chapters that issues of gender difference are central to each of the areas we explore in *Beginning Postcolonialism*. However, some feminist critics have pointed out that postcolonialism can appear a male-centred field. So the title of this chapter partly recognises that postcolonialism and feminism are sometimes seen to share tense relations with each other. And as we shall presently explore, feminists working out of different locations have also questioned the extent to which Western, or 'First World' feminism is equipped to deal with the problems encountered by women in once-colonised countries or those living in Western societies with ancestral connections to these countries (such as migrants and their descendants). So, by using these terms 'postcolonialism' and 'feminism' in conjunction I hope to maintain, on the one hand, a sense of the potential tensions between postcolonial and feminist critical practices, while, on the other, suggest their rapport.

A note on terminology is needed before we look at some of these debates, particularly concerning how to define 'feminism' and 'patriarchy'. As we would expect, it is as challenging to define 'feminism' as it is to define 'postcolonialism'. The variable range of work which can be called 'feminist' makes it difficult to summarise feminism in a sentence. But we need a place to start if we are to use it. In their introduction to *The Feminist Reader: Essays in Gender and the Politics of Literary Criticism* (ed. Belsey and Moore, Macmillan, 1989), Catherine Belsey and Jane Moore argue that a feminist reader is 'enlisted in the process of changing the gender relations which prevail in our society, and she regards the practice of reading as one of the sites in the struggle for change' (p. 1). They suggest that a feminist reader might ask of a text questions such as 'how [it] represents women, what it says about gender relations, how it defines sexual difference' (p. 1). In addition, those texts which do not mention women at all are interesting for this very reason.

In talking of 'the struggle for change', we can understand that feminist reading practices are involved in the contestation of patriarchal authority. The term 'patriarchy' refers to those systems – political, material and imaginative – which invest power in men and marginalise women. Like colonialism, patriarchy manifests itself in both concrete ways (such as disqualifying women a vote) and at the level of the imagination. It asserts certain representational systems which create an order of the world presented to individuals as 'normal' or 'true'. Also like colonialism, patriarchy exists in the midst of resistances to its authority. Furthermore, as a singular term, 'patriarchy' can be misleading. As much feminist criticism has shown, there are many different forms of patriarchy, each with its own specific effects: indeed, this latter point is particularly important in postcolonial feminist criticism. So, feminism and postcolonialism share the mutual goal of challenging forms of oppression.

Two further terms require comment before we proceed: 'First World' feminism and 'Third World' women. These terms relate to a system of ways of mapping the global relationships of the world's nations which emerged after the Second World War. The 'First World' referred to the rich, predominantly Western nations in Europe, America and Australasia; the 'Second World' denoted the Soviet Union and its communist allies; while the 'Third World' consisted in the main of the former colonies such as countries in Africa and South Asia which were economically under-developed and dependent upon the wealthy nations for their economic fortunes. This mapping of the world has remained influential, for better or worse, in a variety of discourses. In terms of postcolonialism and feminism, the phrase 'First World' feminism is an unhappy generalisation which glosses over the variety of feminisms, and the debates within and between them, in Europe and America. As with 'race', I think it is worthwhile keeping the quotation marks to remind us continually that it is *not* a transparent term. Yet the naming of a 'First World' feminism has proved a productive means of acknowledging and questioning the limits of feminist scholarship in the West, particularly its relations with 'Third World' women. Of course, this latter phrase is also problematic for similarly conflating the experiences and representations of a diverse body of people often in once-colonised countries, as we will be discovering presently, yet it too has acted at times as an enabling conceptual category. So, although such phrases will be used in this chapter, they remain provisional *categories of convenience* rather than factual denotations of fixed and stable groups.

In what follows, we will begin by locating the various kinds of patriarchal authority to which women from countries with a history of colonialism may be subjected, and address the concept of 'double colonisation'. Then we will look at postcolonial critiques of 'First World' feminism in thinking about the problems and possibilities when using 'First World' feminism in postcolonial contexts. This will involve examining some important and challenging essays by Gayatri Chakravorty Spivak. Finally, we shall apply some of the ideas and concepts introduced in this chapter when reading Sally Morgan's autobiographical text, *My Place* (Virago, 1988).

The 'double colonisation' of women

Kirsten Holst Petersen and Anna Rutherford have used the phrase 'a double colonisation' to refer to the ways in which women have *simultaneously* experienced the oppression of colonialism and patriarchy. In the 'Foreword' to their edited collection *A Double Colonisation: Colonial and Post-Colonial Women's Writing* (Dangaroo, 1986), Peterson and Rutherford argue that colonialism celebrates male achievement in a series of male-oriented myths such as 'mateship, the mounties, explorers, freedom fighters, bushrangers, missionaries' (p. 9), while women are subject to representation in colonial discourses in ways which collude with patriarchal values. Thus the phrase 'a double colonisation' refers to the fact that women are twice colonised – by *colonialist* realities and representations, and by *patriarchal* ones too. Much postcolonial feminist criticism has attended to the representations of women created by 'double colonisation', and questioned the extent to which both postcolonial and feminist discourses offer the means to challenge these representations.

Let's consider this 'double colonisation' in more detail, because it affects women from *both* the colonised and colonising cultures in various ways. In her book *Imperial Fictions: Europe's Myths of Orient* (Pandora, rev. 1994) Rana Kabbani looks at the production of the Eastern female as a figure of licentiousness, and Western heterosexual male desire, in travel writing and paintings of the 'Oriental' woman and the harem. Kabbani shows how the depiction of Eastern women in the eighteenth and nineteenth centuries objectified them as exotic creatures who epitomised and promised the assumed excessive sexual delights of the Orient. She shows how in reading these representations we must be aware of the mutually supportive processes of colonialism and patriarchy which produce Eastern women in eroticised terms. In addition, as Vron Ware explains in her book *Beyond the Pale: White Women, Racism and History* (Verso, 1992), colonial representations in the Victorian period tended to traffic in iconic representations of white women as epitomising the West's perceived higher moral and civil standards. Thus, as she explains, 'one of the recurring themes in the history of colonial repression is the way in which the threat of real or imagined violence towards white women became a symbol of the most dangerous form of insubordination' (p. 38). You may like to consider E. M. Forster's novel *A Passage to India* (1924) in the light of this statement, particularly the expatriate British community's reaction to the alleged rape of the newly arrived Adela Quested by Dr Aziz. So patriarchal values in colonial discourses impacted upon both *colonised* and *colonising* women, albeit in different ways.

Of course, this does *not* mean that colonised and colonising women were placed in the same position through their 'double colonisation'. Rana Kabbani makes reference to Victorian Western colonial travellers who also depicted the Orient in patriarchal terms. She argues that these women were 'token travellers only, who were forced by various pressures to articulate the values of patriarchy' (*Imperial Fictions*, p. 7). Kabbani draws our attention to the presence and complicity of Western women in the colonising mission, and the ways in which they were also subject to the patriarchal imperatives of colonial discourses. Although Kabbani sees Western women as complicit with colonial discourses, in *Imperial Eyes: Travel Writing and Transculturation* (Routledge, 1992) Mary Louise Pratt has explored the extent to which some Western women represented the colonies in different ways. In her criticism of Mary Kingsley's *Travels in West Africa* (1897), Pratt demonstrates that Kingsley's work distances itself from some of the masculinist tropes and narrative set-pieces prevalent in men's writing about Africa during the period through the use of 'irony or inversion' (*Imperial Eyes*, p. 213). Yet, Kingsley's 'feminised' narrative cannot escape complicity with colonialism and in its turn constructs a different form of mastery over Africa entirely in keeping with colonialist values. As Pratt's work shows, Western women's relationship with the dual workings of colonialism and patriarchy is often particularly complicated as they can be placed in contradictory positions, empowered as members of the 'civilised' colonising nation yet disempowered under a Western patriarchal rubric (you might also like to recall here Sara Mills's work on women's travel writing which we looked at in Chapter 2).

For colonised women in 'settled' colonies, Western patriarchal values had profound effects on indigenous gender roles. In her essay 'White Woman Listen! Black Feminism and the Boundaries of Sisterhood' (in Centre for Contemporary Cultural Studies, *The Empire Strikes Back: Race and Racism in 70s Britain*, Hutchinson, 1982, pp. 212–35), Hazel Carby argues that in many colonised countries British colonialism interrupted indigenous familial and community structures and imposed its own models instead. 'Colonialism attempted to destroy kinship patterns that were not modelled on nuclear family structures, disrupting, in the process, female organisations that were based upon kinship systems which allowed more power and autonomy to women than those of the colonising nation' (p. 224). This had a significant impact on gender roles in indigenous communities, whose established traditions, customs and social systems were irreparably broken, sometimes to the detriment of women. Carby's argument suggests that indigenous gender roles could be more equitable than the sexist and chauvinist gender stereotypes and social roles brought from the colonising culture.

However, we must also take a more critical view of indigenous gender roles, not least because many postcolonial writers have explored the oppression of women *within* native communities. Colonialism can *add* other kinds of patriarchal systems to an already unequal situation; it is not always the sole or primary source of patriarchy. For example, in her novel *The Joys of Motherhood* (Heinemann, 1979) Buchi Emecheta depicts the life of Nnu Ego, an Igbo woman from village of Ibuza in Nigeria. Her father, Agbadi, chooses to marry her to Amatokwu, who duly pays her 'bride price' and sends Agbadi an additional six kegs of palm wine when he finds that Nnu Ego's virginity is intact. However, when Nnu Ego does not become pregnant she is seen to be 'failing' by Amatokwu in her primary task as a woman: to provide male children for her husband. Her inability to conceive causes her much personal distress. Soon she learns from Amatokwu that she must leave their house and move to a hut kept for older wives because a younger wife has been found for him by his father, who is desperate to preserve the male line.

When Nnu Ego complains to him that she misses their former inti-
macy, his answer leaves her in no doubt as to her value:

> 'What do you want me to do?' Amatokwu asked. 'I am a busy man. I
> have no time to waste my precious male seed on a woman who is infer-
> tile. I have to raise children for my line. If you really want to know, you
> don't appeal to me any more. You are so dry and jumpy. When a man
> comes to a woman he wants to be cooled, not scratched by a nervy
> female who is all bones.' (p. 32)

This moment demonstrates how Nnu Ego is significant to Amatokwu only as a means by which the male line of the family can be
preserved. His demands concerning how a woman should act clini-
cally reveal that male power is in the ascendancy in this Igbo community. As an object of exchange between men and the guarantor of
the survival of their hereditary line, her identity and social role are
male-constructed and she suffers if she does not comply. After the
birth of Amatokwu's younger wife's child, Nnu Ego privately takes
to suckling the child at her breast when it cries. But Amatokwu discovers this and beats her for daring to perform the task of a mother
when she has failed to fulfil this role. He then 'returns' her to her
father Agbadi, who says that he does not blame him for beating Nnu
Ego and acknowledges that she has brought shame on the family.
Eventually another husband is found for her in Lagos.

Nnu Ego's plight is culturally and historically specific, but
women in other countries with a history of colonialism would recognise her subservience to indigenous forces of compulsion. Gender
inequalities exist in both the indigenous and the colonial culture:
both often simultaneously oppress women during colonialism and in
its wake. Thus, as Susheila Nasta puts it in her introduction to
*Motherlands: Black Women's Writing from Africa, the Caribbean and
South Asia* (Women's Press, 1991), '[t]he post-colonial woman
writer is not only involved in making herself heard, in changing the
architecture of male-centred ideologies and languages, or in discovering new forms and language to express her experience, she
has also to subvert and demythologise indigenous male writings
and traditions which seek to label her' (p. xv).

This beckons an important general question: do *postcolonial* representations perpetuate or question patriarchal values? Or can they

be complicit in oppressing women? Petersen and Rutherford argue that a male ethos 'has persisted in the colonial and post-colonial world' (*A Double Colonisation*, p. 9). They crucially point out that both colonialism *and* resistances to it can be seen as male-centred. This complicates the extent to which they offer freedom to women.

For example, Ketu H. Katrak has argued in 'Indian Nationalism, Gandhian "Satyagraha," and the Engendering of National Narratives' (in *Nationalisms and Sexualities*, ed. Andrew Parker et al., Routledge, 1992) that Mahatma Gandhi's resistance to British colonial rule in India during the 1920s and 1930s used specifically gendered representations for the purposes of Indian nationalism but ultimately did little to free Indian women from their patriarchal subordination to men. According to Katrak, Gandhi appropriated images of passive women to promote his campaign of 'passive resistance' to British colonial rule. Both men and women were encouraged to adopt a passivity exclusively associated with femininity, although *only* for the purposes of breaking colonial authority and *not* patriarchal authority:

> Gandhi's involvement of women in his 'satyagraha' (literally, truth-force) movement – part of his political strategy for national liberation – did not intend to confuse men's and women's roles; in particular, Gandhi did not challenge patriarchal traditions that oppressed women within the home. Furthermore, his specific representations of women and female sexuality, and his symbolising from Hindu mythology of selected female figures who embodied a nationalist spirit promoted ... a 'traditional' ideology wherein female sexuality was legitimately embodied only in marriage, wifehood, domesticity – all forms of controlling women's bodies. (pp. 395–6)

Katrak's critique invites us to consider at a more general level the extent to which resistances to colonialism bear the traces of unequal gender relationships. (It is worth reminding ourselves here of the chauvinism in many nationalist representations which we explored in Chapter 4).

A similar charge has been levelled at forms of postcolonial theory which have emerged in the wake of Said's *Orientalism*. Said's book may have pointed to the importance of gender in the discourse of the Orient, but it has been up to others such as Sara Mills to pursue this issue in depth. Homi K. Bhabha's work on the ambivalence of colonial discourses explores the relationship between a 'colonising subject' and a 'colonised subject' in highly abstract terms without reference to how the specifics of gender might complicate his model. Do colonial discourses interact with colonised men and women in the same way? As we considered, Bhabha's concepts of 'ambivalence' and 'mimicry' do not prove useful in answering this question.

Perhaps because the work of Fanon, Said, Bhabha and others has become so prominent in discussions of postcolonial theory, Carole Boyce Davies has become suspicious of the male-centred bias of postcolonial critique, and asks 'where are the women in the theorising of post-coloniality? Although there are growing numbers of titular identifications of post-colonial feminist discussions, it seems so far that the discourses of post-coloniality are not, at this point in history, overly populated by "postcolonial women"' (*Black Women, Writing and Identity: Migrations of the Subject*, Routledge, 1994, p. 80). Davies reminds postcolonial critics that they must remain sensitive to issues of gender difference in their work if postcolonialism is significantly going to challenge male-dominance. Otherwise, postcolonialism will, like colonialism, be a male-centred and ultimately patriarchal discourse in which women's voices are marginalised and silenced.

STOP and THINK

If postcolonialism is involved in the necessity of, in Ngugi's famous phrase, 'decolonising the mind', we must ask ourselves: who decolonises? And for whom? It is easy to speak of decolonisation as an abstract process, the wheels of which are kept turning by the various forms of postcolonial critique. But the feminist critiques of postcolonialism demand that we consider exactly *who* undertakes this task, *whose* interests decolonisation serves, and *who* the main beneficiaries are. Do women have substantially more freedom after colonialism, or do they remain subservient to forms of patriarchal power and familiar gendered representations? Do postcolonial representations sustain these unequal gender differences or offer the means to challenge them? Is postcolonialism a male-centred field?

Postcolonial critiques of 'First World' feminism

In this section, we shall consider the extent to which Western feminist discourses are able to address the double colonisation of women living in once-colonised societies and in Western locations. As we shall see, Western or 'First World' feminism has come in for much criticism from postcolonial critics due to the lack of attention paid to the problems suffered by women with links to countries with a history of colonialism. In opening up these debates, we can also think about issues such as female agency, the articulation of women's voices, and the relationship between feminist critics and their subject matter, as well as recognise the creative dialogues that are enabled by the encounters between 'First World' feminism and women from once-colonised countries. We shall attend to three important issues: Feminism and 'race', the limits of 'First World' feminism, and the problems in thinking about 'Third World' women.

Feminism and 'race'

How do differences in women's 'racial' identity impact upon feminism? In the early 1980s several critics explored the difficulties black women faced in working with popular feminist discourses. To what extent was feminism sensitive to their double colonisation?

Helen Carby explores these issues in her influential essay 'White Woman Listen! Black Feminism and the Boundaries of Sisterhood' (cited previously). In identifying and discussing the condition of 'Western feminism' in the 1970s, Carby explains that black and Asian women are barely made visible within its discourses. And when they *are* addressed, their representation remains highly problematic. Western feminism is criticised for the Orientalist way it represents the social practices of other 'races' as backwards and barbarous, from which black and Asian women need rescuing by their Western sisters. In so doing it fails to take into consideration the particular needs of these women, or consider different cultural practices *on their own terms*. The different meanings made by black and Asian women in their narratives (which Carby calls 'herstories' as opposed to 'histories') remain unheard. Carby gives the example of Western feminist horror concerning the arranged marriages of Asian women. In advocating an end to arranged marriages for Asian women because they are deemed oppressive, Western feminists do not consider Asian women's views and assume instead that their 'enlightened' outlook is the most progressive and liberating:

> The 'feminist' version of this ideology presents Asian women as being in need of liberation, not in terms of their own herstory and needs, but *into* the 'progressive' social mores and customs of the metropolitan West. The actual struggles that Asian women are involved in are ignored in favour of applying theories from the point of view of a more 'advanced', more 'progressive' outside observer. (p. 216)

In Carby's view, Western feminism frequently suffers from an ethnocentric bias in presuming that the solutions which white Western women have advocated in combating their oppression are equally applicable to all. As a consequence, issues of 'race' have been neglected which has hindered feminists from thinking about the ways in which racism and patriarchy interact. In addition, white women have failed to see themselves as the potential oppressors of black and Asian women, even when adopting benevolent positions towards them.

As Laura Donaldson helpfully summarises, 'a predominantly white middle-class feminism exhibits not an overt racism that conjures active dominance and enforced segregation but a more subtle "white solipsism" that passively colluded with a racist culture' (*Decolonising Feminisms: Race, Gender and Empire-Building*, Routledge, 1993, p. 1). How can this be changed? Hazel Carby argues that the answer is *not* simply grafting black and Asian women into the current models of Western feminist analysis, nor situating black women as the new 'objects' of research. Rather, Carby asks us to recognise the ways in which white women have oppressed black and Asian women in the past, and explore how Western feminism excludes black and Asian women in the present. White women must listen and learn from black and Asian women, and be willing to transform their prevailing attitudes so that their use of the collective pronoun 'we' (as in 'we women') is no longer imperious.

Learning the limits of 'First World' feminism

In urging white women to listen to black and Asian women, Hazel Carby makes an important intervention in feminist discourse. But her essay raises recurring questions: who is able to speak *for* or *about* 'Third World' women? Can Western women ever adequately deal with the experiences of others? Or do only 'Third World' women occupy this position? How can 'Third World' women intervene in 'First World' feminist debates? These questions have been recurrent preoccupations in the deconstructive criticism of Gayatri Chakravorty Spivak, which we will look at closely in what follows.

In Chapter 5 we considered Spivak's critique of Gilbert and Gubar's *The Madwoman in the Attic* as ignoring the colonial contexts of *Jane Eyre* when celebrating Jane as a proto-feminist heroine. The essay raises important theoretical questions: to what extent is the work of Western, or 'First World', feminists useful in addressing 'Third World' concerns? Might 'First World' feminism suffer from its own complicity with some of the assumptions of colonial discourses? Spivak's work offers some of the most insightful and challenging explorations of these questions which have impacted upon many areas of postcolonialism. She sees her task as a deconstructive one, where conceptual categories such as 'First World' and 'Third World' are brought to crisis by exposing their limits, shortcomings and blind-spots.

Before reading Spivak's work, a word of caution is required. Spivak's writing can, at first, seem sophisticated to the point of impenetrability. She works closely with the insights of poststructuralist thinkers such as Jacques Derrida and Jacques Lacan, and her own writing displays much of the slipperiness with language associated with their deconstructive texts. This is not merely for appearance's sake. Spivak's attention to detail, the range of her scholarship and her remarkable ability to expose the limitations in various forms of knowledge are enabled by her semantically compact prose style. Yet, inevitably, this is at the cost of a certain clarity and accessibility, especially for the beginner, and she cannot escape the charge that she sometimes presumes her readers will be as theoretically expert as herself. So, in what follows, I by no means claim to relay her ideas in embryo, as each of her essays is difficult to reduce to a central or key idea, such is their richness. Rather, I wish to extrapolate from them certain ideas relevant for our purposes at the moment. Hopefully this will function as a useful means of orienting your own reading of Spivak's work. And don't be discouraged if you struggle at first. Spivak's writings reward patient, repeated readings and continually yield new ideas, directions and problems.

In her chapter 'French Feminism in an International Frame' in *In Other Worlds: Essays in Cultural Politics* (Routledge, 1987), Spivak problematises the relationship between 'Third World' women and their representation via 'First World' scholarship. The essay begins with Spivak recording her surprise on meeting a young Sudanese woman in the Faculty of Sociology at a Saudi Arabian university who claimed to have written 'a structural functionalist dissertation on female circumcision in the Sudan' (p. 134). Although Spivak is a little disconcerted that the Sudanese woman uses the term 'female circumcision' rather than 'clitoridectomy' (the removal of the clitoris is not commensurate with the removal of the foreskin in male circumcision), she is particularly surprised by the 'structural functionalist' approach taken. Structural functionalism claims to be disinterested in its subject matter and to applaud all systems which operate successfully. But, asks Spivak, could this young Sudanese woman ever take a 'disinterested' approach to clitoridectomy? Does she mean to applaud the practice of clitoridectomy? Spivak is doubtful. The example raises two fundamentally important methodological questions. First, what is the relationship between the investigator, their methodology, and the object they study – can the researcher ever be 'disinterested'? Something must motivate and limit research. Second, are concepts drawn primarily from Western scholarship suitable to contexts which are culturally divergent?

In pursuing these questions, Spivak reflects on her own Western education as an upper-class woman from Calcutta who studied French avant-garde philosophy in America. In examining her own training in 'International Feminism' (which she describes as the aggregation of feminist thinking from England, France, West Germany, Italy and Latin America), she records how as a younger woman she laboured under a particular assumption when applying International Feminism to 'Third World' women. 'When one attempted to think of so-called Third World women in a broader scope', she remarks, 'one found oneself caught, as my Sudanese colleague was caught and held by Structural Functionalism, in a web of information retrieval inspired at best by: What can I do *for* them?' (pp. 134–5). Spivak is pointing out here the problematic assumption that systems of knowledge can be generally applicable around the globe. Furthermore, the position of the critic is also raised as a problem. The younger Spivak believed that she could complete meaningful work *on the behalf* of oppressed women. Her privileged situation as a well-educated woman made her feel empowered, that she was in a position to help less privileged women. This was an error. Spivak suggests that her younger self should have been asking self-critical questions such as: is my approach best suited to reading and writing 'Third World' women? How might engaging with 'Third World' women reveal the limits of my approach? What can *they* do for *me*?

So, Spivak is demanding that the relationship between the critic and her research must be more *interactive*; she must be willing to explore how divergent cultural contexts may reveal hitherto unseen problems in her approach. Or, as she sardonically puts it, '[t]he academic feminist must learn to learn from them, to speak to them, to suspect that their access to the political and sexual scene is not merely to be *corrected* by our superior theory and enlightened compassion' (p. 135). Note too how Spivak complicates the idea of a 'First World' feminist. As an Indian working in America skilled in European philosophy, and like the Sudanese woman using structural functionalism in Saudi Arabia, the younger Spivak is entirely complicit with 'First World' feminism in her intellectual approach to 'Third World' women.

Spivak proceeds to provide a detailed example of the problems involved when a 'First World' feminist attempts to deal sympathetically with 'Third World' women, by looking at French feminist Julia Kristeva's work on Chinese women. Spivak argues that a 'First World' feminist is often mistaken in considering that her gender authorises her to speak for 'Third World' women. She must 'learn to

stop feeling privileged *as a woman*' (p. 136). (I shall note only in
passing the problematic assumption here that the 'First World' feminist is female.) In indulging in this erroneous privilege, Kristeva's
attempts to offer a feminist account of women in Chinese culture
fails to engage dynamically with the specifics of her subject-matter.
Instead, she indulges in a 'wishful use of history' (p. 138) where her
own ethnocentric speculations into Chinese culture masquerade as
historical fact. Chinese culture becomes *appropriated* in order to
serve Kristeva's particular feminist ends, and her priorities remain
firmly self-centred. Ultimately, argues Spivak, Kristeva is less interested in Chinese women *per se* as she is concerned with how the
exploration of a 'Third World' culture allows her to raise questions
about the 'First World'. In taking a voyeuristic detour through
women in Chinese culture, Kristeva's terminus is in reality a self-
centred critique of Western philosophy. Questions are raised such as
'who then are we (not), how are we (not)' (p. 137), with the 'we' relat-
ing exclusively to 'First World' feminists. We might want to consider here the uncomfortable resemblances which Spivak exposes
between Kristeva's work and the project of Orientalism.

So, using a phrase at the end of Spivak's essay, we can describe the
appropriation of 'Third World' women to serve the self-centred
ends of 'First World' feminists as a compelling example of 'the
inbuilt colonialism of First World feminism toward the Third' (p.
153). In attempting to discover what 'they can do *for* them', Kristeva, the Sudanese woman and the younger Spivak stand accused of
this charge. Feminists must learn to speak *to* women and not *for*
women; they must be willing to *learn the limits* of their methodologies through an encounter with women in different contexts, rather
than assimilate differences within a grander design.

It is important to notice that Spivak's argument avoids the charge
of *ethnocentrism* by refusing the logic that, for example, only Indian
women can speak for other Indian women. Spivak has consistently
advocated that critics must always look to the specifics of their own
positions and recognise the political, cultural and institutional contexts in which they work. The space from which we speak is always
on the move, criss-crossed by the conflicting and shifting discourses
of things like our social class, education, gender, sexuality and ethnicity. It is very difficult to assume that the critic can ever speak 'on

behalf' of anybody, because the position of both the critic and their 'object' is never securely fixed.

'Third World' women

As we noted earlier, 'First World' feminism and 'Third World' women are inadequate phrases which traffic in untenable generali- sations and ring-fence internally various voices. Yet, as Spivak's work shows, their *strategic* deployment can be supported in so far as it enables critics to point out how even the most benevolent and sup- portive attempts on the part of some feminists to engage with dif- ferent groups of women are not always empowering. However, other critics can be less sensitive to the inadequacies of the term, and there always remains the danger that some feminists will use the term 'Third World' women not as a useful *figure of speech*, but as a clearly- defined empirical group.

Chandra Talpade Mohanty warns against precisely this in her important essay 'Under Western Eyes: Feminist Scholarship and Colonial Discourses' (in *Colonial Discourse and Post-Colonial Theory*, ed. Williams and Chrisman, pp. 196–220). In this essay, Mohanty exposes the production of a singular category of 'Third World' women in Western feminism which damagingly creates the 'discursive homogenisation and systematisation of the oppression of women in the third world' (p. 198). She recognises that Western feminism's attention to 'Third World' women is valuable and laud- able, not least in its attempts to forge international links between dif- ferent women. Yet the means by which this scholarship has proceeded remain problematic. For a variety of reasons, 'Third World' nations remain subservient to the West, at the levels of eco- nomic wealth, scientific development and technological resources. Mohanty argues that Western feminism cannot escape implication in these global economic and political frameworks and must be care- ful not to replicate unequal power relations between the 'First World' and 'Third World'. Yet Western feminism is in danger of doing this in its analysis of 'Third World' women.

Mohanty discovers worrying analytical presuppositions in 'First World' analyses of 'Third World' women. First, it is presumed that all women exist as a 'coherent group with identical interests and

desires, regardless of class, ethnic or racial location' (p. 199). This
coherency is established by assuming that all women in divergent
contexts are first and foremost *victims* of different kinds of oppression: male violence, the structure of the family, economic structures
and so on. Although an attention to context might appear sensitive
to difference, context always remains secondary to the universal
assumption of victimage. 'Women are taken as a unified "powerless"
group prior to the historical and political analysis in question. Thus,
it is then merely a matter of specifying the context *after the fact*' (p.
202). Furthermore, if women are eternally cast as victims then men
are posited as perpetual victimisers. There is little attempt to consider the different types of social relations *between* men and women
which might be possible, or to look closely at the relations *between*
women created by social and ethnic differences (although Mohanty
doesn't mention it, we might add sexuality here too).

The second presumption concerns the ways by which 'universal
womanhood' is proved. Mohanty deals with three different methods
of such proof. The first, the 'arithmetic method', presumes that certain forms of oppression are universal if they circumscribe large
numbers of women. Mohanty uses the veiling of Muslim women as
an example of the 'arithmetic method'. It is assumed that because
Muslim women in places such as Saudi Arabia, Iran, Pakistan, India
and Egypt wear the veil, they all suffer from the same form of
oppression. Yet, is the symbolic significance of the veil in each of
these locations necessarily the same? Might there be political circumstances when women *choose* to wear the veil, as an important act
of political empowerment for themselves? The second methodology
concerns the point Spivak made in her critique of international feminism, namely the assumption that concepts (such as patriarchy,
reproduction, the family etc.) are often used 'without their specifi-
cation in local cultural and historical contexts' (p. 209). There may
well be a sexual division of labour in families living in America and
India, but is it tantamount to the same thing in different locations?
Mohanty asks: 'how is it possible to refer to "the" sexual division of
labour when the *content* of this division changes radically from one
environment to the next, and from one historical juncture to
another? (p. 210).

Lastly, Mohanty makes the rather complicated assertion that

some critics 'confuse the use of gender as a superordinate category of organising analysis with the universalistic proof and instantiation of this category' (p. 211). By this she means that there is an important difference between the ways we construct patterns or systems of representations, and the empirical, lived order of societies – for convenience's sake we might simplify this as a difference between imagined order and lived experience. All systems of representations need patterns to work; they posit fundamental differences which function as a centre of reference for all other differences in the system. For example, the fundamental opposition of nature/culture underpins other patterning like wild/domestic or biology/technology. These are the convenient aesthetic distinctions *we make* to conceptualise the world. Mohanty argues that some critics mistakenly go searching for the empirical proof of these patterns in lived experience. They try to squeeze societies into preconceived frames or patterns of reference, rather than consider that their imaginary models of order might be inappropriate. Thus, in a feminist context, although it might be strategically and politically productive to imagine sometimes a difference between 'First World' and 'Third World' women, it is a mistake to believe that these categories exist securely at the level of lived experience and can be empirically 'proved' through field work. The lived experiences of women in countries with a history of colonialism cannot be easily fitted into the homogenising, imaginary category of 'Third World' women.

So, by conceiving of 'the average third-world woman' (p. 199), Western feminists construct a template for female identity in the 'Third World' based on a series of questionable conceptual and methodological manoeuvres, with scant regard for context. This is tantamount to a colonial act, in the imposition of a homogeneous identity on 'Third World' women without regard to the historical and cultural differences which inevitably exceed this category. Furthermore, the assimilation of 'Third World' women *within* Western feminist discourse suggests that *Western* feminism remains the primary means by which patriarchy, sexism and chauvinism are challenged. As objects of Western feminist analysis, 'Third World' women are robbed of their agency.

STOP and THINK

Mohanty's problematisation of the category of 'Third World' women accomplishes much, but her essay creates some problems of its own.

First, is a 'First World' feminist critique of women in 'Third World' locations possible? Mohanty gives an example of one by looking briefly at Maria Mies's book *The Lace Makers of Narsapur: Indian Housewives Produce for the World Market* (Zed, 1982). By attending closely to the economic and ideological specifics of an Indian lacemaking industry in terms of its female workers, Mohanty argues that Mies successfully produces a 'careful, politically focused' study ('Under Western Eyes', p. 207). However, Mies deals with the power relations of the lacemaking industry through a series of familiar approaches and concepts derived from Western materialism. Is Mies's approach *conceptually* different? Mohanty does not say.

The example of Mies's study partly answers a second problem: how does Mohanty avoid asserting an ethnocentric feminism in her privileging of exploring context? It seems that Mohanty accepts that 'First World' women *can* write constructively about 'Third World' contexts. Also, Mohanty advocates the forging of 'strategic coalitions' (p. 211) between different groups of women at apposite moments when contesting the many forms of oppression, although she does not explore this at length.

However, one serious problem remains. How do critics working in one context gain access to the cultural, historical and social specificities of another context? If the Western analyses of 'Third World' contexts always run the risk of misrepresentation by approaching them through a series of concepts or methodologies which are ill-equipped to bear witness to the specifics of other times and places (as Spivak also exposed in her reading of Kristeva's approach to Chinese women), then how can 'First World' feminists ever write about 'Third World' women without imposing their own conceptual systems? Mohanty's repeated stress on context is in danger of making it seem rather transparent, easily rendered by those critics who do some appropriate research. But is cultural difference so easily accessible? Is it always available to those approaching from other contexts?

Can the subaltern speak?

It should be clear from the ideas we have explored so far, that the category of 'Third World' women is an *effect of discourse* rather than an existent, identifiable reality. It does not approximate to any stable, collective body. Similarly the singular 'Third World' woman is an ideological construct wholly produced within 'First World' intellectual debates, and *not* an individual subject. As we have considered, the concepts and methodological approaches used to bear witness to 'Third World' experiences may be inappropriate to the task and result in generalisation, falsification and conjecture. But this leaves a problem: how *does* one bear witness to the agency of those women throughout history who are today inadequately represented as 'Third World' women?

This is an issue which Spivak has explored in one of her most challenging and intellectually rich essays, 'Can the Subaltern Speak?' (reprinted with abridgements in *Colonial Discourse and Post-Colonial Theory*, ed. Williams and Chrisman, pp. 66–111). This essay, published in 1988, is a complex critique of the representation of human subjectivity in a variety of contexts, but with particular reference to the work of the *Subaltern Studies* scholars (which we encountered in Chapter 4). To recap: these scholars were interested in the representation of 'the subaltern' in colonialist texts, with subalterns defined as those who did not comprise the colonial elite – such as the lesser rural gentry, impoverished landlords, rich peasants and upper-middle-class peasants. As a way of mounting her critique of the scholars' assumptions concerning the subaltern in colonialist texts, Spivak begins by turning first to the work of poststructuralist thinkers such as Michel Foucault and Gilles Deleuze who have challenged the notion that human individuals are 'sovereign subjects' with autonomous agency over their consciousness (summed up in the Cartesian dictum 'I think therefore I am'). As poststructuralism would have it, human consciousness is constructed *discursively*. Our subjectivity is constituted by the shifting discourses of power which endlessly 'speak through' us, situating us here and there in particular positions and relations. In these terms we are not the authors of ourselves. We do not construct our own identities but have them written for us; the subject cannot be 'sovereign' over the construction of selfhood. Instead, the subject is 'de-centred' in that its consciousness is always being constructed from positions outside of itself. It follows, then, that the individual is *not* the point of origin for consciousness, and human consciousness is *not* a transparent representation of the self but an effect of discourse. Spivak argues that, surprisingly for these figures, when Foucault and Deleuze talk about oppressed groups such as the working class they fall back into precisely these uncritical notions of the 'sovereign subject' by restoring to them a full 'centred' consciousness – or to use her terms, they are guilty of 'a clandestine restoration of subjective essentialism' (p. 74). In addition, they also assume that the writing of intellectuals such as themselves can serve as a transparent medium through which the voices of the oppressed can be represented. The intellectual is cast as a reliable mediator for the voices of the oppressed, a mouthpiece through which the oppressed can clearly speak.

Spivak is concerned that these two theoretical failings also problematise the study of colonised subjects as in the work of Ranajit Guha and other *Subaltern Studies* scholars. As we have already noticed, these critics read documents recording subaltern insurgency produced by colonial authorities in order to retrieve from them the hitherto absent perspectives of the oppressed subalterns. Spivak is entirely sympathetic to the aims of the scholars and supportive of their politics. But she urges that critics must always beware of attempting to retrieve a 'subaltern consciousness' from texts, as this will merely replicate the two problems in the work of Foucault and Deleuze: perceiving of the subaltern as a 'sovereign subject' in control of his or her own consciousness, and assuming that the intellectual is a transparent medium through which subaltern consciousness can be made present. Representations of subaltern insurgency must *not* be trusted as reliable expressions of a sovereign subaltern consciousness; like 'Third World' women, 'subaltern consciousness' is fiction, an effect of Western discourse. To retrieve the unruly voice of a 'subaltern subject' from the colonial archives is to risk complicity in an essentialist, specifically Western model of centred subjectivity in which 'concrete experience' is (mistakenly) preserved.

These problems are further compounded by the issue of gender, because representations of subaltern insurgency tend to prioritise men. 'As object of colonialist historiography and as subject of insurgency, the ideological construction of gender keeps the male dominant. If, in the context of colonial production, the subaltern has no history and cannot speak, the subaltern as female is even more deeply in shadow' (pp. 82–3). This point raises the following questions: can oppressed women's voices ever be recovered from the archive? Can the subaltern as female, confined in the shadows of colonial history and representation, ever be heard to speak? The answer, it seems, is no, so long as intellectuals go searching for an originary, sovereign and concrete female consciousness which can be discovered and readily represented with recourse to questionable assumptions concerning subjectivity. Rather than hunting for the 'lost voices' of women in the historical archives in an act of retrieval, intellectuals should be aware that this kind of work will continue to keep the subaltern as female entirely muted.

Let us think carefully about this argument, in order to avoid some common misconceptions about 'Can the Subaltern Speak?' which have arisen in the wake of its publication. As Robert Young puts it in his reading of the essay, the problem which Spivak identifies is 'not that the woman cannot speak as such, that no records of the subject-consciousness of women exist, but that she is assigned no position of enunciation [and therefore] everyone else speaks for her, so that she is rewritten continuously as the object of patriarchy or of imperialism' (*White Mythologies: Writing History and the West*, Routledge, 1990, p. 164). She is always being written with recourse to a form of representation which is incapable of bearing adequate witness to her subject-position. Spivak gives examples of these silenced subaltern women by looking at the documentation of *sati* or widow sacrifice in colonial India. Ultimately, she suggests, it is better to acknowledge that the subaltern as female exists as the unrepresentable in discourse, a shadowy figure on its margins. Any attempt to retrieve her voice will disfigure her speech. So, she concludes, intellectuals must instead critique those discourses which claim to rescue the 'authen-

tic' voices of the subaltern as female from their mute condition, and
address their complicity in the production of subalterneity. Simply
inserting subaltern women into representation is a cosmetic exercise
as long as the *system* of representation endorses discredited models
of essential, centred subjectivity. As Spivak memorably concludes,
'[t]here is no virtue in global laundry lists with "woman" as a pious
item' (p. 104).

To summarise: in 'Can the Subaltern Speak?' Spivak complicates
the extent to which women's voices can be easily retrieved and
restored to history. Rather than making the subaltern as female seem
to speak, intellectuals must *bring to crisis* the representational systems which rendered her mute in the first place.

By rendering the subaltern as female as a discursive construct and
not a 'sovereign subject', Spivak's essay potentially derails the work
of critics like the *Subaltern Studies* scholars. Their attention to
subaltern insurgency is part of an important political project which
opposes the false images of Indian history constructed in elite historiography. But after reading 'Can the Subaltern Speak?', critics
might be discouraged from pursuing subalterns if their voices are
forever lost inside colonial discourses. Why bother? Spivak seeks
to get round this *impasse* in another piece from *In Other Worlds*,
'Subaltern Studies: Deconstructing Historiography' (also available
in *The Spivak Reader*, ed. Donna Landry and Gerald MacLean,
Routledge, 1996). In exploring how the subaltern scholars attempt
to retrieve subaltern consciousness from history, Spivak argues in
her typically verbose fashion that their work can be described as 'a
strategic use of positivist essentialism in a scrupulously visible political interest' (*In Other Worlds*, p. 205). By this, she suggests that
although it is theoretically improper to assume the existence of a
sovereign or essential subaltern consciousness, it is none the less
important to continue to use the concept of an essential subject as
part of a wider political project. In other words, in trying to change
things we sometimes have to use ideas or tools which we know are
problematic. For example, think about the idea of Negritude which
we looked at in Chapter 3; although an essential black self is more
fiction than fact as critics have shown, the investment in an essentialising black identity in the 1950s and 1960s had a revolutionary
impact and contributed valuably to resisting colonialism. Spivak's

influential notion of *strategic essentialism* works something like this; we choose to use a concept which we know is flawed. However, she does open herself to the charge of having things both ways by dismissing on theoretical grounds the subaltern subject while supporting elsewhere those projects which still subscribe to notions of essential subjectivity.

More recently, Spivak has reflected on the ideas raised in 'Can the Subaltern Speak?' and the responses they provoked, in an interview printed as 'Subaltern Talk' in *The Spivak Reader* (pp. 287–308). An important point she makes concerns the use of the term 'speak' in the title of her essay, which has been misunderstood. In discussing the silence of the subaltern as female, she explains that she was not using the term literally to suggest that such women never *actually* talked. Rather, she wanted to consider the inability for their words to enable *transactions* between speakers and listeners. Their muteness is created by the fact that even when women uttered words, they were still interpreted through conceptual and methodological procedures which were unable to understand their interventions with accuracy. It is not so much that subaltern women did not speak, but rather that others *did not know how to listen*, how to enter into a transaction between speaker and listener. The subaltern cannot speak because their words cannot be properly interpreted. Hence, the silence of the female as subaltern is the result of a failure of *interpretation* and not a failure of articulation.

'Going a piece of the way': creative dialogues in postcolonial feminism

Of course, not all critics have subscribed to Spivak's views and have found problems with her argument. This is sometimes as a result of misconceptions that exist concerning the finer points of her argument – although, for some, Spivak's complex and adventurous style must shoulder some responsibility for this. One of the shrewdest readers of Spivak is Bart Moore-Gilbert who, in his book *Postcolonial Theory: Contexts, Practices, Politics* (Verso, 1997), makes the important point that 'the more the subaltern is seen as a "theoretical" fiction ... the more the suffering and exploitation of the subaltern becomes a theoretical fiction, too' (p. 102). In other words, by

regarding the subaltern as an effect of discourse and not an actual
individual, Spivak treats material realities as purely textual or theoretical phenomena. (Note too that exactly the same might be said of
positing 'Third World' women as an entirely discursive category.)
Moore–Gilbert has also suggested that one major implication of
'Can the Subaltern Speak?' is the way it leaves the non–subaltern
critic in an impossible position, unable to do anything positive on
behalf or in support of the subaltern as female. '[T]he non–subaltern
must either maximally respect the Other's radical alterity, thus leaving the status quo intact, or attempt the impossible feat of "opening
up" to the Other without in any way "assimilating" that Other to
his/her own subject-position, perspectives or identity' (p. 102).

Spivak's conclusions can indeed leave the critic feeling ham-
strung. What is the point in trying to engage with oppressed voices
if these voices are eternally doomed to perish due to the methods
and concepts we use? The simpler option might be to leave the subaltern as female well alone, beyond representation and lost in the
shadows of the text. Furthermore, after reading Spivak and
Mohanty, we might be left doubting if 'First World' feminism can
be used purposefully in 'Third World' contexts at all, and be
tempted to dismiss it as a contemporary form of colonial discourse.

But other ways of thinking about the relationship between 'First
World' feminism and 'Third World' women are available. As we
have seen, the work of Spivak and Mohanty demanded that we must
be vigilant in using certain kinds of approach to subaltern and
'Third World' texts. But, taking a different view, the dismissal of
'First World' feminism at a stroke because of these problems might
risk losing its resources which *can* contribute to feminist critique, as
well as deny the possibilities for the coalitions between 'First World'
and 'Third World' feminists that Mohanty advocates. Spivak herself
would never wish to dismiss entirely 'First World' feminism on
these grounds. Rather, other kinds of relationships might be built,
more equitable, vigilant and transformative for all involved.

The possibility of building such new, vigilant and transformative
relations between women *across* 'First' and 'Third World' feminism
is evidenced by a book of literary critical essays edited by Susheila
Nasta titled *Motherlands: Black Women's Writing from Africa, the
Caribbean and South Asia* (Women's Press, 1991). In her introduc-

tion, Nasta argues that a 'creative dialogue' is possible (p. xvi) where 'First World' and 'Third World' voices both contribute to and learn from each other. This is not at all a convenient compromise between positions – far from it. Rather, Nasta argues that the insights of 'First World' feminism can illuminate postcolonial texts which, in their turn, enable women readers in the 'First World' to 're-evaluate the cultural assumptions which inform their own readings' (p. xvii). The relationship is mobile, dialogic and *mutually* transformative. Nasta's argument is borne out by the essays in the collection written by a variety of scholars, many of whom have links to once-colonised countries and work in British and American universities. The critics' explorations of representations of motherhood in a variety of postcolonial texts emerge from the intersections between 'First World' and 'Third World' work on this subject and others, and is in part facilitated by many of the critics' own relations with both 'First World' and 'Third World' locations. Thus, Jane Bryce-Okunlola uses the work of a diverse body of thinkers which include Micere Mugo, Julia Kristeva, Carole Boyce Davies, Alice Walker, Sandra Gilbert and Susan Gubar in her reading of the novels of Flora Nwapa, Rebeka Njau and Bessie Head. As these essays demonstrate, 'First World' and 'Third World' voices need not always construct antagonistic relationships with each other.

The creative writers studied in *Motherlands* all use various forms of English in their work, and Nasta acknowledges how as a 'father tongue' English remains a problematic language for these women in that it houses both colonial and patriarchal values. None the less, language is also 'both source and womb of creativity, a means of giving birth to new stories, new myths, of telling the stories of women that have been previously silenced' (p. xiii). Language is both disabling and enabling. Although many of the women writers studied in *Motherlands* could not be described as subaltern in the strict sense used by Guha, Spivak and others, Nasta's words none the less act as a corrective to the potential denial of agency for women's speech in 'Can the Subaltern Speak?'. Nasta reminds us that we must attend to the ways in which women from once-colonised countries are transforming English to enable *new* kinds of representation through which they *can* speak. Similarly, critical approaches are being negotiated which bear better witness to the specificities of this speech. In attending to the ways in which our critical practices render the subaltern as female unable to speak, Spivak's work perhaps comes too close on occasions to denying women the *possibility* of changing the dominant modes of interpretation, an agency which the essays in *Motherlands* variously demonstrate with memorable verve. In showing how a 'creative dialogue' is possible, *Motherlands* makes an important contribution to the debates concerning postcolonialism and feminism while also calling readers' attention specifically to the agency and voices of black women from Africa, the Caribbean and South Asia.

In terms of postcolonial theory, a similar 'creative dialogue' can be discovered. For all of their attention to the problematics of Western concepts and methodologies, we must remember that the work of Mohanty, Spivak and others is facilitated by their own creative dialogues between Western theory and postcolonial contexts. A good example is Spivak herself. In recent years she has translated the fiction of the Bengali writer Mahasweta Devi (see *Imaginary Maps: Three Stories by Mahasweta Devi*, trans. Gayatri Chakravorty Spivak, Routledge, 1995). Her commentaries on Mahasweta's work, and the challenges it poses for the translator, have intervened in a wealth of academic debates about postcoloniality, nationalism, the subaltern, ethics and ecology. Spivak admits that these interventions are born out of a 'habit of mind' which 'may draw a reader to Marx, to Mahasweta, and to Derrida, in different ways' (*The Spivak Reader*, p. 274). The directions and tensions engendered by this eclectic group of thinkers bear witness to the valuable possibilities enabled by bringing diverse materials into dialogue with each other and revealing new directions and limits, as Spivak's body of often brilliant work aptly evidences.

Carole Boyce Davies makes a valuable point in *Black Women, Writing and Identity* when she uses the phrase 'going a piece of the way with them' to explain her own encounters with Western theory. Davies argues that it is impossible for her to work fully with the various theoretical schools available, such as feminism and Marxism, because they have the potential to marginalise her as a black woman in their methodological assumptions. None the less, existing schools of thought can be engaged in a process of negotiation which yields useful critical tools. Davies proposes 'a kind of *critical relationality* in which various theoretical positions are interrogated for their specific applicability to Black women's experiences' (p. 46). In negotiating with existing schools of thought, black women become active agents in intervening in dominant discourses and producing enabling conceptual frames. Davies stresses that black women must be ever mobile, departing from and returning to different critical positions in a migratory movement. Although some might be concerned about the itinerant aspects of this theory (sometimes it is important to take a 'fixed' position as a critic) her notion of 'going a piece of the way with them' bears witness to the ways in which black women (and, I would argue, others) have the agency to unsettle received ideas and challenge the biases of 'First World' theory and male-centred postcolonialism, as well as transforming each in the process.

Representing women in Sally Morgan's *My Place*

Let us conclude by considering a literary text in 'critical relationality' to some of the ideas we have met in this chapter.

Set in Australia, *My Place* is an autobiographical text which explores the history of Sally Morgan's family in the wider context of Australian history. Sally records her childhood as a time of difficulty. The family are often short of money. Her father, a veteran of the Second World War, suffers from illness and dies while Sally is a young girl. Her mother, Gladys, has a variety of cleaning jobs to make ends meet. Sally spends most of her young life with her brothers and sisters, and her grandmother Daisy. During the course of her youth she begins to realise that she is not always regarded by others in the same way as white children. On pressing her mother about her family background she is told that she is an Indian. However, she learns later that this is a lie, and she is instead descended from Australia's Aborigines. This sets Sally on a determined quest to discover the hitherto hidden Aboriginal branches of her family tree. Her mother and especially her grandmother are frequently reluctant to talk about their pasts, but gradually Sally pieces together a story of her Aboriginal inheritance. This involves her travelling to the places where her mother and grandmother grew up and meeting Aboriginal peoples whom she had no idea existed, as well as tape-recording the voices of other Aboriginal members of her family which she transcribes and includes in her autobiography.

At one level, *My Place* offers a corrective to historical representations of Australian history. As Sally reflects, 'there's almost nothing written from a personal point of view about Aboriginal people. All our history is about the white man. No one knows about what it was like for us. A lot of our history has been lost, people have been too frightened to say anything' (p. 163). The writing of Australian history privileges the white (and the) male. In opposition to this, Sally's narrative calls attention to the experiences of women and records the exploitation of Aboriginal peoples by white settlers, who often broke up Aboriginal families and employed Aboriginal women as domestic servants without paying them a wage. The text evidences what we have been calling the 'double colonisation' of women on many occasions, as many characters find themselves subservient to colonialist and patriarchal values. It exposes how Aboriginal women could become objects of sexual desire for white men who compelled them to have intercourse and cared little for the devastating effect this could have on them, particularly as concerns pregnancy. Throughout the text there is uncertainty as to the identity of Daisy's father who could be one of several possible white men. In addition, Gladys's narrative records how the children fathered by white men and born to Aboriginal women were taken from their mothers and forced to grow up separately. As a child she was placed in a boarding-school and rarely saw her mother, who was in service to a white family in Perth. *My Place* enables a feminist critique of the patriarchal values enshrined in historical representations of Australia, and in the institutions which impacted devastatingly on many women's lives

The position of white women is also an issue. On the one hand, *My Place* shows how they are subject to the patriarchal authority of white men and have to endure the men's sexual encounters with Aboriginal women. They suffer their own, distinct forms of oppression. Yet they are also complicit in the marginalisation of Aboriginal women due to the ways that colonial discourses position them in relation to the Aboriginals. For example, Gladys remembers one incident as a child while staying in Perth with Daisy. The mother of the white family, Alice, comes into the kitchen with her daughter June, who is carrying a beautiful doll with golden hair and blue eyes.

Gladys is captivated by the doll as it reminds her of a princess. Alice proceeds to give her a doll of her own, but this one is 'a black topsy doll dressed like a servant. It had a red checked dress on and a white apron, just like Mum's. It had what they used to call a slave cap on its head' (p. 261). Gladys is devastated:

> That's me, I thought, I want to be a princess, not a servant. I was so upset that when Alice placed the black doll in my arms, I couldn't help flinging it onto the floor and screaming, 'I don't want a black doll, I don't want a black doll.' Alice just laughed and said to my mother, 'Fancy, her not wanting a black doll.' (p. 262)

Alice has internalised a patriarchal set of values which secure a differential hierarchy between white and Aboriginal women. These values in their turn help to buttress the colonialist attitudes which endure in Australian constructions of 'race'. It is crucial to grasp that, at this moment, both Alice and Gladys remain doubly colonised in different ways, despite the fact that Alice seems to occupy a position of authority and privilege. None the less, this example shows how white women were complicit in constructing subservient roles and racialised identities for Aboriginal women, and exposes the difficulties faced by advocating a universal notion of sisterhood when contesting patriarchal representations in Australian history.

My Place is also fascinating to consider in terms of the issues raised by the debates surrounding Spivak's essay 'Can the Subaltern Speak?'. Of course, Spivak's focus is nineteenth-century India and her essay cannot be freely mapped onto Morgan's text. Yet the problems of accessing and representing the consciousness of doubly colonised women otherwise silent in received historical representations are central in *My Place*, and we might (to borrow Carole Boyce Davies's phrase) 'go a piece of the way' with some of the conceptual vocabulary gleaned from our exploration of Spivak's work when looking at *My Place*.

Of particular interest is Sally Morgan's identification of an 'Aboriginal consciousness'. In the latter stages of the book, Sally takes a journey with her family to her grandmother's birthplace, Corunna Downs. After a series of emotional meetings with her Aboriginal relations, she describes how their tentative search for family knowledge

had 'grown into a spiritual and emotional pilgrimage. We had an Aboriginal consciousness now, and were proud of it' (p. 233). What does
she mean by 'Aboriginal consciousness' here? What is the relationship
between Sally's 'Aboriginal consciousness' and the Aboriginal characters she meets at Corunna Downs, many of whom speak Aboriginal
languages and communicate with Sally through an interpreter? Are
the subject-positions of these women correspondent? Do they occupy
the same 'place'? In constructing an 'Aboriginal consciousness' and
laying claim to it, Sally Morgan could be criticised for fictionalising a
form of essentialised, sovereign subjectivity which homogenises all
Aboriginals and papers over the important historical and cultural
specifics of Sally's position. Her version of 'Aboriginal consciousness', like Spivak's subaltern as female, is perhaps a convenient fiction
of her own making.

However, we might read this novel from a different direction too.
Sally's Aboriginality is not easily fixed, and significantly she inherits Aboriginality from a maternal line. Her father was a white Australian, while her mother Gladys was born to an Aboriginal mother,
Daisy, and white father. To complicate things further, Daisy's Aboriginality is also at issue as she was born to a white father and Aboriginal mother. It is clear that in the text 'Aboriginality' is more than
a description of physiological 'race'. Sally could choose to conceal
her Aboriginality and claim a non-Aboriginal identity. Indeed, this
was the approach her mother Gladys had taken by telling the children they were Indian and keeping their Aboriginal heritage a
secret. So we might argue that Sally's firm decision to embrace and
explore an Aboriginal identity is *an important political decision*,
despite the problems of her claims to 'Aboriginal consciousness'
examined in the previous paragraph.

The importance of this act can be measured in one particularly
moving moment at Corunna Downs, when Sally is told by an old
Aboriginal woman that her explorations into her past mean a great
deal to Aboriginals because Sally is so proud to acknowledge and
treasure (rather than conceal) her Aboriginal past: 'You don't know
what it means that you, with a light skin, want to own us' (pp.
228–9). Figured in this quotation are, first, the differences between
the women – Sally cannot ever *know* the meaning of her actions for
the Aboriginals – which splits a sense of a homogeneous 'Aborigi-

nal consciousness' connecting these women; and second, the vital political significance of Sally's quest which potentially overrides these conceptual problems. We might go so far as to think about Sally's acknowledgement of an 'Aboriginal consciousness' as an exercise in 'strategic essentialism', which enables her to build affiliations with Aboriginal peoples and involve herself in bringing their lives to bear upon Australian history, despite the fact that their experiences will remain out of reach of her knowledge. Read in these terms, *My Place* is both a feminist and a postcolonial text in its contestation of the mutually supportive projects of patriarchy and colonialism.

Selected reading

Alexander, M. Jacqui and Chandra Talpade Mohanty (eds), *Feminist Genealogies, Colonial Legacies, Democratic Futures* (Routledge, 1997).
  A wide-ranging collection of essays which examine the challenges for different groups of feminists in an often neo-colonial and patriarchal world.
Davies, Carole Boyce, *Black Women, Writing and Identity: Migrations of the Subject* (Routledge, 1994).
  A sustained and conceptually sophisticated critique which challenges some orthodox positions in postcolonial theory and negotiates new theoretical frames for reading black women's writing.
Donaldson, Laura E., *Decolonising Feminisms: Race, Gender, and Empire-Building* (Routledge, 1992).
Kabbani, Rana, *Imperial Fictions: Europe's Myths of Orient* (Pandora, rev. 1994).
  An excellent critique of the gender politics of Orientalist art and writing.
Lionnet, François, *Postcolonial Representations: Women, Literature, Identity* (Cornell University Press, 1995).
McClintock, Anne, *Imperial Leather: Race, Gender and Sexuality in the Colonial Context* (Routledge, 1995).
  An exciting and thought-provoking critique of colonial discourses and their intersections with 'race', gender and sexuality.
Mohanty, Chandra Talpade, 'Under Western Eyes: Feminist Scholarship and Colonial Discourses' in Williams and Chrisman (eds), *Colonial Discourse and Post-Colonial Theory*, (Harvester Wheatsheaf, 1993), pp. 196–220.

Mohanty's influential and important essay is required reading for discussions of postcolonialism and feminism.

Moore-Gilbert, Bart, *Postcolonial Theory: Contexts, Practices, Politics* (Verso, 1997).

Moore-Gilbert's chapter on Spivak is perhaps the finest to date in rendering and critiquing her influential ideas.

Nasta, Susheila (ed.), *Motherlands: Black Women's Writing from Africa, the Caribbean and South Asia* (Women's Press, 1991).

An excellent collection of critical essays which exemplifies the manifold voices of postcolonial and feminist criticism.

Petersen, Kirsten Holst, and Anna Rutherford (eds), *A Double Colonization: Colonial and Post-Colonial Women's Writing* (Dangaroo, 1986).

A landmark text which features creative and critical writing that addresses the 'double colonisation' of women.

Rajeswari, Sunder Rajan, *Real and Imagined Women: Gender, Culture, and Postcolonialism* (Routledge, 1993).

Spivak, Gayatri Chakravorty, 'Can the Subaltern Speak?', reprinted with abridgements in Williams and Chrisman (eds), *Colonial Discourse and Post-Colonial Theory* (Harvester Wheatsheaf, 1993), pp. 66–111.

Probably one of the most important essays in postcolonialism, 'Can the Subaltern Speak?' has proved influential in feminist criticism and theories of colonial discourses. A very difficult essay at times, but one which rewards patient reading.

Spivak, Gayatri Chakravorty *The Spivak Reader*, ed. Donna Landry and Gerald MacLean (Routledge, 1996).

This collection features some of Spivak's most influential and groundbreaking work, and includes highly valuable introductions to her essays. Also included is a full bibliography of Spivak's work.

Trinh, T. Minh-ha, *Woman, Native, Other: Writing Postcoloniality and Feminism* (Indiana University Press, 1989).

A ground-breaking and challenging study of postcoloniality and feminism which explores the role of writing in contesting dominant patriarchal representations.

7

Diaspora identities

What is a 'diaspora'?

It seems an obvious point that the British Empire was an international affair. Through the work of colonialism countless people voyaged *out* from Britain, often settling around the world in a variety of different places. But less well-known today, perhaps, were the voyages *in* by colonised peoples from around the world who travelled to Britain where they remained for the rest of their lives. Often these voyages took place under duress, as in the instances of plantation owners taking slaves to put to work as servants in their British homes, or the use of South Asian women as 'ayahs' by families employed by the East India Company during and after their return to Britain. If the British Empire changed life in colonised countries, then Britain too was changed forever by its colonial encounters.

It is remarkable that relatively few people today are aware that the populations of most Western nations have consisted *for centuries* of people from many different 'races' and cultures. For example, the existence of African peoples in Britain can be traced back to Elizabethan times, as testified by Peter Fryer's books *Staying Power: The History of Black People in Britain* (Pluto, 1984) and *Black People in the British Empire: An Introduction* (Pluto, 1988). Anna Marie Smith has recorded that '[t]he black population in London numbered between 15,000 and 20,000 in the late eighteenth century – almost 3 per cent of the total population of the city' (*New Right Discourse on Race and Sexuality: Britain*

1968–1990, Cambridge, 1994, p. 134). In recent years much critical interest has grown in the writings of those colonised people who became located in Britain during the colonial period. One example is Ignatius Sancho. Born on a slave-ship and raised in South London, Sancho served as a butler, wrote music, corresponded with many fashionable literary figures and had his portrait painted by none other than Thomas Gainsborough. *The Letters of the Late Ignatius Sancho, An African* were published posthumously in 1782. Another figure is Olaudah Equiano, born in Nigeria and transported to Barbados, later arriving in England at the age of twelve. His book, *The Interesting Narrative of the Life of Olaudah Equiano, or Gustavus Vassa, the African* was published in 1789 and became an important text in the movement to abolish slavery.

Interestingly, editions of both have been published recently by Penguin books in the 'Penguin Classics' series (alongside Jane Austen, Charlotte Brontë and other canonical British writers). The burgeoning interest in these and other 'Black Britons' living before the decline of Empire is partly a consequence of the work of writers and critics from Britain's diaspora communities who are challenging popular ways of thinking about British history, such as the mistaken view that migration from countries with a history of colonialism has only happened since the 1950s. It is a falsehood to think that Britain and other colonising nations were culturally and ethnically homogeneous before the Second World War.

None the less, it is fair to say that since the end of the Second World War the former colonising nations have experienced the arrival of many peoples from once-colonised countries who have established new homes at the old colonial centres. The reasons for migration have been variable. In Britain, colonial peoples were specifically recruited by the Government to cope with labour shortages, such as the drive after the Second World War to employ Caribbeans in public services like health and transport. Others arrived to study, or to escape political and economic difficulties in their native lands. Some followed family members who migrated before them. As a consequence, at the end of the millennium Britain can boast a wide variety of diaspora communities that may trace connections to locations such as Australia, Africa, South Asia, the Caribbean, China or Ireland.

What is a 'diaspora'? In his excellent book *Global Diasporas: An Introduction* (UCL Press, 1997) Robin Cohen tentatively describes diasporas as communities of people living together in one country who 'acknowledge that "the old country" – a notion often buried deep in language, religion, custom or folklore – always has some claim on their loyalty and emotions' (p. ix). The emphasis on collectivity and community here is very important, as is the sense of living in one country but looking across time and space to another. Cohen continues that 'a member's adherence to a diasporic community is demonstrated by an acceptance of an inescapable link with their past migration history and a sense of co-ethnicity with others of a similar background' (p. ix). Note Cohen's careful choice of phrase: 'past migration history'. It is tempting to think of diaspora peoples as migrant peoples, and indeed many living in diasporas certainly are. However, *generational differences* are important here. Children born to migrant peoples in Britain may automatically qualify for a British passport, but their sense of identity borne from living in a diaspora community will be influenced by the 'past migration history' of their parents or grandparents. This is why it is more accurate to talk about 'diaspora identities' rather than 'migrant identities'; not all of those who live in a diaspora, or share an emotional connection to the 'old country', have experienced migration. This also should make us aware that diasporas are *composite* communities. As Avtar Brah puts it in *Cartographies of Diaspora: Contesting Identities* (Routledge, 1997), distinct diaspora communities are created out of the 'confluence of narratives' of different journeys from the 'old country' to the new which create the sense of a shared history (p. 183). Yet we must not forget that 'all diasporas are differentiated, heterogeneous, contested spaces, even as they are implicated in the construction of a common "we"' (p. 184). Differences of gender, 'race', class, religion and language (as well as generational differences) make diaspora spaces dynamic and shifting, open to repeated construction and reconstruction.

The experiences of migrancy and living in a diaspora have animated much recent postcolonial literature, criticism and theory. Indeed, the slippages between the terms 'diaspora', 'migrant' and 'postcolonial' have been frequent and are not free from problems, as we shall consider. The literature produced by 'diaspora writers', such as Buchi Emecheta, Amitav Ghosh, Hanif Kureishi, Bharati Mukherjee, Caryl Phillips and Ben Zephaniah, has proved immensely popular in Western literary criticism. Similarly, in the work of academics such as Homi K. Bhabha, Avtar Brah, Rey Chow, Carole Boyce Davies, Paul Gilroy and Stuart Hall, the new possibilities and problems engendered by the experience of migrancy and diaspora life have been readily explored. These possibilities include creating new ways of thinking about individual and communal identities, critiquing established schools of critical thought, and rethinking the relationships between literature, history and politics.

But diaspora communities are not free from problems. Too often diaspora peoples have been ghettoised and excluded from feeling they belong to the 'new country', and suffered their cultural practices to be mocked and discriminated against. In addition, in more recent years critics such as Avtar Brah, Stuart Hall and Kobena Mercer have interrogated the shared sense of diaspora collectivity as potentially marginalising certain groups inside their limits, such as lesbian and gay people.

In this chapter we will explore such possibilities and problems with specific attention to the theme of identity. In so doing we will meet and define a range of conceptual terms, such as 'hybridity', 'borders', 'new ethnicities' and 'cultural diversity'. We will think critically about these conceptual tools and use them to help us read Beryl Gilroy's novel of diaspora identities, *Boy-Sandwich* (1989).

Living 'in-between': from *roots* to *routes*

Let's begin by looking at a memorable moment in V. S. Naipaul's memoir 'Prologue to an Autobiography' (in *Finding the Centre: Two Narratives*, Penguin, 1984). Now living in Britain, Naipaul grew up in the Caribbean island of Trinidad and came from a family descended from Indian migrants to the Caribbean. He records an incident which occurred in the Summer of 1932, when Indian indentured labourers were promised the passage back to India from Trinidad by the government once their contracts had expired. This had also happened in the previous year, when the *S. S. Ganges* collected a number of Indian labourers in Trinidad and sailed for India.

The ship returned to Trinidad in 1932, collected more immigrant Indians and set off for Calcutta once again:

> Seven weeks later the *Ganges* reached Calcutta. And there, to the terror of the passengers, the *Ganges* was stormed by hundreds of derelicts, previously repatriated, who wanted now to be taken back to the other place. India for these people had been a dream of home, a dream of continuity after the illusion of Trinidad. All the India they had found was the area around the Calcutta docks.
>
> Our own past was, like our idea of India, a dream. (p. 53)

Note how often the word 'dream' is repeated, as well as the reference to 'illusion'. Naipaul points out that migration alters how migrants think about their *home* and *host* countries. Trinidad has been an illusion for the Indian migrants because it has not lived up to its promises. When viewed from India, it seemed a place of opportunity and promise, but the experience of the miserable working conditions meant it did not live up to the myth. But note too how, due to migrancy, India *also* becomes illusory, like a dream. When viewed from the poverty of Trinidad, India can seem to the migrants a refuge from their miserable conditions. Yet, their voyage home reveals this view of India similarly to be more imaginary than true, as the return does not alleviate their hardships. The indentured labourers have in Trinidad constructed a different, imaginary India which is *discontinuous* with the real location. It exists primarily in the mind, and no act of actual, physical return can facilitate it. The *idea* of the home country becomes split from the *experience* of returning home. Naipaul's example helps us understand Avtar Brah's statement that '"home" is a mythic place of desire in the diasporic imagination. In this sense it is a place of no-return, even if it is possible to visit the geographical territory that is seen as the place of "origin"' (*Cartographies of Diaspora*, p. 192).

Importantly, Naipaul regards this episode as capturing his dream-like view of India as somebody born in Trinidad into an Indian family; and thus, strictly speaking, *not* an Indian migrant. For him, India is also an illusory place from which he is fractured in both time and space, but which retains an emotional influence over his life. His example invites us to think about migrancy as constructing certain ways of seeing that impact upon *both migrants and their descendants* in a number of ways (although the response of different generations is not always the same). To be blunt, migrancy has effects which last long after the act of migrating has finished. As Russell King, John Connell and Paul White argue in the preface to their edited collection *Writing Across Worlds: Literature and Migration* (Routledge, 1995), '[f]or some groups, migration is not a mere interval between fixed points of departure and arrival, but a mode of being in the world – "migrancy"' (p. xv). In talking of migrancy, then, we are looking at the problems and new possibilities that result from a particular mode of existence.

Let us probe deeper the ways in which 'home' is *imagined* in diaspora communities. The concept of 'home' often performs an important function in our lives. It can act as a valuable means of orientation by giving us a sense of our place in the world. It tells us where we originated from and where we belong. As an *idea* it stands for shelter, stability, security and comfort (although actual experiences of home may well fail to deliver these promises). To be 'at home' is to occupy a location where we are welcome, where we can be with people very much like ourselves. But what happens to the *idea* of 'home' for migrants who live far from the lands of their birth? How might their travels impact upon the ways 'home' is considered?

In considering these questions, we can turn usefully to Salman Rushdie's essay 'Imaginary Homelands' (in *Imaginary Homelands: Essays and Criticism 1981–1991*, Granta, 1991, pp. 9–21). Rushdie was born in 1947 in Bombay, where he spent his childhood. He moved to England as a young man to attend Rugby School and later Cambridge University, and he eventually settled in London. In his essay Rushdie reflects upon the process of writing his novel *Midnight's Children* (1981) which is set in India and Pakistan, while living in north London. He records that on the wall of his London study was a black-and-white photograph of his childhood home in Bombay. Rushdie reveals that one of the reasons which motivated his writing of the novel was an attempt to restore the world of his childhood home, distant in both time and space, to the present. But it proved an impossible task to 'return home' via the process of writing. In a sense, we all leave home at one time or another in our lives and feel a sense of loss for doing so; but, as Rushdie argues 'the writer who is out-of-country and even out-of-language may experience this loss in an intensified form. It is made more concrete for him by the physical fact of discontinuity, of his present being in a different place from his past, of his being "elsewhere"' (p. 12). This disjunction between past and present, between here and there, makes 'home' seem far-removed in time and space, available for return only through an act of the imagination. Speaking of Indian migrants, Rushdie writes that 'our physical alienation from India almost inevitably means that we will not be capable of reclaiming precisely the thing that was lost; that we will, in short, create fictions, not actual cities or villages, but invisible ones, imaginary homelands, Indias of the mind' (p. 10). In this formulation, home becomes primarily a mental construct built from the incomplete odds and ends of memory that survive from the past. It exists in a fractured, discontinuous relationship with the present.

So, if we take these remarks as applicable to other acts of migration (not just Indian), we can argue that the migrant occupies a *displaced* position. The imagination becomes more and more the primary location of home but the mind is notoriously unreliable and capricious. Rushdie remarks that when thinking back to his Bombay childhood, he could recall only fragmentary, partial memories, often of small, mundane occurrences. In a useful turn of phrase, he records that his reflections were made 'in broken mirrors, some of whose fragments have been irretrievably lost' (p. 11). As his essay evidences, migrants envision their home in fragments and fissures, full of gaps and breaches. The transformations wrought by the experience of migrancy make impossible the recovery of a plenitudinous sense of home. Reflections of home seize it in pieces only; a sense of displacement always remains.

If imagining home brings fragmentation, discontinuity and displacement for the migrant, can new homes be secured in the host country? In migrating from one country to another, migrants inevitably become involved in the process of setting up home in a new land. This can also add to the ways in which the concept of home is disturbed. Migrants tend to arrive in new places with baggage; both in the physical sense of possessions or belongings, but also the less tangible matter of beliefs, traditions, customs, behaviours and values. This can have consequences for the ways in which others may or may not make migrants feel 'at home' on arrival in a new place. In Chapters 3 and 4 we looked in detail at the ways in which nationalist discourses attempt to construct 'deep, horizontal comradeship' by setting 'norms and limits' for the nation's people. Although migrants may pass through the *political* borders of nations, crossing their frontiers and gaining entrance to new places, such 'norms and limits' can be used to exclude migrants from being accommodated inside the *imaginative* borders of the nation. The dominant discourses of 'race', ethnicity and gender may function to exclude them from being recognised as part of the nation's people. Migrants may well live in new places, but they can be deemed not to belong there and disqualified from thinking of the new land as their home. Instead, their home is seen to exist elsewhere, back across the border.

Rushdie's remarks about the Indian writer in Britain inevitably speak of the migrant as an adult who has experienced enough of India as a child to have memories of home to explore in retrospect. But what of those who migrated to Western countries as small children, or those born in the West to migrant parents, who (like the young Naipaul in Trinidad) have little or no memories of a 'home' overseas? How do they deal with the issues of 'home' and 'belonging'?

Naipaul's use of the incident of the *S. S. Ganges* demonstrated an affinity between two generations: Indian migrants to Trinidad and 'Indian–born' Trinidadians. Yet, the descendants of migrants are not always in the same position. Consider for a moment the photograph of Rushdie's childhood home hanging on his wall. At the beginning of 'Imaginary Homelands' Rushdie recalls re-visiting the house in Bombay after many years in Britain and being amazed at how different it looked, both to the photograph on his wall and to his memory. The visit affords Rushdie the opportunity to indulge a childhood memory, even as it underlines the fact this return does *not* eliminate feelings of displacement. Standing outside, he prefers not to announce himself to the new owners as he 'didn't want to see how they'd ruined the interior' (p. 9). We can borrow this remark to suggest that migrants in positions similar to Rushdie with their childhood memories of a distant place, have a certain degree of 'interior knowledge' no matter how fragmentary and fissured it may be. But to the children of migrants, the 'interior knowledge' of a distant place is unavailable. Thus, their reflections about these places in terms of 'home' are often differently constructed.

These *generational differences* are not absolute. Migrants can share both similarities and differences with their descendants, and the relationship between generations can be complex and overlapping, rather than forming a neat contrast. To get a sense of this, let us turn to an essay called 'The Rainbow Sign' by Hanif Kureishi, a writer born in Britain with a Pakistani father and English mother (the essay is collected in *My Beautiful Laundrette and The Rainbow Sign*, Faber, 1986, pp. 7–38). This essay records Kureishi's experiences as a boy growing up in London, a visit to Pakistan as young man, and some comparisons between life in both locations. As a child, Kureishi admits to having 'no idea of what the sub-continent was like or how my numerous uncles, aunts and cousins lived there' (p. 9). His relationship with Pakistan is obviously different to his father's. Yet at school he was mistakenly identified as an Indian by his teachers, one of whom placed pictures of Indian peasants in mud huts before his class in order to show the others Kureishi's 'home'. 'I wondered: did my uncles ride on camels? Surely not in their suits? Did my cousins, so like me in other ways, squat down in the sand like little Mowglis, half-naked and eating with their fingers' (p. 9). The reference here to the figure of Mowgli from Rudyard Kipling's *The Jungle Book* suggests how Kureishi's identity was similarly fictionalised by others as an outsider who belonged to a land overseas, despite the fact that Kureishi was born, like his mother, in Britain. He was not readily permitted to 'belong' to Britain like his classmates. This is an example of the ways in which the descendants of migrants can suffer similar experiences to their parents or grandparents.

On a visit to his relations in Karachi as a young adult, Kureishi also found it difficult to think of this place in terms of 'home'. He admits to 'a little identity crisis' (p. 17). His uncles' anti-British remarks make him feel uncomfortable and strangely patriotic towards Britain, feelings he had not previously experienced. Although he does not try to indulge in feeling 'Pakistani', as this would be a dubious act of sentimentality, his identity crisis is outlined when an acquaintance declares to him: 'we are Pakistanis, but you, you will always be a Paki – emphasising the slang derogatory name the English used against Pakistanis, and therefore the fact that I couldn't rightfully lay claim to either place' (p. 17).

This observation serves as a pivotal moment when thinking about migrancy, which we might spend a moment considering. On the one hand, and without wishing to ignore generational differences, this comment indicates the perilous intermediate position that *both* migrants and their children are deemed to occupy: living 'in-between' different nations, feeling neither here nor there, unable to indulge in sentiments of belonging to either place. Kureishi feels devoid of the 'rightful' claims to belong. But on the other hand, and more productively perhaps, this moment shows that the conventional ways we use to think about ideas such as 'belonging' no longer work. Conventional ideas of 'home' and 'belonging' depend upon clearly-defined, static notions of being 'in place', firmly rooted in a community or a particular geographical location. We might think of the discourses of nationalism, ethnicity or 'race' as examples of models of belonging which attempt to root the individual within a clearly-defined and homogenised group. But these models or 'narratives' of belonging no longer seem suited to a world where the experience and legacy of migration are altering the ways in which individuals think of their relation to place, and how they might 'lay claim' to lands that are difficult to think of in terms of 'home' or 'belonging'. Instead, new models of identity are emerging which depend upon reconsidering the perilous 'in-between' position of someone like Kureishi as a site of excitement, new possibilities, and even privilege.

Let us approach these new models of identity by returning for a moment to Salman Rushdie's essay 'Imaginary Homelands'. In registering his displacement from the Bombay home of his childhood, Rushdie does not dwell nostalgically upon this loss, although he registers loss in his remarks. Instead, he makes a virtue from necessity and argues that the displaced position of the migrant is an entirely valuable one. In learning to reflect reality in 'broken mirrors', he or she comes to treasure a *partial, plural* view of the world because it reveals *all* representations of the world are incomplete. 'Meaning is a shaky edifice we build out of scraps, dogmas, childhood injuries, newspaper articles, chance remarks, old films, small victories, people hated, people loved; perhaps it is because our sense of what is the case is constructed from such inadequate materials that we defend it so fiercely, even to the death' ('Imaginary Homelands', p. 12). The migrant seems in a better position than others to realise that all systems of knowledge, all views of the world, are never totalising, whole or pure, but incomplete, muddled and hybrid. To live as a migrant may well evoke the pain of loss and of not being firmly rooted in a secure place; but it is also to live in a world of immense possibility with the realisation that new knowledges and ways of seeing can be constructed out of the myriad combinations of the 'scraps' which Rushdie describes – knowledges which challenge the authority of older ideas of rootedness and fixity.

In these terms, the space of the 'in-between' becomes re-thought as a place of immense creativity and possibility, as Kureishi's essay 'The Rainbow Sign' also goes on to testify. Kureishi recalls seeing a photograph in his uncle's house in Pakistan of his father as a young boy. This fragment from the past, like the photograph in Rushdie's study, becomes a valuable 'scrap' which he can use when stitching together new ways of thinking about his identity and his place in the world. He cannot ever think of his uncle's house as his 'home', but it is a vital treasure-house of manifold possibilities. Kureishi describes it as 'a house full of stories, of Bombay, Delhi, China; of feuds, wrestling matches, adulteries, windows broken with hands, card games, impossible loves, and magic spells. Stories to help me see my place in the world and give me a sense of the past which could go into making a life in the present and the future' ('The Rainbow Sign', p. 35). Notice here how Kureishi must become actively involved in *forging new narratives* which will accommodate his position more adequately than older, totalising (or 'holistic') narratives. To borrow some terms from Paul Gilroy's book *The Black Atlantic* (Verso, 1993), he does not have secure *roots* which fix him in place, in a nation or an ethnic group; rather, he must continually plot for himself itinerant cultural *routes* which take him, imaginatively as well as physically, to many places and into contact with many different peoples. This forges a relationship between past, present and future, but does not presume an even, continuous passage through time. The grounded certainties of *roots* are replaced with the transnational contingencies of *routes*. Kureishi's family's history in South Asia may appear to him as just stories, the fragments of lives

and experiences very removed from his own; yet they are vital
resources which he can use to orient his way into the future.
Although Kureishi does not occupy the same position as the
Bombay-born Rushdie, and lacks what we called 'interior' knowledge, he is also displaced. So it is safe to argue that the constructions of new narratives or *routes* can be a possibility, if not a necessity,
for migrants and those born to them.

Let us pause for a moment and review the ideas we have encountered so far:

- Migrancy constructs modes of existence and ways of seeing that
  last beyond the actual journey between countries.
- Migrancy can expose the migrant and their children to displacement, fragmentation and discontinuity.
- Home is a problematic concept, both in the past and in the present.
- Living 'in-between' can be painful, perilous and marginalising.
- Migrants and their children occupy different positions due to
  generational differences, but they can have similar experiences of
  feeling rootless and displaced.
- The dominant narratives of belonging and identity cannot
  accommodate those who live 'in-between'.
- But new, transnational models of identity and belonging are possible which, in Paul Gilroy's terms, challenge the certainty of
  roots with the contingency of *routes*.

Hybrid identities at the 'in-between'

Several of the issues and ideas raised in Rushdie's and Kureishi's
essays have preoccupied postcolonial theories of identity. In particular, the 'in-between' position of the migrant, and his or her errant,
impartial perceptions of the world, have been used as the starting
point for creating new, dynamic ways of thinking about identity
which go beyond older static models, such as national identity and
the notion of 'rootedness'. These frequently merge the circumstances of migration with the theoretical ideas and languages of
poststructuralism.

One particularly enthusiastic exponent of this line of thought has
been Homi K. Bhabha, himself a migrant from Bombay to Britain

who now lives in America. Some of the essays collected in his book *The Location of Culture* (Routledge, 1994) advocate new, exciting ways of thinking about identity born from 'the great history of the languages and landscapes of migration and diaspora' (p. 235). Bhabha specifically describes these as new forms of *postcolonial* identity, making a slippage between 'migrant' and 'postcolonial' which, as we shall presently consider, is not free from problems. We are going to focus in detail upon the introductory chapter, called 'Locations of Culture' as it contains many ideas concerning identity which are elaborated at many points in the text.

'Locations of Culture' addresses those who live 'border lives' on the margins of different nations, in-between contrary homelands. For Bhabha, living at the border, at the edge, requires a new 'art of the present'. This depends upon embracing the contrary logic of the border and using it to rethink the dominant ways we represent things like history, identity and community. Borders are important thresholds, full of contradiction and ambivalence. They both separate and join different places. They are intermediate locations where one contemplates moving beyond a barrier. As Bhabha defines it, the 'beyond' is an in-between site of transition: 'the "beyond" is neither a new horizon, nor a leaving behind of the past ... we find ourselves in the moment of transit where space and time cross to produce complex figures of difference and identity, past and present, inside and outside, inclusion and exclusion' (p. 1). The space of the 'beyond' is often described in terms which emphasise this transitory, in-between sense: such as 'liminal', 'interstitial' or 'hybrid'. Look how, in the quotation just given, the emphasis is placed on *crossing*, or shuttling between seemingly opposed states. For Bhabha, the border is the place where conventional patterns of thought are disturbed and can be disrupted by the possibility of crossing. At the border, past and present, inside and outside no longer remain separated as binary opposites but instead commingle and conflict. From this emerge new, shifting complex forms of representation that deny binary patterning. So, it is argued that *imaginative* border-crossings are as much a consequence of migration as the *physical* crossing of borders.

Bhabha turns the possibility of such imaginative crossings against received notions of identity and subjectivity which precisely depend upon fixed, binary definitions: such as native/foreigner and master/slave. These are contested as ideologically suspect and inappropriate; the 'art of the present' requires a habit of mind in which movement and crossing are paramount. Bhabha urges that we must 'think beyond narratives of originary and initial subjectivities and ... focus on those moments or processes that are produced in the articulation of cultural differences. These "in-between" spaces provide the terrain of elaborating strategies of selfhood – singular or communal – that initiate new signs of identity' (p. 1). There are three things to notice here. First, like Gayatri Chakravorty Spivak whose work we explored particularly in Chapter 6, Bhabha also opposes the idea of a 'sovereign' or essentialised subject. For Bhabha and Spivak, identity is a discursive product. Second, because subjectivity is discursively produced, it is possible for it to be remade and remodelled in new and innovative ways – hence his attention to the processes of 'articulation' and 'elaboration' in the quotation. The border is a place of possibility and agency for new ideas. Third, the new 'signs' of identity which are possible impact upon both individuals *and* groups. Rethinking identity is not a solipsistic activity but is bound up in group identity, group formation and group hostilities. So, the imaginative crossings at the 'beyond' offer ways of thinking about communal identity that depart from older ideas, such as the 'deep, horizontal comradeship' of the nation which can fall foul of the binary logic of same/different, inside/outside, citizen/stranger.

A crucial manoeuvre in this line of thought is the refusal to think of cultures as pure or holistic, with received wisdom handed down from generation to generation in a way which preserves knowledge. Instead, culture is regarded as intermingled and manifold. As in his essay 'DissemiNation', Bhabha stresses the importance of *performance* as the means by which new, hybrid identities are negotiated. We saw above how both Rushdie and Kureishi claimed that meaning could be made from the discontinuous scraps and fragmentary remains of their different Indian and Pakistani inheritances, bringing the resources of the past to bear upon their lives in the present. Bhabha makes a similar point, in an albeit more compact and dense fashion. Standing at the border, the migrant is empowered to intervene *actively* in the transmission of cultural inheritance or 'tradition' (of both the home and host land) rather than *passively* accept its venerable customs and pedagogical wisdom. He or she can question, refashion or mobilise received ideas. The migrant is empowered to act as an agent of change, deploying received knowledge in the present and transforming it as a consequence, just as Kureishi could make the photograph of his father mean something new and important in a unpredictable context. As this example demonstrates, this does *not* mean that received or traditional knowledge becomes dismissed. Rather, inherited knowledge can be reinscribed and given new, unexpected meanings. Bhabha calls this action 'restaging the past'. From a migratory, minority position, the restaging of the past 'introduces other, incommensurable cultural temporalities into the invention of tradition. This process estranges any access to an originary identity or a "received" tradition' (p. 2).

This quotation has two important consequences. First, the subject becomes produced from the process of *hybridisation*. His or her subjectivity is deemed to be composed from variable sources, different materials, many locations – demolishing forever the idea of subjectivity as stable, single, or 'pure'. The concept of hybridity has proved very important for diaspora peoples, and indeed many others too, as a way of thinking beyond exclusionary, fixed, binary notions of identity based on ideas of rootedness and cultural, racial and national purity. Hybrid identities are never total and complete in themselves, like orderly pathways built from crazy-paving. Instead, they remain perpetually in motion, pursuing errant and unpredictable routes, open to change and reinscription.

Second, in using the term 'incommensurable cultural temporalities', Bhabha anticipates the next stage in his argument where he traces how an aesthetics of the border impacts upon received binary knowledges. These ideas, exciting and challenging, need contextualising first in terms of Bhabha's influence by the psychoanalytical work of Sigmund Freud and Jacques Lacan. In his Introduction, Bhabha turns to Freud's writings on the *unheimlich*: often translated as the 'unhomely' or 'uncanny'. As Freud uses the term, an uncanny experience can be prompted when something that we have hitherto regarded as imaginary appears before us in reality, or when something that has been previously concealed or forgotten disturbingly returns. In Bhabha's thinking, the disruption of received totalising narratives of individual and group identity made possible at the 'border' can be described as an 'uncanny' moment, where all those forgotten in the construction of, say, national groups return to disturb and haunt such holistic ways of thinking. This uncanny disruption brings with it trauma and anxiety. It serves as a reminder that exclusive, exclusionary systems of meaning are forever haunted by those who are written out and erased. At the limits of conventional knowledge, these figures return as disruptive 'unhomely' presences that cannot be articulated through existing patterns of representation. It is this uncanny presence which Bhabha seizes upon as having the power to disrupt the exclusive binary logic upon which a range of discourses – nationalist, colonialist, patriarchal – depend.

This is where literature plays an important part. Bhabha suggests that literature concerning 'migrants, the colonised or political refugees' (p. 12) could take on the task of unhousing received ways of thinking about the world and discovering the hybridity, the difference that exists within. However, and importantly, these internal differences are displaced, existing beyond representation. This is why Bhabha calls them 'incommensurable'. This term refers to the existence of something that cannot be measured or described by the prevailing system of language. Cultural differences are figured as unrepresented, uncanny presences which bear witness to displaced experiences, histories, and lives. As Bhabha argues, 'As literary creatures and political animals we ought to concern ourselves with the understanding of human action and the social world as a moment when *something is beyond control, but it is not beyond accommodation* … the critic must attempt to fully realise, and take responsibility for, the unspoken, unrepresented pasts that haunt the historical present' (p. 12). 'Accommodation without control': this is the challenge for new hybrid forms of knowledge, one which the binary discourses of fixed individual and group identity failed. Bhabha gives examples of this new literature by referring, amongst others, to Toni Morrison's novel *Beloved* (1987), in which the uncanny, ghostly appearance of a young black girl on the outskirts of Cincinnati in 1873 points to the unspoken histories of American slaves. These unspoken alternative histories return to haunt the received history in which they find no voice.

It is worth comparing Bhabha's ideas with those in Spivak's essay, 'Can the Subaltern Speak?' (explored in Chapter 6). Whereas as both Spivak's subaltern as female and Bhabha's unhomely presences are beyond conventional modes of representation, Bhabha's use of Freud's sense of the 'uncanny' keeps open the possibility that oppressed voices maintain the agency to make their (absent) presence felt, to menace the scene of representation. Can the same be said for Spivak's subalterns?

It would be useful to pause here and make a summary. We have been thinking about how Bhabha's attention to the border, the 'beyond', considers the opportunity for new, hybrid forms of knowledge, but does not fix or prescribe them. An element of incommensurability always remains. As Bhabha declares early in the piece with deliberate ambiguity, the boundary is the place 'from which *something begins its presencing*' (p. 5). To secure exactly what this 'something' is, would be to fall back on a logic which demands fixity, limitation, definition. Rather, we must attend to what is incommensurable and unhomely in conventional systems of thought. Suitably, an uncanny, incommensurable presence is eerily registered in the choice of the italics which animate the quotation and reveal the possibility of that 'something' half-hidden inside Bhabha's characteristically cryptic sentence.

STOP and THINK

Bhabha's work moves from the crossing of physical borders to imaginative borders, where new ways of thinking about identity, community and knowledge suitable to a changed world can be fashioned. This changed world is specifically named as 'postcolonial'. But we might wish to beware of the generalising tendency in this argument. Bhabha's declaration that the experience of migrants encapsulates the common 'contemporary compulsion to move beyond' (p. 18) seems to position the migrant as a late-twentieth-century universal 'everyman' (the gender is not inappropriate here, I think). Bhabha has been accused of neglecting cultural and historical specifics in his work by abstracting a general theory from particular experiences. As

Aijaz Ahmad points out in his essay 'The Politics of Literary Post-coloniality' (in *Race and Class*, 36 (3), 1995, pp. 1–20), the image of the postcolonial subject which results from Bhabha's work 'is remarkably free of gender, class, [and] identifiable political location' (p. 13). This is not always a fair criticism, but the swift movements in Bhabha's work, (between nineteenth-century India to nineteen-eighties South Africa, for example) does reveal a globetrotting tendency in his writing that threatens to decontextualise the experiences of different times and places.

Other problems present themselves too. Bhabha is often called a cosmopolitan due to his transnational terms of reference. His work is itself in perpetual motion, facilitated by border crossings and hybrid combinations at the level of ideas. Yet, is this hybrid mixture *definitive* of postcolonialism? Bhabha seems to suggest that it is, such is the ease with which the logic of the 'beyond' is described as 'postcolonial'. As he bluntly puts it in one essay, '[t]he postcolonial perspective resists the attempt at holistic forms of social explanation' (*The Location of Culture*, p. 173). This formulation, however, ignores the per-spectives of those in countries with a history of colonialism who have never migrated. Are their perspectives wrong if they do not fit Bhabha's formula? What would happen to Ngugi's arguments (which we encountered in Chapter 4) concerning the need to protect and enrich Gikuyu, if we accept Bhabha's ideas? For a thinker as subtle and exciting as Bhabha, it is disappointing to come across totalising representations of the 'postcolonial perspective'. As we have seen throughout this book, such moves are perilous.

New ethnicities

In thinking about these problems, it might be useful to look at a comparable essay first published in 1989 by Stuart Hall called 'New Ethnicities' (in *Critical Dialogues in Cultural Studies*, ed. David Morley and Kuan-Hsing Chen, Routledge, 1996, pp. 441–9). This piece also deals with the transformations wrought by migration in similar ways to Bhabha, but avoids the generalising tendencies of

Bhabha's work in part because it deals specifically with changes made by Britain's black community. Whereas Bhabha's writing is situated more within the realm of literary theory and criticism, Hall's work emerges from the fields of sociology and cultural studies, although the work of both figures bears witness to the increasing interdisciplinarity of postcolonialism since the 1980s.

In 'New Ethnicities' Stuart Hall considers the ways in which members of the black British diaspora have represented themselves in response to the 'common experience of racism and marginalisation in Britain' (p. 441). He identifies two separate yet overlapping phases or moments. In the first, the term 'black' was used as a way of uniting people of different ethnic or racial backgrounds and organising them into communities of resistance. In asserting a common black experience, black Britons created a 'singular and unifying framework based on the building up of identity across ethnic and cultural difference between the different communities' (p. 441). These communities could be from African, Caribbean or South Asian locations, yet they were united through the representation of a common 'black' community. This served two purposes: first, it raised the question of rights of access to representation by black writers and artists, and second, it enabled the stereotypical and derogatory representations of black people at large to be contested by positive images of the black community, often through the coherence of an essentialised black subject who typified black experience in general.

But in the second moment these unifying modes of representation become contested from *within* the black community, as individuals begin to question the existence and purpose of believing in an essential black subject. In its place, the 'extraordinary diversity of subjective positions, social experiences and cultural identities' (p. 443) are asserted and explored. Diaspora identities are presented instead as multiple and mobile, with their own inner tensions. This 'inevitably entails a weakening or a fading of the notion that "race" or some composite notion of race around the term black will either guarantee the effectivity of any cultural practice or determine in any final sense its aesthetic value' (p. 443). In other words, black artists and writers no longer work *on behalf* of the black community, because that community cannot be easily homogenised. Furthermore, the work they produce cannot be celebrated simply because it comes from the diaspora. Instead, more critical and conflictual responses become possible. This creates a challenge for the black community: how can a politics be constructed 'which works with and through difference, which is able to build those forms of solidarity and identification which make common struggle and resistance possible but without suppressing the real heterogeneity of interests and identities' (p. 444).

In his description of the first 'moment' of black representations, Hall shows how diaspora communities have used unifying and homogenising modes of representation in response to some of the less welcome experiences of diaspora. This gives the lie to Bhabha's work on the 'border lives' of migrant individuals who concern themselves with the critique of totalising systems of representation, by showing that this need not be the only kind of response engendered by their 'border' position. Hall's work shows that, for historical and cultural reasons, the construction of a generalised black community and an essentialised black subject has, in one context, served an important political purpose, despite the fact that we might want to question some of the assumptions upon which these representations rest.

Speaking more generally, this point also beckons questions concerning the production of community by diaspora peoples. *How* are they organised, and *who* organises them? In addition, it is tempting to regard Hall's 'two moments' as bearing witness to the responses of different generations in Britain, yet Hall warns against this. These phases of response are 'of the same movement, which constantly overlap and interweave. Both are framed by the same historical conjuncture and both are rooted in the politics of anti-racism and the post-war black experience in Britain' (p. 441). Hall's essay demonstrates that these different responses to the experience of living in a diaspora are *simultaneously* possible. It is not wise to make generalisations about a typical 'migrant perspective' or a 'diaspora experience'.

In speaking of a 'second' moment, Hall's work opens up debates concerning the variety of different subject positions within diaspora communities. By focusing on representations of gay and lesbian peoples in the black British diaspora, Hall calls attention to the ways in which the generalising images of a diaspora community or typical subject may not be representative of all those who would consider themselves as living in a diaspora. In addition, attention must be given to the power relations *within* diaspora communities which can often favour certain groups over others. In his discussion of black British cultural studies during the 1980s, Kobena Mercer points out how black lesbian and gay groups helped effect a paradigm shift from the essentialised, generalised notion of a black community to a situation similar to Hall's notion of 'new ethnicities', where 'mobile and flexible frameworks for studying the shifting landscapes of diaspora' became the norm (in *Welcome to the Jungle: New Positions in Black Cultural Studies*, Routledge, 1994, p. 16). These 'new ethnicities' – fluid, contingent, multiple and shifting – can be compared to Bhabha's 'border lives', where the concepts of overlapping, hybridity, *routed* identity, and shifting subjectivity become enthusiastically promoted as the new 'art of the present' and are seen as 'crucial and vital efforts to answer the "possibility and necessity of creating a new culture": *so that you can live*' (*Welcome to the Jungle*, p. 4).

In concluding this section, it is important to realise that the possibilities engendered by rethinking identity in terms of fluidity and hybridity (*routes* rather than *roots*) have the propensity to alter the ways in which identities are formed for *all* people in one location, not just those who are constructed as 'diaspora communities'. Indeed, *all* oppositional divides between 'native inhabitants' and 'diaspora peoples', 'majority' and 'minority' communities, are threatened with dissolution. Avtar Brah captures this idea in her concept of 'diaspora space' (*Cartographies of Diaspora*, p. 209). A diaspora space is an intersection of borders where all subjects and identities become 'juxtaposed, contested, proclaimed, or disavowed; where the permitted and the prohibited perpetually interrogate, and where the accepted and the transgressive imperceptibly mingle even while these syncretic forms may be disclaimed in the name of purity and tradition' (p. 208). It is important to understand that this space is *not* some kind of postmodern playground of 'anything goes', where all kinds of identities are equally valuable and available as if in a 'multicultural supermarket'. Discourses of power which seek to legitimate certain forms of identity and marginalise others by imposing a logic of binary oppositions remain operable and challenge new forms of identity from emerging. We must not forget the troublesome politics of diaspora identities when promoting their possibilities. None the less, the transformative propensity of 'diaspora space' remains potent not just for those *within* diaspora communities but those who, in Brah's words, 'are constructed and represented as indigenous' (p. 209). New routes are opened for all.

STOP and THINK

The enthusiastic support for the new forms of fluid, hybrid identity can often mask a number of difficulties with these 'new ethnicities'. First, are fluid hybrid identities always a favourable option? As Hall's attention to the first moment of black British representations evidences, there may be circumstances when the representation of an essentialised diaspora subject or homogeneous diaspora community may serve important purposes: such as offering support and a sense of belonging for migrant peoples, or as a way of uniting people against acts of discrimination. Also, does everybody experience diaspora life in the same fashion? How do differences of class, gender, sexuality, region and age all impact upon diaspora communities?

Cultural diversity, cultural difference and the 'Black Atlantic'

Brah's concept of 'diaspora space' recognised the ways its possibilities are contested by established discourses of power, which attempt to organise people into communities of 'us' and 'them'. Indeed, one of the dangers in too-quickly celebrating hybridity as a solution to all problems is that it stops us thinking about the divisive ways in which *reactionary* responses to diasporic cultural practices can operate. Individual and collective identities are things which we fashion for ourselves to a degree; but they are also fashioned by others for us, whether we like it or not. In terms of diaspora identities, the dominant discourses of 'race', nation, ethnicity, class and gender in the West can militate against the possibility of embracing and exploring hybrid forms of identity, by seeking to fix diaspora peoples into certain positions and indigenous peoples into others, in such a way that recalls to an extent the stereotypical representation of colonised peoples into discourses such as Orientalism. Throughout this book we have seen how the imaginative legacy of colonialism remains after the colonialism has formally ended in once-colonised countries. But the same is also true of Western colonial nations, where the discursive apparatus of colonialism remains available to members of the host nation as a means by which diaspora peoples can be represented.

As R. Radhakrishnan has pointed out in *Diasporic Mediations: Between Home and Location* (University of Minnesota Press, 1996), critical theories of diaspora identities which celebrate hybridity and difference can be 'completely at odds with the actual experience of difference as undergone by diasporic peoples in their countries of residence' (p. 174). Although *theories* of migrant or diaspora identities emphasise new emergent forms of thinking about identity in terms of fluidity and hybridity, these often clash with dominant ways of representing cultural difference in Western locations that have been inherited from colonial discourses that depend upon constructing borders which are traversed only on special occasions. Phrases like 'cultural diversity', 'pluralism' and 'multiculturalism' are frequently used these days to bear witness to the fact that Western countries like Britain and America have a variety of different diaspora communities whose values, cultural practices or religious beliefs differ from those of the majority. These terms would seem to depict Western nations as locations of tolerance, where all cultural practices are happily accommodated. However, some critics have interrogated representations of 'cultural diversity' as convenient fictions which mask the continuing economic, political and social inequalities experienced by migrants from countries with a history of colonialism, and their descendants.

For example, in his essay 'On Cultural Diversity' (in *Whose Cities?*, ed. Mark Fisher and Ursula Owen, Penguin, 1991, pp. 97–106) the British-based Guyanese writer David Dabydeen comments that '[c]ultural diversity can be a cosy term, evolved out of a blend of European post-colonial guilt and enlightenment, to justify tolerance of our presence in the metropolis' (p. 101). He contends that 'a sizeable segment of the British people of a certain generation, those above forty, say, would prefer it if we went away and never came back' (p. 101). Dabydeen uses the image of a beehive when talking about the 'cultural diversity' of a city like London. Although there may be a number of different cultural groups present in one place, each is confined to its own 'cell' with little communication between different groups taking place. White Britons 'don't spend long enough in the West Indian cells to appreciate the syntax, metre, chords, daubs, noises and smells created in these cells (p. 104), nor do they invite West Indians to *their* cells either. Dabydeen concludes that 1990s London 'is culturally diverse, but there is little cross-fertilisation of cultures taking place' (p. 104). The engagement with 'cultural diversity' becomes purely recreational, like visiting an Indian or Chinese restaurant or spending an afternoon at an annual carnival. Very little happens by way of cultural *exchange*; people cross back to their cells having had a brief, diversionary encounter with 'cultural diversity'. In these terms, uses of 'cultural diversity' can mask the continuing separation of cultures in Western locations into separate cells, rather than encourage the border-crossings which make possible cultural exchange, interactive experiences and new kinds of relationships for all.

Homi K. Bhabha deals with this issue in more theoretical terms in his chapter 'The Commitment to Theory' in *The Location of Culture*. He also takes issue with the term 'cultural diversity' as a misleading one which depicts the separate, equitable co-existence of many cultures. In his typical style, Bhabha attacks cultural diversity as giving the false impression that cultures are holistic, separated and static with 'pre-given cultural contents and customs' (*The Location of Culture*, p. 34). Instead, we must recognise the *porous* borders between cultures, the fact that they are always leaking into each other, criss-crossing supposed barriers. Bhabha uses the phrase 'cultural difference' to advocate this second way of thinking about cultures as hybridised and fluid, where 'cultural interaction emerges only at the significatory boundaries of cultures, where meanings and values are (mis)read or signs are misappropriated' (p. 34). For Bhabha, the subscription to a notion of culture as interactive, constantly recomposed from a wide variety of possible sources becomes an important *political* act. It *matters* how we conceptualise difference. This is why Bhabha is so enthusiastic about using 'the cultural and historical hybridity of the postcolonial world ... as the paradigmatic place of departure' for his theoretical work (p. 21). If the *experience* of diaspora communities in Western nations may be one of segregation and ghettoisation rather than border-crossings and cultural exchange, then the need to rethink how cultures inter-relate becomes even more urgent. For this reason, Bhabha's work has tended to contain a utopian element which has not always been well received by his critics.

Yet, the problem posed in 'New Ethnicities' by Stuart Hall remains: how are new communities forged which do *not* homogenise people or ignore the differences between them; communities based on crossings, interactions, partial identifications? Can there be 'solidarity through difference'? One response to this question can be found in the work of Paul Gilroy, especially in his transnational concept of the 'Black Atlantic' which he explores in his influential book *The Black Atlantic: Modernity and Double Consciousness* (Verso, 1993). In the opening chapter, 'The Black Atlantic as a Counterculture of Modernity', Gilroy explores the transnational connections, crossings, tensions and affiliations between black people located in and moving between Africa, the Caribbean, America and Britain. Part of his purpose is to oppose ideas such as ethnic or 'racial' particularism and nationalism on the grounds that they are falsifications. In looking at a number of black radical thinkers in Britain and America in the nineteenth and twentieth centuries, Gilroy shows the extent to which their work was bound up with, and contributed to, the development of Western modernity. This makes a nonsense *both* of a sense of the West as ethnically and racially homogeneous, and of ideas concerning an essentialised, common 'black' community separated from Western influence. Black peoples in history have been travellers: brought from Africa to America and the Caribbean on the slave-ships across the 'Middle Passage' of the Atlantic Ocean; migrating to Britain after the 1950s due to the shortage in British labour; throughout the nineteenth and twentieth centuries making journeys between the Americas, Britain and Africa. These crossings created myriad ways of thinking which drew from and contributed to the prevailing ideas in each of these places. For these reasons, Gilroy pits the *transnational* quality of black history and experience against those ideas of community grounded in mistaken ideas of purity or cultural essentialism. He suggests that 'cultural historians could take the Atlantic as one single, complex unit of analysis in their discussions of the modern world and use it to produce an explicitly transnational and intercultural perspective' (p. 15). The prefixes 'trans-' and 'inter-' in this sentence call our attention to Gilroy's attempt to expose all borders as porous, across which ideas move and are changed as a consequence.

In the spirit of the untidy journeys and crossings of the 'Black Atlantic' which disturb the neat borders of ethnicity, 'race' and nation, Gilroy fixes on the image of the ship as a way of symbolising a new form of politics based on a transformed idea of community. The ship symbolises 'a living, micro-cultural, micro-political system in motion' (p. 4) which bears witness both to the history of black oppression (in recalling the slave-ships of the middle passage) but also the possibility of putting ideas and cultural practices 'on the move', circulating them across different places in perpetual motion. The ships which criss-crossed the Atlantic Ocean in the nineteenth century may have trafficked in the sordid history of slavery, but they also provided the means by which radical, oppositional ideas could be spread transnationally. For Gilroy, these transnational *routes* provide a better way of thinking about black identities in the present than notions of *roots* and rootedness, which merely recapitulate the absolutist principles common to colonialist, nationalist and racist discourses. However, Gilroy also worries that the eager embracing of 'new ethnicities' which emphasise the constructed, hybrid nature of all identities tends to forget the ways that racism still operates in the present. There is still the necessity for a black politics of resistance. How, then, is one created without falling foul of the problems of the two ways of thinking about identity we have just considered?

Gilroy's answer lies in the ways in which different cultural practices circulate in the black Atlantic between groups in different locations, creating *contingent* transnational forms of community. 'Solidarity through difference' can be built by plotting the ways in which diaspora peoples in any one location draw upon the resources and ideas of other peoples in different times and places in order to contest the continuing agency of colonialist, nationalist or racist discourses at various sites. These mobile, transitory circuits of transnational solidarity help formulate acts of local resistance.

An example of this concerns uses of black popular music. Music is not simply a form of recreation or cultural diversion from the world of politics; as evidenced by the songs of black slaves, music can be the means of 'communicating information, organising consciousness, and testing out or deploying the forms of subjectivity which are required by political agency, whether individual or collective' (p. 36). In his essay 'It Ain't Where You're From, It's Where You're At: the Dialectics of Diaspora Identification' (in *Small Acts: Thoughts on the Politics of Black Cultures*, Serpent's Tail, 1993, pp. 120–45), Gilroy describes the fortunes of the hit song 'I'm So Proud', originally written and performed by the Chicago vocal trio The Impressions. Later it was re-released in Britain by Macka B and Kofi, and titled 'Proud of Mandela'. In a rather breathless sentence which bears superb witness to the untidy, manifold routes of the 'Black Atlantic', Gilroy describes the song as 'produced in Britain by the children of Caribbean and African settlers from raw materials supplied by black Chicago but filtered through Kingstonian sensibility in order to pay tribute to a black hero whose global significance lies beyond his partial South African citizenship' (*Small Acts*, p. 141). Notice how the plotting of this transnational route *belies* an essentialised sense of identity, and the view that meaning is forever fixed, closed and static.

The continual transformations of 'I'm So Proud' engendered by its reproduction by black peoples in different locations underlines the fact that the black diaspora is discontinuous, historically contingent, locally variable and internally heterodox. Yet, the purpose for reproducing 'I'm So Proud' emphasises the *political* character of the 'Black Atlantic' as a webbed space which makes available important political resources to black peoples for new uses that, in the process, transform the received materials. So, Gilroy proclaims that '[f]oregrounding the role of music allows us to see England, or perhaps London, as an important political junction point on the web of black Atlantic political culture' (p. 141). Thus, forms of culture circulate with and between black diasporas in various locations, promoting a sense of a protean collective culture and set of mutual experiences which forge contingent transnational communities. Yet the notion of a *singular* transnational black community is resisted due to the emphasis on the localised, discontinuous and unpredictable ways in which cultural resources are put to new uses.

We can clarify this idea by concluding with an example of our own, this time from Hanif Kureishi's memoir 'The Rainbow Sign'. Kureishi remembers a 'great moment' as a child when he visited a sweet-shop and saw a television in the backroom showing the 1968 Olympic Games: 'Thommie Smith and John Carlos were raising their fists on the victory rostrum, giving the Black Power salute as the "Star Spangled Banner" played. The white shopkeeper was outraged. He said to me: they shouldn't mix politics and sport' ('The Rainbow Sign', p. 13). As a British-born Londoner with one Asian parent, Kureishi is at some remove from the struggle against racism by the Black Power movement in America in the 1960s, to which the gesture refers. But the gesture becomes *routed* transnationally from black American politics to the Mexico Olympics, and onwards via television to the sweet-shop in London into which Kureishi chanced. Conjoined to his avid reading of black Americans such as James Baldwin and Richard Wright, this momentary gesture becomes a valuable political resource for Kureishi in his contest against London's racism, exemplified all too clearly by the outraged white sweet-shop owner. The 'solidarity through difference' forged here is contingent, discontinuous and transnational, bringing together for a moment oppressed peoples in disparate locations. Yet it is of immeasurable value to the young Kureishi's attempt to think beyond the prevailing discourses of power which fix and marginalise his identity, and to construct solidarity with others in both different and similar positions to his own.

Moving pictures: Beryl Gilroy's *Boy-Sandwich*

Let us conclude this chapter by looking briefly at Beryl Gilroy's *Boy-Sandwich* (Heinemann, 1989) in the light of some of the concepts we have explored. Beryl Gilroy was born in Berbice, Guyana in 1924 and moved to Britain in 1951. She has worked as a teacher in both places (indeed, she was London's first black Head Teacher) and has written books for both children and adults.

Set in London in the 1980s, *Boy-Sandwich* is narrated by Tyrone Grainger, a British-born black teenager whose parents and grandparents were born in the Caribbean and migrated to Britain. Tyrone is on the verge of going to Cambridge to study but has taken a year out to help look after his grandparents. The novel opens with his grandparents' eviction from their London home amidst the taunts of a racist crowd, and their removal to an old peoples' home called The Birches. Tyrone spends the vast majority of his time at The Birches listening to his grandparents' stories of 'the Island' (such is the name Gilroy gives their Caribbean home) and battling with the home's authorities to make sure they are properly cared for.

On one of the rare occasions when he ventures to other parts of London, he attends a house-party where his girlfriend Adijah is working with her brother Dante, a D. J. The party is firebombed by racists. Twelve black partygoers are murdered, and Adijah is badly burned. For Tyrone, this incident is another tragedy to add to his list. A couple of years previously, his brother Goldberg had been killed in a racist attack when a brick was thrown from a passing truck. So, when Tyrone comes into an unexpected fortune, he decides to spend it on moving the three generations of his family back to the village of Picktown on the Island, a decision applauded in a local newspaper. But after spending some time away, Tyrone decides to return to Britain as he feels he cannot be readily accommodated in a Caribbean environment. The novel ends at an airport terminal, with Tyrone looking to the future back in London.

At one level, *Boy-Sandwich* paints a sobering picture of black diaspora experience in London. His family have not been accommodated and allowed to settle, as witnessed by the fact that the novel begins with the 'unhousing' of his grandparents. The fire at the party recalls the New Cross fire of 1981 in which thirteen black Londoners were killed, while Goldberg's tragedy references the everyday, seemingly random acts of violence and abuse which historically have overshadowed diaspora experience in Britain. Tyrone also recalls being stopped as a child by a local policeman on the grounds of his 'race'. He remembers the incident 'left me feeling disembodied and anxious and marked me for years' (p. 48).

As a consequence, Tyrone's attitudes to London as 'home' are complex. On the one hand, the continuing experience of racial violence makes him identify strongly with the 'old country' of his grandparents' island home. He spends a large part of the novel looking through their old photographs of the Island, and these become an important means by which his sense of an 'imaginary homeland' overseas is constructed. But on the other hand, the fact that he is British–born complicates matters further. 'I belong', he declares, 'regardless of those who say I don't. Inside me there is an oasis where my identity blooms precariously and my certainties flicker like lights and then die down' (p. 30). The novel explores the ways in which this blooming, precarious identity can be nurtured, one which goes beyond the 'certainties' of fixed roots.

For much of the novel, Tyrone takes refuge in the photographs and stories of his grandparents. These seem to offer him a sense of certainty and rootedness which combats his precarious feelings. Yet he cannot ever have the 'interior knowledge' of his grandparents, whose relationship with this photographic record is different. His almost obsessive pursuit of their past becomes a hindrance to his own 'blooming' identity as he tries to build a fixed self continuous with their memories of the Island's past. This is suggested by the contrast between his grandparents' photograph album and the recurring descriptions of his grandmother's bag, in which she hoards various relics and leftovers from her past:

> The bag in protest spills it contents – buttons, peanuts probably years old, letters, postcards, orange peel, folded-up mini plastic bags, combs of all sizes and coins in ancient cloth purses that the market women of the Island use. In the midst of everything are biscuits, chocolate and clumps of cheese. (p. 28)

There are at least two ways of thinking about this bag. On the one hand, we might describe it in terms of the fragmentary, untidy remains of the 'old country' which signify both the *connection with* and the *displacement from* the Island. Grandma conjures memories of home through these scraps, odds and ends which she refuses to discard. The bag is, then, an important means of orientation for Grandma in London. But from Tyrone's perspective, the bag looks quite different. It remains a point of reference to the Island, to be sure; but without the same kind of 'interior knowledge' which attaches particular emotional associations to these objects, the bag might also look like an arbitrary collection of meaningless junk. This makes us question whether or not the heavy investment in the past which Tyrone makes through his grandparents' memories is his best way of tending his blooming identity.

Later in the novel, a different way of negotiating between past and present is mooted. Tyrone finds in Grandma's bag some gold doubloons. This leads him to root about in his parents' attic for other potential valuable treasures, and by chance he happens across a painting of a group of peasant women and children wearing masks. On taking it for cleaning and valuation, he learns its title is 'The Masks' (which, appropriately enough for novel concerned with colonised identities, recalls Fanon's *Black Skin, White Masks*) and that it was painted by a Spanish artist who travelled to the Caribbean in the early twentieth century. It attracts an extremely large amount of money at auction. This is the money which Tyrone uses to relocate his family in Picktown.

It is worth pausing at this juncture and tracing the transnational crossings upon which this incident turns. The first crossing is of the Spanish artist from Europe to the Caribbean where 'The Masks' is painted; next, the crossing of Grandma and the picture from the Caribbean to London; its storage in an attic and subsequent sale to an unknown new owner; which in turn finances the Graingers' travels back to Picktown (and Tyrone's concluding return to London). Recalling Paul Gilroy's idea of the 'Black Atlantic', we might consider how the continual crossings which surround the painting provide valuable resources which enable Tyrone to rethink his identity in terms of unpredictable *routes* and not secure *roots*. As he puts it, the Spanish artist '[w]hatever he was, cut-throat or priest, black or white, his greed or his sense of beauty now reaches across the decades and touches my life' (p. 97).

In visiting Picktown, Tyrone realises that the villagers regard him as a London-born black and he finds it hard to identify with their community. The *route* from London to Picktown has not established firm *roots*. Rather, it emphasises Tyrone's necessity to move beyond such forms of identity and create new, more precarious forms for himself. (In addition, the return to the Island is not an unproblematic one for his grandparents and particularly his parents, as Picktown creates for them some insoluble challenges born from their continuing displacement.) Tyrone begins to embrace the possibilities, and not just the problems, of thinking of himself as a London-born black. He confesses that he feels trapped on the Island and desires to recover his 'space' in London. It is a space which is both real and imaginary. In concrete terms, Tyrone has previously shunned London spaces as dangerous and intimidating, preferring the insular environment of The Birches. But now, in Picktown, London is reconsidered as an important space in imaginative terms too, a space where he can understand and nurture his difference. This involves putting the past 'on the move'. Like the selling of the painting, pictures from the past offer the means for routeing but cannot be treated as providing order, certainty and identity for Tyrone's generation. As he comments after the fire at the party, 'there is no picture in the album to compare with those that have been taken of the ruins, of the house that has been razed' (p. 84).

So, the family's past is not wholly rejected as rubbish by Tyrone. Grandma's bag has led to a valuable source of treasure. It has opened up new transnational routes which take him back to the 'old country' *and beyond*. But neither has the past remained an obsession for Tyrone, as his grandparents' memories of the Island cannot be used to provide the certainties he wishes for at times. Instead, the past has been *put to work* for the present. Past images have been reinvested with value (both financial and symbolic) in order to put them and Tyrone 'on the move', opening the opportunity for him to think about identity beyond certainties and embrace the precarious possibilities of his life. *Boy-Sandwich* brings to crisis ways of thinking about identity as a 'certainty' with secure roots, an accessible home, and a continuous relationship between past and present. It is no coincidence that the text ends at a border location, among the 'fragments of conversation and the inquisitive glances of passers-by' (p. 121) in the terminal of an airport as Tyrone prepares to travel yet another route. That these will be *imaginative* as well as *geographical* passages is suggested by him finding a copy of *Dylan Thomas in America* left 'fortuitously forgotten' on his seat on the plane – a story of another past route which might also prove a resource for Tyrone's future?

Selected reading

Bhabha, Homi K., *The Location of Culture* (Routledge, 1994).
    Bhabha is often seen as the high priest of diaspora theory. Pay particular
    attention to the introduction and Chapters 8, 9, 11 and 12.

Brah, Avtar, *Cartographies of Diaspora: Contesting Identities* (Routledge, 1997).

An excellent, theoretically sophisticated account of diaspora experiences with particular reference to South Asian diaspora communities in Britain.

Chow, Rey, *Writing Diaspora: Tactics of Intervention in Contemporary Cultural Studies* (Indiana University Press, 1993).

A highly complex and stimulating book which deals critically with the theorising of diaspora.

Cohen, Robin, *Global Diasporas: An Introduction* (UCL Press, 1997).

Perhaps the clearest and best introduction to the different diaspora communities around the globe.

George, Rosemary Marangoly, *The Politics of Home: Postcolonial Relocations and Twentieth-Century Fiction* (Cambridge University Press, 1996).

The introductory chapter on constructions of 'home' is excellent, as is the final chapter, '"Travelling Light": Home and the Immigrant Genre'.

Gilroy, Paul, *The Black Atlantic: Modernity and Double Consciousness* (Verso, 1993).

A ground-breaking and influential work which explores the transnational diaspora aesthetics of black cultures between Africa, America, the Caribbean and Britain.

Gilroy, Paul, *Small Acts: Thoughts on the Politics of Black Cultures* (Serpent's Tail, 1993).

A wonderful collection of essays, often witty and incisive, which build upon some of Gilroy's ideas in *The Black Atlantic*.

Hall, Stuart, 'New Ethnicities' in David Morley and Kuan-Hsing Chen (eds), *Critical Dialogues in Cultural Studies* (Routledge, 1996), pp. 441–9.

Hall is one of the most insightful writers on diaspora communities in Britain. This is one of his most influential essays.

King, Russell, John Connell and Paul White (eds), *Writing Across Worlds: Literature and Migration* (Routledge, 1995).

An excellent collection of essays which looks at diasporic writings in a variety of contexts. Highly recommended.

Mercer, Kobena, *Welcome to the Jungle: New Positions in Black Cultural Studies* (Routledge, 1994).

An enthusiastic critique of diaspora aesthetics in Britain and America with particular reference to film, video and photography.

Radhakrishnan, R., *Diasporic Mediations: Between Home and Location* (University of Minnesota Press, 1996).

Rushdie, Salman, *Imaginary Homelands: Essays and Criticism 1981–1991* (Granta, 1991).

Rushdie is one of the foremost writers to reflect upon the impact of migrancy and diaspora experiences upon literary practices. The essays in this collection deal severally with the issues raised by migrancy.

8

Postcolonialism and the critics

Problematising postcolonialism

This short concluding chapter is designed to allow us to revisit some of the comments we made when defining postcolonialism in Chapter 1, and to think again about the problems and possibilities of the term in the light of the ideas we have encountered throughout *Beginning Postcolonialism*. In addition, it will enable us to collect together the criticisms of postcolonialism we have encountered as we have worked through this book, and add some more. We have an opportunity, then, to reflect critically upon the beginnings we have made. Ultimately, the purpose of this chapter (if not *Beginning Postcolonialism* as a whole) is to assist you in reaching some conclusions concerning the extent to which 'postcolonialism' is an enabling term.

Hence, in this chapter there are no separate 'Stop and Think' sections. Instead, think of this chapter as a single 'Stop and Think' section and work through the criticisms of postcolonialism patiently, stopping at each turn to reflect upon the complaints being raised.

Each problem we encounter comes with a series of responses that we might make. These responses are offered *not* as definitive ways of solving the problems raised, if indeed they can be solved. Rather, they offer resources to stimulate your own ways of thinking critically about the 'pros and cons' of each objection. The conclusions you make concerning each, either in agreement or disagreement, ultimately must be your own.

From 'Commonwealth' to 'postcolonial' and back again?

Although postcolonialism rejects many of the critical assumptions with which critics of Commonwealth literature worked, and has created a wide-ranging critical vocabulary of its own which draws upon the work of other disciplines, for some the shift from 'Commonwealth' to 'postcolonial' is not as pronounced as might be expected. There are two problems we can raise in this context. Both invite us to question the extent to which postcolonialism is significantly different from the older paradigm of Commonwealth literature. They might be summarised as follows:

- Postcolonialism accepts uncritically the *geographical divisions* of Commonwealth literature.
- Postcolonialism does not discriminate adequately between *different experiences* of colonialism.

Let us take first the issue of geographical divisions. William Walsh divided his book *Commonwealth Literature* into six chapters, each dealing with a separate area: India, Africa, the West Indies, Canada, New Zealand and Australia. In postcolonial literary studies, it could be argued that this particular mapping of the field remains. John Thieme's excellent *The Arnold Anthology of Post-Colonial Literatures in English* (Edward Arnold, 1996) divides the field geographically as follows: West Africa, East Africa, Southern Africa, North Africa, Australia, Canada, the Caribbean, New Zealand and South Pacific, South Asia (consisting of India, Sri Lanka, Bangladesh, Pakistan), South-East Asia (consisting of Malaysia, Singapore, the Philippines, Thailand), and 'Trans-Cultural Writing'. Look how in Thieme's anthology there is a greater sensitivity to the differences within particular regions and between them, plus the focus on 'trans-cultural' literature which cannot be contained within national categories. Yet the map of Commonwealth literature such as we find in Walsh's book is still determining to a degree Thieme's subdivisions twenty-three years later, despite his increased nuance and sensitivity to difference. Note how, for example, Ireland remains absent from both Walsh's and Thieme's subdivision of the field.

This mapping of the field can be regarded from two contrasting perspectives, as cause either for complaint or congratulation. To take the criticisms of this mapping first, we can consider two objections. If the study of Commonwealth literature privileged Britain as a central point of reference for the new literatures in English, then postcolonialism also repeats this privileging. It continues the *collecting and tethering of these literatures to the colonial centre* via the use of the term 'postcolonial literatures' which, for some, performs essentially the same task as the study of Commonwealth literature. Furthermore, as the omission of Ireland perhaps indicates, the scope of postcolonialism remains limited to a *selective* number of those countries with a history of colonialism, derivative of the key areas of concern in Commonwealth literature.

There are two ways we might respond to these complaints. First, we might note that postcolonialism *has* expanded in range and focus. Ireland is a case in point. Several critics have argued in recent years that many of the issues raised in postcolonial studies – such as language, representation, resistance, nationalism, gender, migrancy and diaspora – are central in the study of Irish literature, and have suggested that the literature of Ireland be read as 'postcolonial' in its own right, and comparatively with the postcolonial writings of other nations. As Elleke Boehmer has argued, Ireland's struggle against British colonial rule 'was in certain other colonies taken as talismanic by nationalist movements' (*Colonial and Postcolonial Literature*, p. 4). Indeed, in his novel *Troubles* (Fontana, 1970), the Anglo-Irish novelist J. G. Farrell includes in his representation of Irish nationalist resistance in the first decades of the twentieth century newspaper reports concerning anti-colonial activities in such places as India, in order to point out the ways in which Irish nationalism was related to other forms of resistance to colonialism throughout the British Empire. In *Culture and Imperialism*, Edward Said argues that the Anglo-Irish writer W. B. Yeats should be read as an 'indisputably great *national* poet who during a period of anti-imperialist resistance articulates the experiences, the aspirations, and the restorative vision of a people suffering under the dominion of an offshore power' (pp. 265–6). He proceeds to read Yeats's poetry in tandem with the work of the likes of the Chilean poet Pablo Neruda and Césaire's Negritude poetry (which we looked at in Chapter 3). In a similar vein, in his book *Anomalous States: Irish*

Writing and the Post-Colonial Moment (Lilliput Press, 1993), David
Lloyd argues that '[f]or the theory and practice of decolonisation,
however, Ireland is, to a sometimes distressing extent, more exem-
plary than anomalous' (p. 7). Lloyd's own work looks closely at the
likes of Seamus Heaney, Samuel Beckett, W. B. Yeats and James
Joyce in the various contexts which emerge from Ireland's postcolonial 'moment'.

In addition, it has occasionally been pointed out that the literatures from the British isles, such as Wales and Scotland, can be
thought of as postcolonial. These countries have suffered the institutional and cultural authority of England which the writing from
each has attempted to challenge. As Berthold Schoene has provocatively argued in his essay 'A Passage to Scotland: Scottish Literature and the British Postcolonial Condition' (*Scotlands*, 2 (1), 1995,
pp. 107–22),

> [a] discussion of Scottish literature in light of current postcolonial
> theory is bound to lead to interesting results. Here we find not only
> individual works of postcolonial literature but a whole tradition of
> postcolonial writing ... Scottish writers since the early eighteenth
> and perhaps even the early seventeenth centuries are likely to have
> much in common with contemporary writers from the former
> colonised and now independent Commonwealth countries. (p. 110)

Schoene proceeds to look at the work of such writers as Lewis
Grassic Gibbon and Hugh MacDiarmid in terms of the insights of
postcolonial theory.

The focus on Ireland and Scotland in terms of postcolonialism
enables us to respond to the criticism that postcolonialism works too
closely with the map of the Commonwealth, by pointing out that
new contexts *are* being explored productively with the concepts
which postcolonialism has made available. For example, Barker,
Hulme and Iversen's collection *Colonial Discourse/Postcolonial
Theory* features work which engages variously with colonial and
postcolonial representations in Peru, Martinique, South Africa,
Brazil and Mexico; and deals with *various* forms of European colonialism, such as the British and Spanish experiences. In a similar
vein, Deborah L. Madsen's edited collection of essays *Post-Colonial
Literatures: Expanding the Canon* (Pluto, 1999) is a deliberate

attempt to go 'beyond the Commonwealth' and regard the work of (amongst others) Chicano/a and Hispanic writers as postcolonial, calling attention to body of work often neglected in anthologies of postcolonial writing. It seems that postcolonialism has in the 1990s widened its scope and ceased to privilege the British Commonwealth by looking at other relevant colonial contexts. So, we can argue that one of the strengths of postcolonialism is that it has made available a variety of concepts and reading practices that can be productively applied to contexts that go beyond the older, selective areas of concern which preoccupied critics of Commonwealth literature.

That said, from a contrary position, we might regard as a *strength* the fact that the geographical divisions of Commonwealth literature determine mappings of postcolonialism, and be more wary of these attempts to 'expand the canon'. For example, one of the problems of applying postcolonial concepts and reading strategies to a variety of contexts is that postcolonialism becomes detached from its historical and geographical referents: Empire, colonialism, and the once-colonised countries. There is a danger in using terms like 'colonialism' and 'postcolonialism' too sweepingly. Although the experiences of the Irish and Scots, and those who suffered from British and Spanish rule, can be cited as examples of colonialism, are these experiences and versions of colonialism necessarily the same? Problems may arise when words like 'colonialism' and 'postcolonialism' become attached to every example of international or intercultural conflict at the expense of an attention to the specifics of each case. From one perspective the Irish and Scots may appear as colonised peoples, but in other parts of the Empire (such as India, for example) they functioned as agents of colonialism and prospered under colonial rule. Critics such as Edward Said have solid historical and cultural evidence for their claims and contribute much by reading the work of Irish literature in a postcolonial context. But in the hands of a less sophisticated critic, the declaration that 'this or that' nation was colonised and its literature is consequently 'postcolonial' is often a disingenuous way of securing at a stroke the political context of a nation's literature while legitimating the work of the literary critic as 'radical' and 'oppositional'. As a consequence, the term 'postcolonialism' becomes further and further detached from its historical and geographical referents. Benita Parry cites this as a particular problem resulting from the work of colonial discourse analysts such as Bhabha and Spivak who have 'stimulated studies which by extending "colonisation" as an explanatory notion applicable to all situations of structural domination, are directed at formulating a grand theory valid for each and every discursive system' ('Problems in Current Theories of Colonial Discourse', p. 52).

From this position, we can regard the geographical divisions of *The Arnold Anthology of Post-Colonial Literatures in English* in a favourable light. Rather than considering its organisation as privileging certain countries with a history of colonialism over others, we might *commend* this work for its historical and geographical accuracy in collecting only literatures in English from countries which were once colonies of the British Empire. Thieme's deployment of the term is responsible to both geographical and historical referents.

These problems of *reference* lead to the second aspect of the proximity between postcolonialism and the study of Commonwealth literature, which concerns the issue of different *experiences* of colonialism. This is also in part a consequence of the continuing prevalence of the geographical distinctions made by critics of Commonwealth literature. In particular, the continued collecting together of the literature from settler and settled countries under the umbrella term 'postcolonial' smacks of the lack of attention to history for which critics of Commonwealth literature stand accused. One vocal argument which runs along these lines is given by Ella Shohat in an influential essay, 'Notes on the "Post-Colonial"' (*Social Text*, 31/32, 1992, pp. 99–113):

Positioning Australia and India, for example, in relation to an imperial center [*sic*], simply because they were both colonies, equates the relations of the colonised white-settlers to the Europeans at the 'center' with that of the colonised indigenous populations to the Europeans. It also assumes that white settler countries and the emerging Third World nations broke away from the 'center' in the same way. Similarly, white Australians and Aboriginal Australians are placed in the same 'periphery,' as though they were co-habitants vis-a-vis the 'center'. The critical differences between the Europe's [*sic*] genocidal oppression of Aboriginals in Australia, indigenous peoples of the Americas and Afro-diasporic communities, *and* Europe's domination

of European elites in the colonies are levelled with an easy stroke of the
'post'. (p. 102)

Shohat's accusation that postcolonialism levels the 'critical differences' both *within* and *between* nations is perhaps the most common
complaint made against postcolonialism. The equation of diverse
peoples as 'postcolonial' conveniently forgets that their historical
fortunes can be widely different. In these terms, 'postcolonialism' is
a vague, ahistorical, obfuscatory term that merely skates over the
historical and political surfaces of various nations and refuses to
attend to them in depth. Here we must also add the criticisms of
postcolonialism by feminists such as Carole Boyce Davis which we
looked at in Chapter 6, particularly the remark that postcolonialism
continues to privilege men and gives little attention to the multiple
experiences of women.

The generalising tendency of postcolonialism is, perhaps, its
greatest weakness. Shohat's focus on the collapsing together of settler and settled communities is a common cause of complaint. The
thorny issue of the relationships between white settler communities
and Aboriginal or First Nations peoples has made it difficult to refer
unproblematically to the old dominions of the British Empire in
terms of postcolonialism. In his essay 'Postmodernism or Postcolonialism?' (*Landfall*, 155, 1985, pp. 366–80), Simon During has
seen fit to split the term 'postcolonialism' in two, using the phrases
'postcolonising' and 'postcolonised': 'The former fits those communities and individuals who profit from and identify themselves as
heirs to the work of colonising. The latter fits those who have been
dispossessed by that work and who identify with themselves as heirs
to a more or less undone culture' (pp. 369–70). Although this is an
admirable attempt to bear witness to the political differences and
tensions *within* nations, not just between them, During's splitting of
'postcolonialism' reveals just how quickly the term begins to break
up under the pressure of historical accuracy. We might wonder,
then, if the term 'postcolonialism' could be dispensed with entirely
and more accurate concepts discovered.

None the less, we can respond to this issue by noticing how a swift
review of literary criticism in the field suggests that Shohat's fears
concerning vagary need not necessarily result from using 'postcolonialism' in more general contexts. Elleke Boehmer's *Colonial and*

Postcolonial Literatures and Dennis Walder's *Post-Colonial Literatures in English* are scrupulous in separating out different national
and cultural contexts (as well as attending to problems within each).
Edward Said's *Culture and Imperialism* offers a range of exciting
ways to read a variety of literary texts in relation to each other and to
the various forms of anti-colonial resistance around the globe. Thus,
these texts offer the means of thinking *comparatively* about the various representations which occurred throughout the Empire, as well
as noticing how anti-colonial struggles in different places often
resourced each other, as in the 'talismanic' case of Ireland.

As John Thieme argues in the introduction to *The Arnold Anthology of Post-Colonial Literatures in English*, we should reject using
terms like 'postcolonialism' if they suggest 'a prescriptive and
restrictive repertory of common concerns for the various literatures'
(p. 5). But the term can be enabling if it takes 'the issue of language
usage into account and reserves the term for writing in European
languages and related forms' (p. 5). This kind of attention to both
similarity and *difference* might be one way of reserving valency for
'post-colonialism'. Although Shohat sounds a valuable warning to
critics by calling for an attention to the specific, we perhaps should
be careful not to rule out *comparative* modes of thought too.

Postcolonialism and neo-colonialism

The issues which arise under this heading deal with complaints that
are made more commonly against the practitioners and ideas of
postcolonial theory. According to some, postcolonialism may wear a
radical or oppositional face, but this only masks its complicity with
the *continuing* oppression of peoples in the present (what we have
been calling *neo-colonialism*). How can postcolonialism be at the service of the very phenomenon, colonialism, which it seeks to contest?
There are at least five areas in which issues of neo-colonialism arise.
They are:

- The debt to Western theory in postcolonialism
- The new 'ghetto' of postcolonial literary studies
- The problem of 'antifoundationalism'
- The issue of temporality
- The relationship between postcolonialism and global capitalism

Let us take the issue of the Western origins of postcolonial theory first. One good example of this debate can be found in *Interrogating Post-Colonialism: Theory, Text and Context* (eds. Harish Trivedi and Meenakshi Mukherjee, Indian Institute of Advanced Study, 1996). In the opening chapter, 'Interrogating Post-Colonialism' (pp. 3–11), Meenakshi Mukherjee makes the point that the concepts and nomenclature of postcolonialism have been fashioned in Western, especially American, universities and are not always adequate to meet the contemporary needs of countries with a history of colonialism, such as India. The imperatives of postcolonialism are being set elsewhere, particularly by migrant Indian intellectuals who have helped to make postcolonialism the fashion in Western academia by drawing upon the latest advances in literary theory. Think of Bhabha's penchant for Freud and Lacan, or Spivak's indebtedness to deconstruction. According to Mukherjee:

> Several diasporic Indians have been pioneers in the area of post-colonial theory, and the field is now densely populated with academics in American universities who originally came from the ex-colonies. But as of now no major theoretical contribution has come to this discourse from home-based Indian intellectuals. (p. 8)

This leads Mukherjee to argue that countries with a history of colonialism are being colonised again, this time by Western theoretical imperatives and the current focus in Western universities upon cultural difference. In terms of literary studies, the colonies provide literary texts as 'raw materials' which are imported by the West to be 'processed' using postcolonial theory, with the resulting intellectual product shipped back to the erstwhile colonies for academic consumption. For example, Indian literatures are read *exclusively* as postcolonial in their representations and politics, as if this is the only frame within which they can be understood. As Arun P. Mukherjee (not to be confused with Meenakshi Mukherjee) similarly puts it in another essay in the collection called 'Interrogating Postcolonialism: Some Uneasy Conjunctures' (pp. 13–20), much literature from India 'cannot be answered within the framing grid provided by postcolonial theory where readers are instructed solely on how to decode the subtle ironies and parodies directed against the departed coloniser. I think I need another theory' (p. 20).

So, because the West always remains the place of power and privilege with Western-based academics dictating the shape and form of
postcolonial literary studies, we might argue that there is engendered *an unequal neo-colonial relationship* between academics based
inside and outside the Western nations. According to this view, postcolonialism is nothing but a Western practice using Western theories
that is performed in Western (especially American) universities in
the main by privileged migrants from the once-colonised nations
who have been able to secure lucrative academic posts. Thus
defined, the asymmetrical, unequal relationship between the West
and the once-colonised countries resembles too closely colonial
relationships.

There are two ways of responding to this criticism of postcolonialism. First, Meenakshi Mukherjee and Arun P. Mukherjee do
not seem to realise that some of the most popular postcolonial theorists expend a great deal of time interrogating exactly the kind of
neo-colonial relations they describe. An excellent example is Gayatri Chakravorty Spivak's essay 'How to Read a Culturally Different
Book' (collected in both *The Spivak Reader*, pp. 237–66; and *Colonial Discourse / Postcolonial Theory*, pp. 126–50). In this essay, Spivak
argues against those literary critics who teach *The Guide* (1980) by
Indian novelist R. K. Narayan as, variously, typical of Indian literature in English, or the Indian people as a whole, or postcolonialism
in general. In an attempt to stop 'the international readership of
Commonwealth literature' (*The Spivak Reader*, p. 241) from imposing its own agenda onto this novel, Spivak explores the character of
Rosie/Nalini who is a *devadasi* or temple dancer, on the way to
exposing the novel's complicity with patriarchal and neo-colonial
values. So, it seems that Spivak *is* thinking responsibly and critically
about the unequal, neo-colonial relations between postcolonial texts
and their Western readerships. She is concerned with exactly the
issues raised by opponents of postcolonial theory. This makes the
argument about the commodification of postcolonial literature by
Western theory difficult to sustain.

Another response to this line of argument is given by Gareth
Griffiths in his essay in the same volume, 'Representation and Pro-
duction: Issues of Control in Post-Colonial Cultures' (*Interrogating
Post-Colonialism*, pp. 21–36). Objecting to the wave of 'anti-theory',

Griffiths takes issue with Arun P. Mukherjee's argument that only local and specific frames of reference are the appropriate ones for Indian literature. Griffiths wonders if this line of thinking is questing nostalgically for an area of indigenous Indian culture which has remained untouched by colonialism. He accuses Arun P. Mukherjee and others of asserting a 'politics of recuperation which suggests that the recovery of an unproblematic alternative history [as] a simple and sufficient resistant practice in itself, and one which has no inherent dangers' (p. 22). In other words, in demanding that Indian literature is read with recourse to local and historical specifics and not via the niceties of postcolonial reading practices, such critics posit a version of Indian history and culture which has remained untouched by colonialism. Such a cleavage between that which has been influenced by colonialism and anti-colonial resistance, and that which has not, is too neat and tidy for Griffiths. Where does one draw the dividing line? Rather, such critics need to wake up to the 'necessary, indeed inevitable, "hybridity" resulting from the impact of colonisation on both the colonised and, it needs to be said, the coloniser' (p. 23).

It is not for me to resolve this debate one way or the other; rather let us note the existence of an all-too-familiar division which can occur within postcolonialism. On the one side are those who decry postcolonial concepts and modes of analysis as unable to deal with the particular concerns of literature that often exist *outside* the frame of colonialism and resistance to it. On the other side are those who argue that such anterior positions do not exist: 'local' concerns *cannot help but be influenced* by the legacy of colonialism. Each critical position is condemned by the other as 'neo-colonialist'. The anti-theorists are deemed neo-colonial for refusing to learn from the insights of postcolonial theory, while the pro-theorists are seen as Western-oriented, insensitive to historical context and happy to generalise. (For a more complicated and patient description of this kind of division, see Stephen Slemon, 'The Scramble for Post-Colonialism' in *De-Scribing Empire: Post-Colonialism and Textuality*, ed. Chris Tiffin and Alan Lawson, pp. 15–32).

Let us turn next to the argument that postcolonialism creates a 'ghetto' for literature from once-colonised countries within English departments and degree schemes. Arun P. Mukherjee makes this

point in 'Interrogating Postcolonialism: Some Uneasy Conjunctures' when arguing that the Western-constituted field of postcolonialism is little more than a trendy 'grab bag of canonical,
predominantly male, writers from Africa, the Caribbean, South
Asia, south Pacific, and sometimes Canada' (p. 14). Mukherjee
describes the division of labour in the English department where she
works in Canada into fields such as 'Shakespeare', 'Renaissance' or
'Romanticism'. Each focuses squarely upon one nation (Britain) and
is confined to a limited period of time. But academics teaching 'Postcolonial Literature' courses are expected to deal with a much wider
category of literature which can span the globe and range across the
nineteenth and twentieth centuries – an impossible task in one
semester-length course. For Mukherjee, this state of affairs is
another example of neo-colonialism. Courses in 'Postcolonial Literature' are merely fashionable gestures, tacked on to existing degree
schemes in university English departments to make them seem up-
to-date and sensitive to cultural difference. But little thought is
given to the academic reasons and intellectual challenges of the field,
nor the ways in which it might contest the existing division of academic labour within the department as a whole. Instead, postcolonialism neatly ring-fences a wide body of diverse literatures which
conveniently can be added to a department's course provision, without disturbing too much the more conventional approaches to
canonical English literature.

Once again, a response to this point is given by Gareth Griffiths.
It is wrong, he argues, to see the division of labour in some academic
departments as the *result* of postcolonialism (see footnote 3 on p. 34
of his essay). Mukherjee's complaint about having to teach the full
range of postcolonial literatures on one course in her department
tells us more about the department's appointments system and less
about postcolonialism, which is precisely attempting to break down
some of these divisions. The fault lies not with the *theory* but with
the *institution*. This is a fair point, perhaps, but Mukherjee's argument invites us to be suspicious of the current popularity of postcolonialism in English departments, especially in Britain and
America. To what extent are the insights of postcolonialism impact-
ing more centrally on degree schemes and undergraduate curricula?
Whose interests does it serve to construct new glossy courses in

'Postcolonial Literatures' which enable students to sample a handful of 'different' literary products? What status is assigned to these texts?

The third problem regarding postcolonialism as neo-colonial concerns the issue of 'antifoundationalism'. This is a criticism made by, amongst others, Arif Dirlik in his oft-quoted essay 'The Postcolonial Aura: Third World Criticism in the Age of Global Capitalism' (*Critical Inquiry*, 20, 1994, pp. 328–56). 'Antifoundationalism' is a term used to describe the thinking of poststructuralists such as Jacques Derrida, Michel Foucault, Gilles Deleuze, Jean-François Lyotard and others whose work is deemed to interrogate and collapse the distinctions between language and reality. Rather than view language as a medium which reflects reality, antifoundationalists argue that reality is actually an 'effect' of language and the world is first and foremost a *textual* product. In addition, all the old grand theories or 'grand narratives' of knowledge which were once used to *explain and critique* human behaviour, such as the Marxism and nationalism, have broken up, leaving us in a world of fragmented, local knowledges without any 'grand narratives' to adjudicate between them.

According to critics hostile to such views, antifoundationalist thought ignores the ways in which 'concrete' phenomena such as economic and social conditions remain the foundations of reality and determine how we live our lives. The world is much more than a fragmentary 'text'. Also, such thinking confounds the possibility of *resistance* by declaring an end to all metanarratives of knowledge. Because figures such as Said, Bhabha and Spivak draw heavily on Western poststructuralist thought, Dirlik condemns the inevitable antifoundational thrust of their theory. (We might like to recall at this point Spivak's representation of the subaltern as female as an effect of language in her essay 'Can the Subaltern Speak?', which we explored in Chapter 6.) The following moment from Dirlik's essay gives a good example of the antifoundational critique being made here:

Within the institutional site of the First World academy, fragmentation of earlier metanarratives appears benign (except to hidebound conservatives) for its promise of more democratic, multicultural, and cosmopolitan epistemologies. In the world outside the academy, however, it shows in murderous ethnic conflict, continued inequalities

among societies, classes, and genders, and the absence of oppositional
possibilities that, always lacking in coherence, are rendered even more
impotent than earlier by the fetishisation of difference, fragmentation,
and so on. (p. 347)

According to this line of argument, postcolonial theory has con-
ceded too much ground by questioning oppositional discourses
such as nationalism and Marxism *at the very moment* when we need
these discourses more than ever to combat conflicts around the
world. For Dirlik, postcolonialism is practised by a select few 'Third
World' intellectuals who have taken up 'First World' fashionable
theory. From their elite, privileged position as intellectuals, and
empowered by their command of the cosmopolitan languages of
transnational academic theory, this select few construct the world in
their own hybridised self-image by projecting globally 'what are but
local experiences' (p. 345). Meanwhile, outside the ivory tower
oppressed people continue to kill each other, oblivious to the
'hybridity' of their decentred subjectivities and their mistaken pursuit of discredited metanarratives.

In responding to this critique, we might argue that Dirlik is perhaps rather disingenuous in his collapsing of the work of postcolonial theorists with each other, and with Western poststructuralist
thinkers. Postcolonial theorists have an uneasy relationship with
'antifoundational' thought at the best of times. As we have witnessed, Gayatri Chakravorty Spivak has written at length about the
problems in poststructuralism (as in 'French Feminism in an International Frame'), as well as exploring the possibilities in forms of
knowledge such as Marxism for a changed and changing world. The
same argument could be made about Edward Said. Dirlik's dismissal of all things 'antifoundational' lacks a more nuanced awareness of the work being carried out by postcolonial theorists,
regardless of whether or not one supports their work.

Fourthly, the issue of the 'neo–colonial temporality' of postcolonialism requires comment. This returns us to the 'post' in postcolonialism and the representation of history it suggests. As we defined
the term in Chapter 1, postcolonialism stresses both *continuity* and
change by recognising the continuing agency of colonial discourses
as well as resistances to them. Yet, for some critics the use of the
prefix 'post' brings with it too many troubling associations which

hinder more supple renderings of the term. In particular, these associations have to do with the particular representation of historical time implied by the 'post' in postcolonial. In her 1992 essay 'The Angel of Progress: Pitfalls of the Term "Postcolonialism"' (in *Colonial Discourse/Postcolonial Theory*, pp. 253–66), Anne McClintock takes issue with the 'post' in postcolonial on the following grounds. First, although postcolonial theory often challenges binary oppositions, the use of the 'post' represents global history through a binary division: colonial/postcolonial. Second, by conferring on colonialism 'the prestige of history proper' (p. 255) non-European cultures become historicised with recourse to European chronology. Colonialism becomes the 'determining marker of history' (p. 255); alternative ways of dividing historical epochs or narrating historical time which do *not* privilege colonialism, are ignored. In adding her voice to those who believe that postcolonialism cannot accommodate the multiplicity of histories and experiences it covers, McClintock argues that the term does not allow us to think about how postcolonialism is 'unevenly developed globally' (p. 256). Different countries encounter decolonisation at different times, while others have not experienced it all. In addition, not all forms of decolonisation are the same. By collapsing these different times into one temporality, 'the postcolonial', we lose the opportunity to think about the historical differences that exist between contrasting locations. Ultimately, the 'post' in postcolonial is too celebratory, implying an end to all things colonial. Its celebratory emphasis damagingly directs attention away from the continued, neo-colonial operations throughout the globe.

Similar arguments are raised by Ella Shohat in 'Notes on the "Post-Colonial"'. Shohat shares McClintock's misgivings that the term implies the end of colonialism, and worries about the collapse of chronology which this effects. 'When exactly, then, does the "post-colonial" begin? Which region is privileged in such a beginning? What are the relationships between these diverse beginnings?' (p. 103). It is very difficult to 'begin postcolonialism' if we can never be certain when the postcolonial originates. Like McClintock, Shohat is also concerned about the inability of postcolonialism to address neo-colonialism. In the late twentieth century, it is argued, Western multinational companies are the new 'colonialists', while America continues the military aggression of certain nations. The global economic relationships between the wealthy Western nations and their poorer neighbours reflect 'colonialism's economic, political, and cultural deformative-traces in the present' (p. 105). Hence:

> the term 'post-colonial', when compared with neo-colonialism, comes equipped with little evocation of contemporary power relations; it lacks a political content which can account for the eighties and nineties-style U. S. militaristic involvements in Granada, Panama, and Kuwait–Iraq, and for the symbiotic links between U. S. political and economic interests and those of local elites. (p. 105)

There are three responses that can be made here. First, let us remember that when we addressed postcolonialism in the introduction to this book, we carefully decided that we would use the term to refer specifically to aesthetic practices: representations, discourses and values. 'Postcolonialism' is not a strict historical marker; it does not exclusively denote an epoch. But much of the confusion surrounding the term comes from its use *simultaneously* to describe, on the one hand, historical, social and economic *material conditions* (Marx's 'base', if you like) and, on the other, historically-situated *imaginative* products and practices (Marx's 'superstructure'). To keep this confusion at bay, we reserved 'postcolonialism' to describe the latter of these. Shohat in particular stresses the need for us to be vigilant at all times in defining the term precisely, but 'Notes on the "Post-Colonial"' could be accused of failing to differentiate adequately between 'postcolonial' as a historical marker *and* an aesthetic critical practice. If carefully defined, postcolonialism perhaps *can* recognise the continuing agency of colonial discourses and relations of power in the contemporary world as we have seen at various points in this text.

Second, 'postcolonialism' is a generalising term, to be sure; but all terms must inevitably generalise, such as Romanticism, socialism, Marxism, even neo-colonialism. What word could McClintock and Shohat find which could avoid generalisation? And third, if 'postcolonialism' is too generalising, perhaps one solution is to use the same term in different ways in different contexts. This would reflect contingent historical, cultural and geographical conditions while offering ways of thinking *across* these differences to the *global*, transnational operations such as multinational capitalism and US military aggression which inevitably link together disparate locations. Once again, the ability to think *comparatively* and across differences can be enabling.

The arguments of Shohat and McClintock lead us directly to the fifth and final complaint against postcolonialism we examine in this section: its inability to address issues of economic power and social class. When defining colonialism at the beginning of Chapter 1 we considered its inseparable relationship with the expansion of Western capitalism and imperialism. According to some, postcolonialism services the requirements of Western capitalism in its contemporary global and multinational operations just as surely as colonialism served capitalism in an earlier period. As regards these issues, two essays are especially worth our attention. The first, by Aijaz Ahmad, is called 'The Politics of Literary Postcoloniality' (*Race and Class*, 36 (3), 1995, pp. 1–20). In this essay Ahmad points out that the economic and social situation today in some of the poorer nations of the world reflects the fortunes of many countries with a history of colonialism:

> there have been other countries – such as Turkey which has *not* been colonised, or Iran and Egypt, whose occupation had not led to colonisation of the kind that India suffered – where the onset of capitalist modernity and their incorporation in the world capitalist system brought about state apparatuses as well as social and cultural configurations that were, nevertheless, remarkably similar to the ones in India, which *was* fully colonised. In this context, we should speak not so much of colonialism or postcolonialism but of capitalist modernity, which takes the colonial form in particular places and at particular times. (p. 7)

Ahmad's focus upon capitalist modernity is part of his critique of postcolonialism as having nothing to say about contemporary global economic conditions which can be described as neo-colonial. Multinational capitalist companies are increasingly able to come and go as they please in many of the poorer nations of the world, hiring cheap labour in one location only to move operations to other places if the costs there are lower (this process is sometimes called 'flexible production'). The labour forces are left behind without much afterthought, devoid of a means of living. Meanwhile companies such as

IBM and CNN can electronically circumnavigate the globe imposing a 'regime of electronic pleasures' (p. 12) which bypass national
borders and beam Western ideologies and desires for Western products direct to those peoples in the poorer parts of the world who can
afford television sets, while those less economically advantaged are
left to their own devices 'to obtain conditions for bare survival'
(p. 13). For Ahmad, postcolonial theory is entirely complicit with
the globalising, transnational tendencies of contemporary capitalism. It offers no new ways of criticising the advancement of global
capitalism; and it also discredits older modes of critique such as
Marxism. Ahmad argues that '[p]ostcoloniality is also, like most
things, a matter of class' (p. 16). But issues of class remain absent
from the agendas of much postcolonial theory.

Arif Dirlik, in his essay 'The Postcolonial Aura: Third World Criticism in the Age of Global Capitalism', makes many similar claims to
Ahmad, but goes even further. It is not just that postcolonialism originates in Western theoretical discourse, offers no ways of critiquing
global capitalism, and spreads its theoretical pronouncements
throughout the academic world along the same neo-colonial, transnational routes as global capitalism. Dirlik claims that postcolonial intellectuals *are actually trying to hide* their complicity with global
capitalism. We noted above Dirlik's critique of postcolonial intellectuals as projecting globally their specific cosmopolitan, privileged position in their constructions of postcolonialism. But also, he argues, such
figures are trying to stop us thinking about the relationship between
intellectual debate and economic power because they do not want to be
exposed as profiting from global capitalism: 'To put it bluntly, postcoloniality is designed to *avoid* making sense of the current crisis and,
in the process, to cover up the origins of postcolonial intellectuals in a
global capitalism of which they are not so much victims as beneficiaries' (p. 353). Dirlik's suspicions are raised by the sudden interest in
transnationalism and multiculturalism of people working within capitalist industries. A little local knowledge of cultural 'otherness' and difference can go along way to assisting capitalism's flexibility in
establishing itself in different times and places. Dirlik concludes by
hoping that the postcolonial intelligentsia 'can generate a thoroughgoing criticism of its own ideology and formulate practices of resistance
against the system of which it is a product' (p. 356).

In responding to the relationship between postcolonialism and global capitalism let us deal first with Dirlik's assault on postcolonial intellectuals. His argument is perhaps not greatly helped by the conspiracy theory it builds against postcolonial intellectuals, conjuring bizarre images of the likes of Said, Spivak and Bhabha gathered in American hotel rooms anxiously shredding their IBM-sponsored expense-account statements. This, of course, is a gross trivialisation of Dirlik's argument, but it is a trivialisation engendered in part by the oddly paranoid tone of his essay. Second, if postcolonialism is caught within the transnational operations and movements of global capitalism, does that necessarily condemn it to *total* complicity? It is useful perhaps to revisit Paul Gilroy's work on the 'Black Atlantic' at this juncture. As we saw in Chapter 7, the slave-ships which took millions of Africans across the seas to a life of servitude and misery also carried dissident ideas from place to place, and hence enabled the spread of resources for black peoples in several locations. Could the same resistant opportunities exist today, with global networks such as television, e-mail and the internet, and multinational publishing houses enabling the circulation of oppositional thought? Third, critics working within postcolonialism have seemed *very* aware of the problems with global capitalism and Western economic power. Both Said's *Orientalism* and *Culture and Imperialism* include long sections which explore the neo-colonial dominance of Western nations such as America and contemporary modes of resistance. And as we saw in Chapter 6, postcolonial critiques of 'First World' feminism have been motivated by critics who do *not* want to use problematic neo-colonial forms of thought. So perhaps the self-critique which Dirlik demands is not as absent as it might seem. None the less, the lack of attention to class in postcolonialism can remain a serious blind-spot in the scope of its interests. Although Spivak's work attends closely to class, the same might not be said of Bhabha's *The Location of Culture*.

Where do we go from here?

In the introduction to *Beginning Postcolonialism*, we considered 'postcolonialism' as potentially a vague umbrella term that perhaps lets too much in. Looking back over the many issues we have raised in this book, it remains doubtful if a coherent sense of postcolonialism in general can be found; nor should we be looking for one.

Perhaps articulating 'postcolonialism' can be defended on the grounds that it serves as a constant reminder of the historical contexts of both oppression and resistance which inform literature in the colonial period and its aftermath; it provides us with a challenging, innovative set of concepts which we can bring to bear in our reading practices, perhaps making us change some habits of mind; and it reminds readers that 'English literature' is only a small part of the literatures in English that are available today. Attending to cultural, historical, social, political and geographical differences is paramount; but so is thinking *between* and *across* differences too. Comparative modes of thought remain a valuable means of critique, and need not lead to generality and universalism.

Throughout this book we have concluded each chapter with a selected reading list, and collectively these lists should give you a wide-ranging set of texts from which you can continue your work in postcolonialism. Listed after the Appendix are some good texts, many of which have been mentioned in the previous selections, for you to open next as you develop your thinking on postcolonialism. Like all reading lists, my choices are inevitably selective and inexhaustive. I have divided them into different sections to help you navigate your work. In one sense you will have already begun these texts by finishing *Beginning Postcolonialism*. I hope your enjoyment and critical understanding of postcolonialism will be all the more satisfying for having done so.

Appendix

'The Overland Mail (foot-service to the hills)' (Rudyard Kipling)

In the Name of the Empress of India, make way,
    O Lords of the Jungle, wherever you roam,
The woods are astir at the close of the day –
    We exiles are waiting for letters from Home.
Let the robber retreat – let the tiger turn tail –   5
In the Name of the Empress, the Overland Mail!

With a jingle of bells as the dusk gathers in,
    He turns to the footpath that heads up the hill –
The bags on his back and a cloth round his chin,
    And, tucked in his waistbelt, the Post Office bill: –   10
"Despatched on this date, as received by the rail,
"*Per* runner, two bags of the Overland Mail."

Is the torrent in spate? He must ford it or swim.
    Has the rain wrecked the road? He must climb by the cliff.
Does the tempest cry halt? What are tempests to him?   15
    The service admits not a "but" or an "if."
While the breath's in his mouth, he must bear without fail,
In the Name of the Empress, the Overland Mail.

From aloe to rose-oak, from rose-oak to fir,
    From level to upland, from upland to crest,   20
From rice-field to rock-ridge, from rock-ridge to spur,
    Fly the soft-sandalled feet, strains the brawny, brown chest.
From rail to ravine – to the peak from the vale –
Up, up through the night goes the Overland Mail.

There's a speck on the hillside, a dot on the road –   25
    A jingle of bells on the footpath below –
There's a scuffle above in the monkey's abode –
    The world is awake and the clouds are aglow.
For the great Sun himself must attend to the hail: –
"In the Name of the Empress, the Overland Mail!"   30

Further reading

General introductions

Ashcroft, Bill, Gareth Griffiths and Helen Tiffin, *The Empire Writes Back: Theory and Practice in Post-Colonial Literatures* (Routledge, 1989).

An important book when it first appeared in 1989, this much-quoted text has since been subjected to some rather strong criticism (as we saw in Chapter 1) and now appears a little dated.

Boehmer, Elleke, *Colonial and Postcolonial Literature* (Oxford University Press, 1995).

Probably the best critical history of the literatures in the field.

Childs Peter, and Patrick Williams, *An Introduction to Post-Colonial Theory*, (Harvester Wheatsheaf, 1997).

An excellent, thorough, if not always an *introductory* text which deals with the theoretical writings of Said, Bhabha, Spivak, Gilroy and others; and also engages with the problems of postcolonialism. Highly recommended.

Gandhi, Leela, *Postcolonial Theory: An Introduction* (Edinburgh University Press, 1998).

A reasonably clear introduction, if rather disorganised and idiosyncratic. Includes a useful chapter on 'Postcolonial Literatures' in relation to postcolonial theory. One of the few texts that cites Mahatma Gandhi as an influential figure on forms of postcolonial resistance (indeed, the book as whole deals most frequently with Indian postcoloniality).

King, Bruce (ed.), *New National and Post-Colonial Literatures: An Introduction* (Clarendon Press, 1996).

Features a variety of short, strong critical essays by leading scholars in the field, firmly focused on literary texts.

Loomba, Ania, *Colonialism/Postcolonialism* (Routledge, 1998).

Examines the theoretical influences in postcolonial theory and attends particularly well to the issue of identity. Also very useful for those attending in particular to theories of colonial discourses.

Moore-Gilbert, Bart, *Postcolonial Theory: Contexts, Practices, Politics* (Verso, 1997).

An exhaustive and sophisticated critical account of the emergence of Commonwealth literature and the shift to postcolonialism, with expert chapters on the work of Said, Bhabha and Spivak. Its high level of analysis means that it is not always operating at an 'introductory' level. Required reading.

Skinner, John, *The Stepmother Tongue: An Introduction to New Anglophone Fiction* (Macmillan, 1998).

A useful introduction to the various literatures which preoccupy postcolonialism, although Skinner's narrative is determined by the conventional map of Commonwealth literature. The focus on writers' differing uses of language is most illuminating.

Walder, Dennis, *Post-Colonial Literatures in English: History, Language, Theory* (Blackwell, 1998).

An excellently clear introduction, recommended for newcomers to the field. Features sensible chapters on the issues of history, language and theory in postcolonialism, through which Walder reads a variety of literary texts (such as Indo-Anglian fiction and Black British poetry) in imaginative and thought-provoking ways.

Reference books

Ashcroft, Bill, Gareth Griffiths and Helen Tiffin (eds), *Key Concepts in Post-Colonial Studies* (Routledge, 1998).

Contains many useful definitions of the key terms in the field, with suggestions for further reading.

Benson, Eugene and L. W. Conolly (eds), *Encyclopedia of Post-colonial Literatures in English*, 2 Volumes (Routledge, 1994).

Has useful, short entries on a wealth of writers, concepts and nations. Excellent reference tool.

General readers: theory, criticism and literature

Ashcroft, Bill, Gareth Griffiths and Helen Tiffin (eds), *The Post-Colonial Studies Reader* (Routledge, 1995).

A large and wide-ranging volume which collects together a variety of essays under such headings as 'Nationalism', 'Language' and 'Hybridity'. One of the strengths of this collection is its attention to the settler colonies in the context of postcolonialism. However, many of its collected essays have been severely cut, sometimes at the cost of their sophistication.

Childs, Peter, *Post-Colonial Theory and English Literature: A Reader* (Edinburgh University Press, 1999).

Collects together several important and influential postcolonial critiques of eight literary texts: William Shakespeare's *The Tempest*, Daniel Defoe's *Robinson Crusoe*, Charlotte Brontë's *Jane Eyre*, Rudyard Kipling's *Kim*, Joseph Conrad's *Heart of Darkness*, James Joyce's *Ulysses*, E. M. Forster's *A Passage to India* and Salman Rushdie's *The Satanic Verses*.

Moore-Gilbert, Bart, Gareth Stanton and Willy Maley (eds), *Postcolonial Criticism* (Longman, 1997).

A recent and wide-ranging anthology of postcolonial criticism which features work by Ahmad, Bhabha, Said and Spivak, as well as a lengthy and highly informative introduction.

Mongia, Padmini (ed.), *Contemporary Postcolonial Theory: A Reader* (Arnold, 1996).

An excellent volume which includes essays not often collected elsewhere, such as work by Arif Dirlik and Aijaz Ahmad.

Parker, Michael and Roger Starkey (eds), *Postcolonial Literatures: Achebe, Ngugi, Desai, Walcott* (Macmillan, 1995).

Collects together some illuminating essays on four important postcolonial writers. Also features a clear, focused introduction.

Thieme, John (ed.), *The Arnold Anthology of Post-Colonial Literatures in English* (Arnold, 1996).

A superb and wide-ranging collection of Anglophone postcolonial literature from around the world, sensibly organised and sensitive to cultural specifics.

Williams, Patrick and Laura Chrisman (eds), *Colonial Discourse and Post-Colonial Theory* (Harvester, 1993).

An excellently-structured volume which includes many important essays by the likes of Said, Spivak, Bhabha, Hall, Mohanty and others. More challenging than *The Post-Colonial Studies Reader*, but ultimately more useful and intellectually rewarding. This book also benefits from its excellent introductory essays written by the editors which preface each section, and the focus on postcolonialism in its economic and historical contexts. Highly recommended.

Postcolonial theory: some key texts

Ahmad, Aijaz, *In Theory: Classes, Nations, Literatures* (Verso, 1992).
A detailed and polemical critique of postcolonial theory which argues for the continuing valency of Marxism and nationalism as political and analytical weapons.

Bhabha, Homi K. (ed.), *Nation and Narration* (Routledge, 1990).
An influential collection of essays which interrogates literature and nationalism from a variety of positions.

Bhabha, Homi K., *The Location of Culture* (Routledge, 1994).
This book collects together many of Bhabha's influential essays on 'the discourse of colonialism', cultural difference and postcoloniality.

Fanon, Frantz, *Black Skin, White Masks*, trans. Charles Lam Markmann (Pluto, [1952] 1986). Foreword by Homi K. Bhabha.
Fanon's ground-breaking and polemical critique of the psychological consequences of French colonialism remains an important interrogation of colonised identities. Highly influential in contemporary postcolonial theory, especially the earlier work of Bhabha.

Fanon, Frantz, *The Wretched of the Earth*, trans. Constance Farrington (Penguin, [1961] 1967).
Includes Fanon's important discussions of colonial violence, national culture, and the pitfalls of national consciousness.

Gilroy, Paul, *The Black Atlantic: Modernity and Double Consciousness* (Verso, 1993).
Gilroy's influential and ground-breaking text which examines the aesthetics of transnationality in the context of black migration.

Lazarus, Neil, *Nationalism and Cultural Practice in the Postcolonial World* (Cambridge University Press, 1999).
A wide-ranging and sophisticated text which explores social movements, ideas and cultural practices which have migrated from the 'First' to the 'Third' world over the course of the twentieth century.

McClintock, Anne, *Imperial Leather: Race, Gender and Sexuality in the Colonial Context* (Routledge, 1995).

An exciting and thought-provoking critique of colonial discourses and their intersections with 'race', gender and sexuality.

Parry, Benita, 'Problems in Current Theories of Colonial Discourse', *Oxford Literary Review*, 9 (1–2), 1987, pp. 27–58.

An early and influential critique of the work of Bhabha and Spivak, which remains 'required reading' for any student of postcolonialism.

Pratt, Mary Louise, *Imperial Eyes: Travel Writing and Transculturation* (Routledge, 1992).

Pratt's study of different kinds of travel writing has proved influential in part due to her work on the aesthetics of transculturation created out of the encounter between diverse peoples.

Said, Edward W., *Orientalism* (second edition) (Penguin [1978] 1995).

The second edition includes an important 'Afterword' in which Said addresses the major criticisms of his work and discusses the relationship between *Orientalism* and postcolonialism.

Said, Edward W., *The World, The Text and the Critic* (Vintage, [1984] 1991).

An influential book of essays which cover literature, politics and the intellectual.

Said, Edward W., *Culture and Imperialism* (Vintage, 1993).

An interrogation of the relations between culture and imperialism throughout the world, as well as a critique of forms of anti-colonial resistance.

Spivak, Gayatri Chakravorty, *In Other Worlds: Essays in Cultural Politics* (Routledge, 1987).

Includes a variety of challenging and important essays, such as 'French Feminism in an International Frame' and 'Subaltern Studies: Deconstructing Historiography'.

Spivak, Gayatri Chakravorty, *The Post-Colonial Critic: Interviews, Strategies, Dialogues*, ed. Sara Harasym (Routledge, 1990).

A book of interviews in which Spivak elaborates on several of her critical positions. An approachable if challenging text, and a good place to begin reading Spivak.

Spivak, Gayatri Chakravorty, 'Can the Subaltern Speak?', reprinted with abridgements in Williams and Chrisman (eds), *Colonial Discourse and Post-Colonial Theory*, (Harvester Wheatsheaf, 1993), pp. 66–111.

Probably one of the most important essays in postcolonialism, 'Can the

Subaltern Speak?' has proved influential in feminist criticism and theories of colonial discourses.

Spivak, Gayatri Chakravorty, *Outside in the Teaching Machine* (Routledge, 1993).

This book of essays includes reflections upon theory, pedagogy and cultural texts by the likes of Hanif Kureishi and Salman Rushdie.

Spivak, Gayatri Chakravorty, *The Spivak Reader*, ed. Donna Landry and Gerald MacLean (Routledge, 1996).

This collection features some of Spivak's most influential and groundbreaking work, and includes highly valuable introductions to her essays. Also included is a bibliography of Spivak's work.

Trinh, T. Minh-ha, *Woman, Native, Other: Writing Postcoloniality and Feminism* (Indiana University Press, 1989).

A ground-breaking and challenging study of postcoloniality and feminism which explores the role of writing in contesting dominant patriarchal representations.

Young, Robert, *Colonial Desire: Hybridity in Theory, Culture, and Race* (Routledge, 1995).

A critique of the vogue of hybridity in postcolonial theory which traces the origins of the term to nineteenth-century scientific racism.

Selected collections of essays dealing with 'postcolonialism'

Adam, Ian and Helen Tiffin (eds), *Past the Last Post: Theorising Post-Colonialism and Post-Modernism* (Harvester Wheatsheaf, 1991).

Has several useful essays on the intellectual affiliations of postcolonial theory and its relation to postmodernist aesthetics.

Barker, Francis, Peter Hulme and Margaret Iversen (eds), *Colonial Discourse/Postcolonial Theory* (Manchester University Press, 1994).

An extremely useful, if rather advanced, book of essays, each of which deal critically with several key ideas in postcolonialism – such as 'transculturation', 'hybridity', 'nationalism' and 'minority discourse' – by the likes of Mary Louise Pratt, Annie E. Coombes, Neil Lazarus, Benita Parry and David Lloyd.

Chambers, Iain and Lidia Curti (eds), *The Post-Colonial Question: Common Skies, Divided Horizons* (Routledge, 1996).

Includes stimulating essays by several leading figures in the field and is divided into the following sections: Critical Landscapes; Post-Colonial Time; Frontier Journeys; Whose World, Whose Home?

Gates, Henry Louis jnr. (ed.), *'Race', Writing and Difference* (University of Chicago Press, 1986).

An early, highly influential collection which includes essays by Gayatri Chakravorty Spivak, Mary Louise Pratt, Homi K. Bhabha and others.

Madsen, Deborah L. (ed.), *Post-Colonial Literatures: Expanding the Canon* (Pluto, 1999).

A thought-provoking collection which attempts to deal with hitherto neglected literatures as postcolonial.

Rutherford, Anna, *From Commonwealth to Post-Colonial* (Dangaroo, 1992)

A large and varied collection of essays on postcolonial literatures.

Slemon, Stephen and Helen Tiffin (eds), *After Europe: Critical Theory and Post-Colonial Writing* (Dangaroo, 1989).

Features essays which explore the problems and possibilities of literary theory in postcolonialism.

Tiffin, Chris and Alan Lawson, *De-Scribing Empire: Post-Colonialism and Textuality* (Routledge, 1994).

Includes essays concerning the theorising of postcolonialism, and some stimulating readings of various literary texts in the light of theoretical concerns.

Trivedi, Harish and Meenakshi Mukherjee (eds), *Interrogating Post-Colonialism: Theory, Text and Context* (Indian Institute of Advanced Study, 1996).

A collection of short, readable critical essays which deal with postcolonialism from a variety of positions.

White, Jonathan, *Recasting the World: Writing After Colonialism* (Johns Hopkins University Press, 1993).

A series of thoughtful and considered essays on a variety of writers, such as George Lamming, Salman Rushdie and Toni Morrison.

Journals

ARIEL: A Review of International English Literature.

Published at the University of Calgary, Canada, *ARIEL* features a high standard of critical essays on a wealth of contemporary literary texts (not just postcolonial ones), as well as review articles and book reviews.

Interventions: The International Journal of Postcolonial Studies.

This new journal publishes interdisciplinary essays often partially collected around a specific theme (such as 'Ideologies of the Postmodern' and 'South Asia and Partition'), as well as book reviews.

Journal of Commonwealth Literature.

Established at the University of Leeds in 1965, and still going strong under the editorship of John Thieme. Publishes lots of literary criticism from around the world as well as an invaluable annual bibliography of Commonwealth literature.

Kunapipi: Journal of Post-Colonial Writing.

Kunapipi was established by Anna Rutherford in Australia in 1979; its title refers to the Australian Aboriginal myth of the Rainbow Serpent which is a symbol both of regeneration and creativity. This journal is valuable not least because it features the latest postcolonial creative writing alongside critical essays and interviews.

SPAN: Journal of the South Pacific Association for Commonwealth Literature and Language Studies.

Based at the University of Waikato, New Zealand, *SPAN* often features theoretically exciting critical essays as well as new creative writing.

Wasafiri: Caribbean, African, Asian and Associated Literatures in English.

An exciting journal which features critical essays, interviews and a comprehensive book review section. A leader in its field.

World Literature Written in English.

A wide-ranging journal, established in 1966, which features in the main literary criticism.

Index

DATE DUE